£6

WITHDRAWN FROM
THE LIBRARY

UNIVERSITY OF
WINCHESTER

Urban Society of Eastern Europe
in Premodern Times

URBAN SOCIETY OF EASTERN EUROPE IN PREMODERN TIMES

Edited by
Bariša Krekić

UNIVERSITY OF CALIFORNIA PRESS
Berkeley • Los Angeles • London

University of California Press
Berkeley and Los Angeles, California

University of California Press, Ltd.
London, England

Library of Congress Cataloging-in-Publication Data

Urban society of Eastern Europe in premodern times.

  Includes index.
  1. Cities and towns, Medieval—Europe, Eastern.
2. City and town life—Europe, Eastern—History.
I. Krekić, Bariša.
HT131.U7 1987   307.7'6'0947   86-24939
ISBN 0-520-05788-0 (alk. paper)

Printed in the United States of America

1 2 3 4 5 6 7 8 9

Contents

Preface

While the life and development of West European medieval cities have attracted much scholarly attention and have been the object of many serious studies for a long time, the history of the East European city, and especially its society in the same period, has encountered less interest, particularly in languages accessible to Western readers. Studies dedicated to the urban society of Eastern Europe are relatively few and focus mostly on only certain aspects of its development, contrary to the variety and thoroughness with which Western European society has been examined. This fact is, of course, largely the result of the difference in the availability of sources. With a few exceptions, the abundance, variety, and quality of information that can be found in many West European archives—especially Italian ones—can hardly be matched by materials existing in the archives of Eastern Europe.

Nevertheless, the study of the history and society of medieval East European cities attracted scholars quite a long while ago and has developed with new vigor after World War II. Most works on the subject were published initially by East European historians in their native languages, something that made access to these works rather difficult for many western scholars.[1]

In the 1960s, however, the situation began changing. Studies written by East European scholars began appearing in western languages and a growing number of western scholars became interested in the topic of East European cities and their societies.[2] Of course, many publications continued to appear in East Eu-

ropean languages as well.[3] The 1970s brought about an increase
in both the number and quality of publications written in East[4]
and West European languages[5] regarding the East European city.
The same is true of the 1980s.[6]

It is obvious from the very limited data mentioned here that
some cities attracted the particular attention of scholars: Novgorod, Kiev, and Dubrovnik, among others, have had their history and society examined much more carefully and thoroughly
than most other East European cities. There are several reasons
for such a concentration of scholarly attention on these particular
places: In some instances they were dealing with cities that
played a major role in the history of their own areas and far
beyond; in other instances, historians were attracted by the
wealth of documentary evidence that has survived. In the best
cases scholars were able to combine the two: important cities
which also possess abundant records of their activities (e.g.,
Dubrovnik).[7]

As has been mentioned, until recent times most books and
articles on East European cities were oriented primarily toward
a study of the cities' political history, economic development,
and cultural life. Little attention was paid to the realities of daily
life and to the ways people tried to cope with problems of everyday survival. Most recently, however, more attention is being
paid to those aspects of city life too.

The purpose of this book—which grew out of a symposium
held at UCLA in March 1983, with the support of the UCLA
Center for Russian and East European Studies—is not to give a
complete overview of the urban society of Eastern Europe but
rather to point out certain contrasts and similarities in its structure.

Distant as they were from each other, Novgorod and Dubrovnik, for example, had some characteristics in common in their
society and government. At the same time, places as close to
one another as the Dalmatian cities and the cities in the immediate Balkan hinterland had more disparities than similarities.
Kraków and Buda were not geographically distant and their
societies and institutions had more than one point in common.
Nevertheless, their political development was considerably dif-

ferent. Buda's fate was affected by the "infidel" powers from the east and southeast, the Tatars and the Ottomans, while Kraków's troubles were related principally to the actions of the Christian powers of Central and Eastern Europe. Thus it is obvious that geographic proximity was not necessarily as much of a unifying element in the history and societal development of eastern European cities as it was, for example, in Italy and Flanders.

In spite of this, the development of East European urban societies did not lag chronologically much behind the advanced cities of the West. The flourishing of Novgorod and Kraków, the growth of the Dalmatian cities and of Balkan mining centers was almost contemporary with the flourishing of West European cities. In fact, until the late fifteenth century and, in some cases, into the sixteenth century, most East European cities and urban societies were basically part of European urban society as a whole. Differences did exist but were not as great as is sometimes assumed.

This is particularly apparent when one examines the presence or absence of a free citizenry and communal autonomy. The presence of a strong free citizenry and of substantial communal autonomy in the West and the absence of both in the East, were considered for a long time the essential indicators of the differences in the development of cities and urban societies in Western and Eastern Europe. More recent detailed research of the East European city and its society have made it necessary to reexamine carefully our assumptions and to broaden the basis of the comparative approach to the study of the medieval European city both in the East and the West.

Indeed, it seems safe to say that most urban centers of Eastern Europe developed in ways very similar to those in the West until the time that many East European cities saw their lives violently disrupted and interrupted by outside forces—in the case of Balkan hinterland cities and of Buda at the hands of the Ottoman Turks and, in the case of many Russian cities, at the hands of the Tatars—while cities such as Kraków and Novgorod were deeply affected by wider political processes in their areas. Their fate under these new circumstances is beyond the scope of this volume, but it could no doubt serve as an excellent case study for the "missed Renaissances," as Robert Lopez once called the phenomenon.

Studies published in this volume should be seen as a modest contribution to our knowledge of East European urban society in a very significant period of its evolution. More importantly, they should serve as a stimulus for further comparative research and publication and for new ideas and discussions on the subject.

NOTES

1. To give just a few examples from the 1950s: S. V. Bakhrushin and others, eds., *Istoriya Moskvy*, Vol. I (Moscow: Akademiya Nauk SSSR 1952). M. N. Tikhomirov, *Drevnerusskiye goroda*, 2d ed., (Moscow: Gosudarstvennoe Izdatelstvo Politicheskoi Literaturi, 1956). Idem, *Srednevekovaya Moskva v XIV–XV vekakh* (Moscow: Moskovskiy Universitet, 1957). M. J. Dinić, "Novo Brdo:kratak istoriski pregled," *Starinar*, n.s. 4–4 (Belgrade, 1954–1955) 247–250. V. Trpkova-Zaimova, "Kreposti i ukrepeni gradove prez prvoto bulgarsko carstvo," *Voenno-istor. Sbornik*, 25/3 (Sofia 1956), 40–60. G. Novak, *Povijest Splita*, Vol. I, Matica hrvatska (Split 1957). Among works published in Western languages at the time one should mention, for example, A. Gieysztor, "Le origini della città nella Polonia medievale." *Studi in onore di A. Sapori* (Milan: Istituto Editoriale Cisalpino 1957) I, 127–145. Idem, "Les origines de la ville slave," *Settimane di studio* (Spoleto 1959), VI: 279–315. G. S. Soulis, "Notes on the History of the City of Serres under the Serbs" (1345–1371), *Afieromena M. Triandafillidi* (Thessalonika 1960), 373–379.

2. For example B. Krekić, *Dubrovnik (Raguse) et le Levant au Moyen Age* (Paris-The Hague: Ecole Pratique des Hautes Etudes 1961). D. Angelov, "Die Stadt im mittelalterlichen Bulgarien," *Zeitschrift Geschichtswissenschafts* 10 (1962) 405–416. A. Voyce, *Moscow and the Roots of Russian Culture*, (Norman: University of Oklahoma Press, 1964). V. Velkov, "Zur Geschichte des Stadt Serdica (Sofia) vom IV bis IX Jahrhundert," *Etudes historiques*, 3 (1966) 53–60. V. Beševliev, "Zur Kontinuität der antiken Städte in Bulgarien," *Neue Beiträge zur Geschichte der alten Welt*, Vol. II (Berlin: Akademie Verlag 1965), 211–221. A. Gieysztor, "Les chartes de franchises urbaines et rurales en Pologne au XIIIe siècle," *Les libertés urbaines et rurales du XIe au XIVe siècle* (Brussels: Pro Civitate 1968) 103–125. K. Zernak, *Die burgstädtischen Volksversammlungen bei den Ost- und*

Westlaven. Studien zur verfassungsgeschichtlichen Bedeutung des Veče (Wiesbaden: Otto Harrassowitz, 1967). Witold Hensel, *Anfänge der Städte bei den Ost- und Westlaven* (Bautzen: Domowina, 1967). I. Dujčev, "Melnik au Moyen Age," *Byzantion*, 38 (1968) 28–41. K. Onasch, *Gross-Nowgorod. Aufstieg und Niedergang einer russichen Stadtrepublik* (Vienna and Munich: A. Schroll & Co., 1969).

3. T. Tomoski, "Ohrid do krajot na XIV vek," *Zbornik na trudovi Nar. Muz.* (Okhrid 1961) 7–14. V. A. Golobutskiy and others, eds., *Istoriya Kiyeva*, Vol. I (Kiev: Akademiya nauk Ukrainskoy SSR, 1963). K. Mijatev, "Carevgrad Trnov," *Arheologija*, 6 (1964) 7–17. J. Ferluga, Drač i Dračka oblast pred kraj X i početkom XI veka, *Zbornik radova Vizantološkog instituta*, VIII: 2 *Mélanges Ostrogorsky* (Belgrade 1964) II: 117–32. I. Dujčev, "Trnovo kato politički i duhoven centr prez kasnoto srednovekovie," *Arheologija* 8/3 (1966), 1–9. Idem, "Problemi iz srednovekovnata istorija na Preslav," *Preslav. Sbornik* (Sofia 1968), 29–38. J. Kalić-Mijušković, *Beograd u srednjem veku*, Srpska književna zadruga (Beograd 1967). S. Ćirković, "Civitas Sancti Demetrii," *Syrmium-Sremska Mitrovica* (Sremska Mitrovica 1969) 59–71. S. N. Lišev, *Blgarskijat srednovekoven grad. Obštestvenno-ikonomičeski oblik* (Sofia 1970).

4. Here are a few examples: J. Lučić, *Povijest Dubrovnika*, Vol. II (Zagreb: Jugoslavenska akademija znanosti i umjetnosti, 1973). P. Andjelić, *Bobovac i kraljeva Sutjeska* (Sarajevo 1973). *Istorija Beograda*, Vol. I (Belgrade: SANU, 1974). S. Vilfan, "Tipologija srednjovjekovnih gradova Slovenije i etnička struktura njihovog stanovništva," *Jugoslovenski istorijski časopis* 1–2 (1975) 19–27. N. Klaić–I. Petricioli, *Zadar u srednjem vijeku* (Zadar: Sveučilište u Splitu, Filozofski fakultet u Zadru, 1976). M. Ya. Syuzyumov, "O funkciyah rannesrednevekovnogo goroda," *Ant. drev. i sred. veka*, 14 (1977) 34–51. T. Raukar, *Zadar u XV stoljeću. Ekonomski razvoj i društveni odnosi* (Zagreb: Sveuč. u Zagrebu, 1977). V. L. Yanin, *Ocherki kompleksnogo istochnikovedeniya. Srednevekovy Novgorod* (Moscow: Vysshaya shkola, 1977). D. Kovačević-Kojić, *Gradska naselja srednjovjekovne bosanske države,* (Sarajevo: Veselin Masleša, 1978). D. I. Polyviannyi, *Bolgarskyi srednevekovyi gorod v XIII–XIV vekakh,* (Moscow: Moskovskiy universitet, 1980). M. M. Freidenberg, "Social Connections and Antagonisms in Dalmatian Towns of the XVth–XVIth Centuries," *Studia Balcanica* (Sofia 1970) III: 117–123.

5. See, among others: W. Knackstedt, *Moskau. Studien zur Geschichte einer mittelalterlichen Stadt* (Wiesbaden: Franz Steiner, 1975). L. A. Langer, "The Medieval Russian Town," *The City in Russian History*, M. F. Hamm, ed., (Lexington: University Press of Kentucky, 1976) 11–33. V. Velkov, *Cities in Thrace and Dacia in Late Antiquity*, (Amsterdam: Adolf

M. Hakkert, 1977). H. Stoob, ed., *Die mittelalterliche Städtebildung in südöstlichen Europa* (Cologne: Bohlau, 1977). K. D. Grothusen, "Zum Stadtbegriff in Südosteuropa," *Zeitschrift für Balkanologie,* 13 (1977) 63–81. V. Velkov, *Roman Cities in Bulgaria, Collected Studies,* (Amsterdam: Adolf M. Hakkert, 1980).

6. A. Kuzev-V. Gjuzelev, *Blgarski srednovekovni gradove i kreposti,* Vol. I (Varna 1981). H. Birnbaum, *Lord Novgorod the Great. Essays in the History and Culture of a Medieval City-State* (Columbus, Ohio: Slavica, 1982). J. Kalić, "Byzanz und die mittelalterlichen Städte in Serbien," *Jahrbuch der österreichischen Byzantinistik,* 32/4 (1982) 595–601. I. I. Artemenko and others, eds., *Drevniy i srednevekovy Kiyev* (Kiev: Naukova dumka, 1982). A. Ducellier, *La façade maritime de l'Albanie au Moyen Âge: Durazzo et Valona du XIe au XVe siècle,* (Thessalonika: Institute for Balkan Studies, 1981). P. P. Tolochko, *Drevniy Kiyev,* (Kiev: Naukova dumka, 1983). L. N. Langer, "The 'Posadnichestvo' in Pskov: Some Aspects of Urban Administration in Medieval Russia," *Slavic Review,* 43 (1984) 46–62. L. Steindorff, *Die dalmatinischen Städte im 12. Jahrhundert: Studien zu ihrer politischen Stellung und gesellschaftlichen Entwicklung* (Cologne and Vienna: Bohlau, 1985). *Le pouvoir central et les villes en Europe de l'est et du sud-est du XIVe siècle aux débuts de la révolution industrielle. Les villes portuaires.* Commission internationale d'histoire des villes—Académie bulgare des sciences, Sofia 1985.

7. For additional information on publications concerning the cities of Eastern Europe, see bibliographies that follow after each article in this volume.

1

Kiev, Novgorod, Moscow

Three Varieties of Urban Society in East Slavic Territory*

Henrik Birnbaum

I

Of all the towns and cities of medieval Russia numbering, according to some estimates, about 300 in Kievan Rus' and more
than 350 around the year 1400 (including those under Lithuanian
rule),[1] only three—Kiev, Novgorod, and Moscow—ever reached
the size and significance of major urban, indeed metropolitan,
centers. Though flourishing to their fullest at largely different
times and under different circumstances, they nonetheless held
certain general characteristics in common. This makes it possible
to consider them in some ways merely three instantiations of
one and the same East Slavic prototype, or paradigm, of a large-
scale urban community, quite distinct, it should be emphasized

*I am indebted to Professor Andrzej Poppe, Warsaw, for having read
an earlier version of this study and having suggested a number of
improvements most of which I have followed and all of which I have
considered.

1

at the outset, from the full-fledged virtually independent commune in some parts of Western and Central Europe during the later Middle Ages and the age of the Renaissance. Yet, in addition to exhibiting some striking similarities, the three large Russian cities also had their specifically individual traits which made each of them unique in the general urban setting of medieval Eastern Europe.

Kiev's heyday was in the early period of Russian, or rather East Slavic, history in the eleventh and twelfth century. Its sacking by the Tatars in 1240 put an end to Kiev's previous growth and continuous development. Though subsequently playing a role of some importance as a provincial center, first under Lithuanian and later under Polish control, the city on the Dnieper was not to recover fully from the Mongol devastation until the sixteenth and seventeenth century, usually considered still the late Middle Ages for that part of the continent or, at most, the dawn of a new era in that particular subregion. At that time, however, Kiev reemerged as an urban community of a markedly different kind, now with a distinctly Ukrainian ethnic identity.

Usually regarded as older than the southern metropolis in terms of its semilegendary historical beginnings (a claim not borne out by the findings of archaeology, however),[2] and aspiring to rival the capital of the Old Russian state from the middle of the eleventh century onward, Novgorod did not reach the peak of its glory, wealth, and splendor until quite some time after the Tatar invasion and the repulsion of Swedish expansionist forces and the Teutonic Knights in the 1230s and 1240s. By then, Kiev had long ceased to be a competitor to be reckoned with and Muscovy had only just started upon its course toward subsequent dominance.

It should be noted further that, even though Novgorodian liberty and independence came to a sudden and tragic end with the annexation in 1478 of the north Russian city-state by the Grand Duchy of Moscow, some facets of the specifically Novgorodian variety of urban life, particularly as regards intellectual, devotional, and artistic activities, continued to thrive for some time beyond the downfall of the Republic of St. Sophia.

Muscovy, in turn, governed by the successors of the grand

princes of Vladimir, did not assert itself and was not in a position to transform its main town into a major political and cultural center before the late fourteenth century and fully only by the fifteenth century under Grand Prince Ivan III. Mentioned for the first time in the chronicle account for the year 1147 in connection with an invitation issued by Yuriy Dolgorukiy, prince of Suzdal' (who surrounded it with a city wall only in 1156),[3] and completely destroyed in the winter of 1237 by the Tatars who besieged and raided it once more as late as 1382, Moscow reached the height of its power and might in the reign of that half genius, half madman Ivan IV, known as the Terrible (though the Russian *Grozny* in this instance is perhaps more properly rendered as the Awesome). It was he who can be said to have completed successfully what in Russian historiography is frequently referred to as the "gathering of the Russian lands," with Moscow their unchallenged center. By that time, the fast-growing city in the region between the Upper Volga and the Oka rivers had long been proclaimed the Third Rome of Orthodox Christianity and the legitimate successor to Constantinople, captured by the infidels.

In terms of Russian medieval history, therefore, Kiev can be viewed as the ranking city of the Early, Novgorod of the High, and Moscow of the Late Middle Ages. Turning now to specifics, what then, aside from their obvious and significant differences, were some of the overall characteristics that these three urban centers of Slavic Eastern Europe in the premodern age can be said to have shared and which, incidentally, also distinguished them in part from the medieval city of the West (as conceived in the classic models of scholars such as Henri Pirenne, Max Weber, and Fritz Rörig)?[4]

II

To begin with—and leaving aside the controversial question as to whether any of the three cities was actually founded, in the strict sense of the word, that is by a specific individual, legends to that effect notwithstanding—it ought to be noted that at least two of them, Kiev and Novgorod, were located on important trade routes, even at the crossroads or end points of such land or water routes. Thus, Novgorod, situated just a mile or two north of the outlet from Lake Il'men' into the Volkhov River, was strategically located on the famous waterway referred to in the Primary Chronicle as the "road from the Varangians to the Greeks" (*put' iz varjag v greki*, i.e., from Scandinavia to Byzantium). In addition, it was a major place of transshipment and distribution of goods coming both by ship and overland, from and to regions on and adjoining the southern shores of the Baltic Sea. These were the Baltic lands of Estonia, Livonia and Lithuania, and until the conquest by the Teutonic Knights, Prussia proper (roughly corresponding to the former German East Prussia) as well as north Germany. From there, connecting routes ran west and southwest, notably to Flanders and the Lower Rhine Valley. When the Hansa—with its base in Lübeck but soon also in regional centers of the Livonian-Estonian towns of Riga, Dorpat (Tartu), and Reval (Tallinn)—established its permanent trade station in the city on the Volkhov toward the end of the twelfth century, it was only regularizing and strengthening trade connections that had long been in existence. In Novgorod the Nemetskiy dvor, or German Yard (frequently also referred to by its German name, Peterhof), at first perhaps merely supplemented but was soon to integrate the foreign-trade establishment of the Gotland merchants, initially both Swedish and German, founded somewhat earlier and known as Gotskiy dvor or, in Swedish, Gutagård. Another route, this one overland, linked Novgorod with the town of Smolensk on the Dnieper and with more distant commercial centers in Lithuania, Poland, Hungary, and the Czech lands.[5]

In a similar way, Kiev was situated at the intersection of at least two major trade routes, one running north to south (and vice versa), the other west to east (and in the opposite direction). The first route was the same, well-established "road from the Varangians to the Greeks," here following the Dnieper and in active use as an artery for the movement of goods in Eastern Europe also long after the trading Northmen had stopped traveling along it on their way to Byzantium and the marvels of the eastern Mediterranean. The other was an equally important track facilitating the overland trade and linking the south German town of Regensburg on the Danube with the southern metropolis of the East Slavs on the Dnieper. Passing through Bohemia, Silesia, Little Poland, and the territories of Galicia and Volhynia this trade link, extending through a central portion of Europe, branched out into several connecting routes at both ends and was intersected as well by other routes running north, along the rivers Elbe (from Bohemia), Oder (from Silesia), and Vistula (from southern Poland).

Things were slightly different as regards Moscow. Obviously, the region between the Upper Volga and the Oka rivers, originally settled by Finnic and partly also by Baltic tribes, had played a significant part since at least the tenth century as a district of transit commerce linking Northern Europe with the area of the Caspian Sea as well as with more faraway Islamic countries beyond that body of water. Here the Volga constituted a natural artery, with the predominantly Turkic Bulgars, who occupied territories on its central course and on the banks of its tributary, the Kama, acting as middlmen in that long-distance trade. The role of the Volga-Oka region remained essentially the same or became even more prominent once Slavic tribes entered it and began to subjugate or replace the indigenous non-Slavic population during the late tenth and throughout the eleventh and twelfth century. Thus, the earliest towns of the Russian northeast, particularly Suzdal' and Rostov but soon also the even more splendid Vladimir (founded by the grand prince of Kiev, Vladimir Monomakh, in 1108), while functioning as military strongholds served as commercial centers as well. Whether this dual role of economic hub and strategically placed fortress can likewise be assumed for the city of Moscow in its initial phase of development (as was suggested already at the turn of the century by I. Ye. Zabelin for example) is more difficult to say. Yet there are at least some indications—mostly archaeological in nature and brought to light only in recent years—to support precisely such a hypothesis. At any rate, once the future capital of Russia had grown in size and significance it also served as the terminus of several major trade routes leading south.[6]

In this general context it should be remembered that the basic
feature of every town, as distinct from the numerous large-size
villages in medieval Russia, was that its people earned their
livelihood primarily in nonagricultural pursuits, even though
many East Slavic towns also encompassed pastures and some
wooded lands within their bounds at at least some point in the
course of their history. But the economic needs of the townspeople were satisfied above all by the market and the most salient
feature of the Old Russian town was a centrally located market
square (*torg*). This also applies to the three urban communities
(or at most four, if we also were to include Pskov) that grew
beyond the average size of mere towns.[7]

The life-style of the urban population naturally also determined its social structure, while the origins and external contacts
of Kiev, Novgorod, and Moscow left some trace in the three
cities' ethnic makeup. To be sure, we cannot talk here about any
full identity or specific shared characteristics but merely about
certain general similarities and parallels ascertainable in the three
metropolitan centers of Rus' conspicuous, in particular, in terms
of the overall size and density of their populations at the times
of each of these medieval cities' respectively greatest flourishing.

As regards the actual size of the population of the three urban
communities discussed, it has been tentatively but it seems real-
istically calculated that toward the end of the pre-Mongol period,
Kiev, including its commercial district, Podol, numbered approximately 35,000 to 40,000 inhabitants. Frequently mentioned
figures of about 100,000 or even more are clearly out of propor-
tion. For Novgorod at the height of its economic flowering the
estimated figure is 25,000 to 30,000. Another, slightly higher
number of about 35,000 is now considered somewhat exaggerated. By comparison, Pskov is believed to have had somewhere
in the neighborhood of 22,000 city dwellers in the sixteenth
century, at the time of its annexation by Muscovy and in the
decades immediately following. This figure is possibly even
slightly low given the high density of the area covered with
buildings. Moscow finally passed the 20,000 mark by the fifteenth century at the latest and soon came to outgrow all the
other urban centers of late medieval Russia.

A few comparative statistics from other parts of Europe may be useful to consider in order to put the sizes of the largest three or four Old Russian cities in proper perspective. Constantinople, during its decline in the first half of the fifteenth century, is thought to have had somewhere between 40,000 or 50,000 and 75,000 inhabitants. For Paris the figure of about 80,000 has been established for the year 1328, and for London 35,000–40,000 for the year 1377. The major cities of Italy—Milan, Venice, Florence, and Naples—all had populations in excess of 50,000 as early as the fourteenth century, and the same applies to the two urban communities of Flanders, Ghent and Bruges. It is interesting to note, by the same token, that of all the German cities only Cologne, with its 30,000–40,000 citizens, seems to have outnumbered Novgorod in population in the fifteenth century while still not reaching the size of the populace of Kiev even a few centuries earlier. Cities like Lübeck, Prague, Valencia, Saragossa, and Lisbon appear to have been roughly the same size as Novgorod in the fifteenth century whereas Nuremberg, Augsburg, Vienna, Strasbourg, and Toulouse, with about 20,000 inhabitants each, did not quite come up to the number of people Novgorod (and Pskov) boasted.[8]

Of the various social strata and professional groups represented in the three East Slavic metropolitan centers, there is reason to assume that the craftsmen and artisans, who were the core of what was known as the *chernye lyudi* (or simply *chern'*), carried the heaviest tax burden and made up the bulk of the population in each center. Another fairly large and economically highly influential group consisted of the affluent merchant class engaged in international trade or in otherwise large-scale, long-distance commerce (*gosti, kuptsy,* also *torgovye lyudi,* terms that were applied somewhat differently in the three cities and at different times). Especially in Novgorod, the line is not easy to draw between the merchant class proper and other well-to-do groups, notably the *zhit'i lyudi* (or *men'shiye muzhi*) as distinct from the class of boyars (*boyare* or *vyatshiye muzhi*), and it is even possible that many of the rich merchants actually belonged to the class of the *zhit'i lyudi.* The boyars, descendants of the original families of city dwellers turned landed aristocracy or indeed patriciate, derived their often substantial wealth primarily from their extensive landownership, while increasingly wielding decisive political power through the organ of the general town assembly (*veche*) and its elected officials, the lord mayor (*posadnik*) and the chiliarch (*tysyatskiy*), offices eventually reserved for members of a number of select boyar clans. In addition to the prosperous merchant class, there existed in Novgorod as well as presumably in the other two Old Russian cities, a rather large group of street traders or peddlers who cannot easily be distinguished from parts of the craftsman population as they would frequently engage in selling the goods they themselves or their fellow professionals had manufactured. At the lower and lowest ends of the societal scale were manual laborers and other people performing menial tasks in various service functions including a sizable number of outright serfs or slaves (*kholopy*). Fairly numerous in Kiev, Novgorod, and Moscow, were members of the privileged clergy, both of the Church and of the many monasteries inside the three cities and their immediate vicinities. Also numerous in varying degrees at different times were retainers and employees serving in the administration, at court, and in the (partly mercenary) military units of the political organs and public officers, including the citywide general assembly (most prominently in Novgorod but in the early period also in Kiev), and serving the ruling prince or his lieutenant (probably decreasingly in Novgorod, increasing greatly in grand-princely Kiev, and after the transfer of the center of power from Vladimir, more and more in Moscow).[9]

While the local administrative structure prevailing in the three cities and their earliest topography to some extent reflected this more or less analogous social stratification of the urban (and suburban) population, there existed by the same token substantial differences in this regard, differences setting Kiev, Novgorod, and Moscow clearly apart. These differences as well as the similarities in the administrative and physical makeup of the three urban communities during their respective times of flourishing in the medieval period are therefore best treated separately in the following pages when discussing some of the peculiarities typical of each of the three varieties of urban society in East Slavic territory.

The ethnic composition of the three cities, only partly and without absolute certainty reconstructible in its details (in particular, in the tentative identification of groups other than the East Slavic bulk of the populations of Kiev, Novgorod, and Moscow), is better brought up in connection with the attempt to determine the specifically foreign elements residing within each of the urban communities discussed (see below).

III

Yet there is of course another vast area of community and shared concern among the three metropolitan centers of medieval Rus' that must not be overlooked in this context. I am referring to the by and large identical general cultural and religious background, granted significant regional variations forming subcultures, as it were, against which the history of these medieval cities ought to be viewed. In other words, it is the impact of Byzantine civilization and of its twin sister, Orthodox Christianity, on the everyday life in Kiev, Novgorod, and Moscow, and their permeation of every facet of it that I have in mind.

Christianity came to Kievan Rus', as we know, from Byzantium, notwithstanding attempts at considering alternative routes by which the new faith might have reached the East Slavs other than those through the Greek outpost of Cherson/Korsun' and through the mediation of largely Byzantinized Bulgaria. In particular, a separate conversion of the people of Novgorod which would have originated in the west or, to be precise, in Bohemia-Moravia, as has been contemplated by some scholars, cannot in actual fact be corroborated.

By adopting Christianity in its Byzantine form the Kievan grand princes, Vladimir (called the Saint for his decision to turn his country Christian), and Yaroslav (known as the Wise, presumably because of his dedication to learning) had opened the gates for the introduction of the highly refined culture of Byzantium, its religiously inspired writing, art, architetcture, and science. Of course the aforementioned water route "from the Varangians to the Greeks" had previously already linked Old Rus' with the major centers of the Byzantine Empire, and Russo-Byzantine or rather Varangian-Slavic-Greek relations were regulated by various political, commercial, and subsequently also ecclesiastical and dynastic agreements. Moreover, the Slavic tribes that had settled in the region during the preceding centuries had long-established contacts with the Greek colonies as well as with the more vaguely defined "Scythian" lands along and adjacent to the northern shores of the Black Sea.

Kiev, the "mother of Russian cities," was the capital of a vast state that included different territories centered around Pereyaslavl', Chernigov, Smolensk, Polotsk, Pskov, Novgorod, and several other towns. Only after the Tatar invasion and with the beginning, around 1240, of the appanage period in Russian history did these territories split into clearly separate principalities, most of them for a considerable time dependent on the khan of the Golden Horde. But prior to that Kiev was the unchallenged capital of the federated Old Russian state (though Novgorod early attempted to assert its relative independence) until the center of real political power shifted more and more to the Russian northeast, to Suzdal' and Vladimir, where the son and grandsons of Vladimir Monomakh, Yuriy Dolgorukiy, Andrey Bogolyubskiy, and Vsevolod the Large Nest established their residences.

In the late tenth-early eleventh century, Grand Prince Vladimir expanded the boundaries of the original site of Kiev to the size of what has become known as Vladimir's Town and reinforced its palisaded fortifications. In the center of that early town a complex of princely palaces was erected. The Cathedral of the Dormition, also called the Church of the Tithe (Desyatinnaya tserkov'), was built between 989 and 996 by invited Byzantine architects and local masons and craftsmen. It is said to have been lavishly decorated with marble, mosaics, and frescoes; several times destroyed and restored, it has not survived to the present. Of all Kievan churches decorated with mosaics, the magnificent Cathedral of St. Sophia in the center of Yaroslav's Town, added by Vladimir's son and successor just south of the earlier settlement, is the only one extant to this day, though it was subsequently reconstructed in the baroque style of the seventeenth century and thoroughly restored after the ravages of World War II. Construction on this metropolitan church began in 1037 and by 1046 all the mosaics and murals of the central nave had been completed. According to one view (recently expressed by Andrzej Poppe), the entire cathedral, including towers and external ambulatories, was in fact constructed and fully decorated between 1037 and 1046 and not, as has been suggested by others, over a period of nearly a century.[10] Most of the rest of the interior decoration of Kiev's chief shrine also was done in Grand Prince Yaroslav's lifetime.

Apparent even from its name, the Kiev cathedral was conceived and designed to emulate the main Christian Orthodox sanctuary in Constantinople, the Hagia Sophia. The diversity of styles in the Kiev St. Sophia's decorations reveals the work to have been that of a team of Byzantine mosaicists and painters brought in from various regions of the Byzantine Empire assisted by local artisans. Several other churches were commissioned and erected during Yaroslav's reign, many of them within the then greatly expanded city limits. The famous Caves Monastery— Pecherskiy monastyr', subsequently Kievo-Pecherskaya lavra— southeast of the city and the most important cultural center of early medieval Rus', was founded in the times of Yaroslav although the monastery's earliest preserved church, dedicated to the Dormition, was not built until the 1070s. The last mosaics produced in Kiev were those in the Cathedral of the Archangel Michael in St. Michael's Monastery, immediately east of Vladimir's and Yaroslav's Towns. (The traditional, though in fact in this context not fully adequate, term "cathedral," is here and in the remainder of this paper retained to render the Russian *sobor*. Strictly speaking, "cathedral" refers only to a church that served as the main house of worship of a bishopric, so that a designation such as "main church," or technically, *katholikon*, would be a more accurate equivalent of the Russian *sobor*, the latter actually being less specific than "cathedral.") These latest mosaics were created between 1111 and 1112; however, the cathedral has not survived and the mosaics are now displayed in St. Sophia.

It should be noted that outside of Kiev (and the Caves Monastery) there are no traces of this distinctly Byzantine art form anywhere in Russia. While no new techniques were employed in the Kievan mosaic designs that could not also be found in the homeland of the mosaic, they were here combined with frescoes to enhance the aesthetic impact, a practice first to be found precisely in Kiev's St. Sophia.[11] All the Kievan churches of later date, beginning with the rule of Vladimir Monomakh, were adorned with frescoes, not mosaics, as were those of other Old Russian towns.

Yaroslav, in addition to being a great patron of the visual arts, is to be credited also, and in particular, with bringing Byzantine learning, that is, literary and scholarly works, usually with a Christian-inspired content, to Kiev. He had them copied or translated into the East Slavic ("Old Russian") recension of Church Slavic. It can thus be assumed that not only Old Church Slavic ("Old Bulgarian") handwritten books found their way to Kiev and Kievan Rus' from Bulgaria in great numbers to be copied and adapted to the needs, if not the norms, of the local East Slavic speakers, but that also quite a few original Greek works reached Kiev at that time. This can be concluded from the account of the Primary Chronicle where we read in the entry for the year 1037 that the grand prince "gathered many scribes and translated from the Greek to Slavic writing" and that "they copied many books." There can therefore be little doubt that if any one individual can be identified as having been instrumental in implementing what may be called the first transplantation of Byzantine civilization to Russian soil—adopting Dimitriy Sergeyevich Likhachev's felicitous coinage, rather than speaking of a first influence, since influence always presupposes the previous existence of a set of readily affectable cultural phenomena and values—it would certainly have to be the Kievan ruler, Yaroslav the Wise.[12] The later Kievan or even Byzantine phase of his life was apparently markedly different from the earlier Novgorodian or Varangian phase.[13]

The third towering figure with a major impact on the cultural as well as the political life of Kiev in the early medieval period was Vladimir Monomakh, previously prince of nearby Pereyaslavl', whose reign in the capital city lasted no longer than twelve years. Yet for most of this period Monomakh was busy with military exploits in regions far away from Kiev. His strong link with Byzantium is perhaps best symbolized by the fact that his mother was the Byzantine princess Maria, a daughter of Emperor Constantine IX Monomachos, and that his byname, Monomakh, echoes this imperial bond. Incidentally, also the nickname of his son Yuriy, Dolgorukiy (literally, Longarm), is but a Slavic calque of the Greek family name Dolychocheiros, borne by a famed Byzantine clan. To be sure, it was hardly in the Byzantine literary tradition that Monomakh authored his very personal Instruction or Testament, written for his sons. His autobiographical sketch pioneered a highly individualistic style and genre in Russian letters.

Finally, it can be mentioned here as further evidence of the great prominence of the Byzantine component in the spiritual and public life of Kievan Rus' and especially of its capital city that of the twenty-three known Kiev-based metropolitans of the Russian Church in the pre-Mongol period as many as seventeen were Greeks, while for only two—Ilarion (fl. 1051–1054) and Kliment Smolyatich (fl. 1147–1155), both great masters of the homiletic genre—can Russian, or rather East Slavic, nationality be claimed with certainty; the ethnic identity for the remaining four has so far not been established.[14] This is not to say, of course, that the whole range of the ecclesiastic hierarchy of Kiev was predominantly Greek. On the contrary, the middle and lower ranks of the clergy must have consisted primarily of native Slavs. But the Byzantine component of the highest echelons of the Church of early medieval Russia with its center in Kiev was probably not negligible either. And it is hardly insignificant for the role of the Russian Church of that period, as viewed from the perspective of the Orthodox Patriarch of Constantinople, that the head, that is, the metropolitan—but not yet the autocephalous patriarch—of the Church of Rus' more often than not was by nationality a stranger to his flock.

In short, medieval Kiev, beginning with the reign of Grand Prince Yaroslav, became a major capital city outshining many political and cultural centers of Europe in its imposing size and its dazzling splendor. Yet the unmatched, indeed unattainable, example which the metropolis on the Dnieper was bent on imitating was, naturally, Constantinople, the Imperial City (in Russian, Tsar'grad) on the Bosporus.

Byzantine culture, with all its trappings and new spiritual values, reached Novgorod in the more distant Russian north with somewhat less force and only with a certain, though minor, delay. Moreover, of the many forms in which Byzantine civilization manifested itself in Novgorod and also in other towns of northern Russia, not all came from or through Kiev and the Russian south. For in addition Novgorod maintained some direct contacts with Byzantium as well as extending its ties with the superior civilization of the eastern Mediterranean also to, and via, the territories of the Orthodox Slavs of the Balkans, the Bulgarians and the Serbs, and, particularly in the earliest phase, through the Czech lands of Bohemia and Moravia. In the latter region the Slavic liturgy, introduced in the second half of the ninth century by Constantine and Methodios, natives of Greek Salonica with its Slavic hinterland, continued, with an admixture of Byzantine elements, through the end of the eleventh century. Yet, as was already indicated, the indeed rather striking traces of Glagolitic writing found especially in Old Novgorodian texts (including inscriptions on the walls of the Novgorod Cathedral of St. Sophia), which point to the Slavic West, as well as what seem to be some other echoes of Czech cultural influences (as, for example, the worship of St. Wenceslas, otherwise focused on Bohemia), still do not necessarily indicate that the Novgorodians, unlike the Kievans, would have embraced Christianity first in its western, Roman Catholic form.

However, we know of some temporary resistance to the advent of the new faith in the Volkhov city. Thus, a relatively recent source, the controversial Joachim Chronicle from the second half of the seventeenth century (known only from the compilation made by the early-eighteenth-century historian Vasiliy Nikitich Tatishchev), tells of the bloody events leading to the imposition of Christianity under Novgorod's first, half-legendary bishop, Akim (probably a distortion of Joachim), who had come from Cherson. Allegedly, paganism resurged and was ultimately subdued in Novgorod only by 1030.[15] At that time, though, the North Russian city which was ruled by Yaroslav until his ascension to the Kievan throne was already part of what Dmitriy Obolensky has so aptly referred to as the Byzantine Commonwealth, in the broad, cultural-historical sense of the phrase, stretching in the north as far as the town of Ladoga, otherwise a main point of contact with the Scandinavian element present in various areas of life in Old Rus' (cf. below).[16]

Replacing a previous wooden structure inside the citadel (*Detinets*) the well-preserved Novgorod Sophia, built in stone in 1045–1050 and patterned generally on its Kievan counterpart, bears eloquent witness to the influence of Byzantine architectural style also in the northern city. Yet it should be noted that although like its prototype an imposing edifice, the northern Sophia is much simpler and more austere than the lavishly adorned and elaborate Kievan cathedral must have been. Thus it is not only smaller, but its overall design is distinguished by a monolithic, monumental quality. Whereas the Kiev Sophia was crowned by thirteen cupolas, Novgorod's main house of worship had but five domes, with only the largest one gilded. And, as mentioned, the interior of the Novgorod cathedral lacked mosaics. Still, this magnificent monument of Old Russian architecture as well as the many mostly more modestly designed church buildings and truly grandiose monasteries that soon crowded the city and dotted its environs (cf. below), all testify on the whole to the impact of the Byzantine form of Christianity and its artistic taste.[17]

When we turn to Novgorodian writing in the earlier Middle Ages it is readily clear that the citizens of the north Russian metropolis, who were practical-minded people pursuing their economic interests and realistic political goals, did not by and large attain the level of literary sophistication that their Kievan counterparts had managed to achieve in emulation of primarily Byzantine or Byzantine-patterned South Slavic hagiographic, homiletic, panegyric, and annalistic texts. Here, while the echoes and reminiscences of Byzantine standards and conventions are certainly descernible in more than one instance and detail, we nonetheless find a rather heavy overlay of mere local-vernacular literacy and frequently indeed semiliteracy which points to an inability fully to absorb and integrate the intellectual and artistic influence exerted by Byzantium and its more adaptable adherents. The considerable body of birchbark letters unearthed in various districts of medieval Novgorod at present approaching if not exceeding 600, does not, in my opinion suggest so much a widespread ability of the local townsfolk to read and write (as has been claimed), as it reveals a lack of stylistic, let alone genuinely artistic, accomplishment.

However, a second wave of Byzantine influence, now largely in guise of South Slavic—Bulgarian and, increasingly, Serbian—ideological concepts and aesthetic forms, was to reach Novgorod at the height of its political might and economic flowering. This occurred in the later fourteenth and throughout the fifteenth century in the course of what, with a less adequate but well-established label, has been termed the Second South Slavic Influence on medieval Russian culture. Many of the manifestations and patterns of this influence, or rather cultural integration (for the influence was by no means unidirectional), marked again by the concerns, symbols, and themes of Orthodox Christianity, are too well known and thoroughly studied to bear repeating here. This is not to overlook the fact, however, that their proper overall interpretation as either a solely enriching or essentially retarding factor in the cultural evolution of Russia as a whole remains highly controversial (I having advocated a compromise position, recognizing both effects of this complex phenomenon).[18] There is also no denying that many relevant details are still in need of further close examination. Suffice it for our purpose to recall that two major figures representing different facets of this cultural impact, the great painter Theophanes the Greek (Feofan Grek) from Byzantium and the skillful writer Pachomius Logothetes (Pakhomiy Logofet, also Pahomije Logotet) from Serbia, who is said to have been the first man of letters in Russia to have lived by his pen alone, spent considerable time in Novgorod and were active there before moving on to Moscow, Vladimir, and the monasteries of Muscovite Rus', Other religious-intellectual phenomena, only indirectly related to but not forming part of the Second South Slavic Influence as such—for example, the heretic movement of the so-called Judaizers (*zhidov-stvuyushchiye*) which probably spread from Novgorod to Moscow, and the activities of their fierce opponents, Archbishop Gennadiy of Novgorod and the circle of humanists with which he surrounded himself, will be touched upon below.

In sum then it may be said that the Byzantium which so thoroughly permeated the higher forms of cultural life in Kiev during the early medieval period (eleventh to twelfth century) also left its traces in some of the pursuits of the clerical and secular elite of Novgorod's citizenry. Yet this kind of Byzantinism never took quite the same hold on even a particular segment of the Novgorod people as it did on the inhabitants of the southern metropolis. This is also not altered by the predominantly Byzantinesque appearance of the north Russian city's densely ecclesiastic (and monastic) cityscape and suburban landscape or by the fact that Byzantine concepts and patterns spread to Novgorod, in contrast to Kiev, in two major waves as it were, an early one (mid-eleventh through early thirteenth century) and a subsequent one (late fourteenth and throughout the fifteenth century). Somehow in Novgorod the slightly ethereal, if frequently calculating, Byzantine style and tendencies were always balanced by a healthy portion of down-to-earth pragmatism, a practical attitude to life reflecting, in part at least, the population's primary commercial concerns and its lively connections with Europe's west and north, notably with Scandinavia and northern Germany.

Turning now from Novgorod, the "father of Russian cities," to what was to become Russia's holy capital, Moscow, the city of almost literally "forty times forty churches," it should be noted that the Byzantine traits in its outward appearance and in certain aspects of its daily life came fully to the fore only from the time the Muscovite ruler Ivan I Kalita assumed the title of grand prince (while keeping the secondary title of prince of Vladimir). Concurrently, he succeeded in making the metropolitan "of Kiev and all Russia" permanently transfer his see to the emerging power center in the Russian northeast (1328). Prior to that, it had been mostly the strictly observed, ceremonial forms of the Eastern liturgy, adhered to in Moscow as elsewhere in Old Rus' and holding a central, highly visible place in urban life from the outset of the northeast Russian city's existence, that may have been perceived as a reflection of the distant splendor of Byzantium. It was thus from that point in time that Moscow, rather than Vladimir, became the capital city of the political entity that had formed in that northeastern region of Russia, even though Vladimir continued to play an important role, particularly in the cultural and religious spheres.

Careful to retain good relations with the Golden Horde, Ivan was a vassal of the Khanate throughout his rule. Muscovy's ascendancy to the central position of power over all of Russia was set on a firm course only after the victory of Ivan's grandson Dmitriy over the Tatars in the battle of Kulikovo beyond the Don in 1380 (earning him the epithet Donskoy), the devastation of Moscow by the Mongols two years later, and after the crushing defeat suffered by Novgorod at the hands of Dmitriy in 1386–1387. It was also now that the Byzantinized nature of much of its urban civilization emerged in earnest to reach its culmination in the reigns of Ivan III (married, incidentally, to Zoe, or Sophia, Palaeologue, a niece of the last Byzantine emperor), Vasiliy III (during whose rule the doctrine of Moscow as the Third Rome was first enunciated), and Ivan IV (whose own complex and shrewd personality embodied simultaneously that of a Byzantine autocrat and a Renaissance prince). In this connection it should be remembered that the newly introduced western, and specifically Italian, element in the otherwise generally Byzantine (or rather Byzantinesque) character of Moscow's architecture in the second half of the fifteenth century and throughout the sixteenth century, reflected the rapprochement between Byzantium and Rome in the final hour of the East Roman Empire's threatened existence in the days of the Council of Ferrara-Florence, and of the influx of Greek literati and artists to Italy. While the work of Italian architects particularly in the Moscow Kremlin, certainly added a western flavor to the Muscovite urban scene there is by the same token no ideological, but at most some purely artistic, contradiction between its appearance and the more traditional Byzantine style of the medieval Russian city. Yet it should be pointed out that the Italian master builders active in Moscow— Aristotele Fioravanti, Alevisio Novi, Marco Ruffo, Pietro Antonio Solario, and Marco Bono, called "the Frank" (Fryazin, i.e., Italian)—actually did not simply introduce the Renaissance architectural style when constructing or radically reconstructing cathedrals and other representative buildings as well as the walls and towers of the Moscow Kremlin. Rather, they attempted to combine and reconcile as best they could some of their aesthetic notions and innovative techniques with the traditional, Byzantine-type structural forms that had previously dominated the face of the Russian capital. This applies to such magnificent edifices as the Cathedrals of the Assumption (Dormition) and of the Archangel Michael and the Chamber of Facets, but also, for example, to the commanding Bell Tower of Ivan the Great and, with some qualifications, the Cathedral of Basil the Blessed (Vasiliy Blazhenny)—formerly of the Intercession-on-the-Moat (Pokrova, chto na Rvu)—in Red Square, all characteristic of the skyline of Moscow's inner city today.[19]

After the fall of Constantinople and with the promulgation of the doctrine of Moscow as the Third Rome, the Muscovite autocrat laid claim to the dual role—temporal and eternal—once played by the ruler of the captured capital of Orthodox Christianity. The Russian tsar was soon to translate many of the consequences of such aspiration not only into the more and more rigorously formal, mannered standards of conduct prescribed by the ceremonial of court etiquette, but also into many pompous conventions of everyday life among the upper strata of Muscovite society.

The Muscovite brand of Byzantinism, while of relatively late date (fourteenth to sixteenth century and even beyond) was therefore much more deeply rooted than its counterpart in Novgorod. Somewhat different in kind—for it was overripe as it were, if not outright decadent—its impact on the ways of life could rather be felt in Moscow to a degree more comparable to the far-reaching effect on public and social life that Byzantinism had had in Kiev during the early period of Russian history. As a matter of fact, the Byzantine element, in all its multifaceted cultural manifestations and ideologically determined choices, constituted a significant component in the overall Kievan legacy which Moscow and the ruler of the new all-Russian state were eager to enter upon. It is another matter, to be sure, that eleventh- and twelfth-century Byzantinism was a vital and fertile force worth emulating, while its wilted offspring in the post-Byzantine era was largely an ossified mold of civilization without a future.

IV

If the Byzantine and with it the Orthodox stamp can thus be counted, along with some other factors, among the roughly analogous traits that lent a certain degree of uniformity to the three major urban communities of premodern Russia, there were, of course, also some features peculiar only to each of the three cities. These were features that determined their particular, individual character; some of them will be considered briefly in the remainder of this paper.

Above all, it should be remembered that the three cities played somewhat different roles in their capacity as political centers. Kiev was occupied, from its beginnings as a Varangian-Slavic stronghold, by the semilegendary Oleg in 882 and destined to serve as the capital of a federated state of vast expanse. In this context we discount not only any role that a previous settlement at the present site of the city may have played in prehistoric times for early Slavs or their predecessors in the area (including, perhaps, even the Ostrogoths) as suggested by archaeological evidence, but also the unsuccessful attempt of Prince Svyatoslav in the 960s and early 970s to move the capital south, to the more hospitable Balkans. We here further disregard the fact that soon after the death of Vladimir Monomakh (in 1125) the center of political power was increasingly shifted, in effect if not yet in name, from Kiev to the Russian northeast of Vladimir-Suzdal'. Formally, though, it was Kiev that was the unquestioned capital of the Old Russian state from its formation up to the capture and devastation of the city by the Mongols.

By contrast Novgorod, while early bent on achieving a measure of independence from the sway of the grand prince of Kiev, never really aspired to become the capital of a federation that would encompass all the East Slavs. Not even an isolated attempt, undertaken in 1067 by Prince Vseslav of Polotsk, to make Novgorod the political center of a separate north Russian tribal federation under the leadership of the Krivichi, amounted to more than a short-lived, unsuccessful effort. Rather, by first securing at least a certain degree of noninterference on the part of the Kievan sovereign (while formally continuing to acknowledge his suzerainty) and subsequently, after the Tatar onslaught and occupation of most of the Russian lands, keeping the invaders at bay and managing never to let them enter their own city in any greater numbers (though soon accommodating to the khan as their formal overlord entitled to collect taxes), the Novgorodians created what amounted to an oligarchically ruled polity.

This was, however, substantially different from city-states known elsewhere in European history primarily because of the sheer size of the "colonial" territories. Whereas, for example, Pskov, Novgorod's "younger brother"—which had formally seceded from the Novgorod Republic in 1347–1348 but maintained de facto independence since the end of the thirteenth century—can be compared very well, say, to the city-republic of Dubrovnik in terms of the overall extent of the land it controlled, Novgorod, with the widespread areas of the Novgorod Land (Novgorodskaya zemlya), though retaining the administrative structure and form of government of a genuine city-state had, in fact, grown into a full-fledged European state. Consequently, at least at the height of its blossoming and the farthest expansion of its domination, Novgorod too had the function of a capital city with the qualification, however, that all political power over the vast area under its rule was in the hands of the urban citizenry alone or rather, ultimately, of its upper strata controlling the general assembly (*veche*) and its elected officials (cf. below). By this, the prince's powers and competences—

whenever a formal claimant to the title of prince of Novgorod was actually in office, which was not always the case—were so rigorously limited as to carry very little weight indeed.

The situation was, again, different in Moscow. Emerged from relative obscurity and with insignificant beginnings, it was not until the decisive victories of Dmitriy Donskoy over the Tatars and the Novgorodians that Muscovy firmly embarked on annexing Russian lands and thus forming a centralized state. As is well known, this task was brought to a preliminary conclusion by Ivan IV.

If the role of the three cities as power centers differed in some significant ways, so also did their overall look and topographic design. To begin with, only two of them, Kiev and Novgorod, were located on major waterways, the Dnieper (a few miles south of where the Desna enters it) and the Volkhov (just north of its outflow from Lake Il'men'). But whereas Novgorod was spread over both banks of the river, dividing the city into two parts, the Sophia Side and the Market Side, Kiev, including its commercial district Podol, was situated on the right (western) bank of the Dnieper only. Moscow, in its turn, overlooked a relatively minor stream, the Moskva River, a tributary of the Oka, at the place where the brook Neglinnaya empties into it.

Furthermore, only at the heart of Novgorod and of Moscow was there a genuine fortified citadel, the Novgorod Detinets and the Moscow Kremlin, while Kiev merely was centered around an original palisaded town including first, Vladimir's and later also Yaroslav's and Izyaslav's Town. Compare the similar topographic profile, for example, of Buda or Zagreb as opposed to, say, Prague or Cracow, the latter two each with a real castle hill. It should be remarked, though, that the line between the two types of medieval towns, or their acropolises (cf. also Slavic Vyshgorod, Vyshegrad, etc.), is not always easy to draw. Thus, in scholarly literature frequent references are made to the Kiev Detinets, by which term different sections of Upper Kiev (on the Old Kiev Mount) are understood however. Thus, this designation can refer merely to the quarters immediately adjoining the Church of the Tithe within Vladimir's Town, all of that earliest town—which, incidentally, is the most common usage[20]—or even all three of the ancient settlements on the Old Kiev Mount, Vladimir's Town, Izyaslav's Town (also known as the Mikhaylovskiy sector of town, dominated by St. Michael's Monastery), as well as Yaroslav's Town. From this it follows that the Kiev Detinets, no matter how defined, also included a substantial residential district and not only purely administrative and ecclesiastic quarters. Moreover, Kiev also had a Castle Hill of its own, northwest of Vladimir's Town—Zamkovaya gora (now Zamkova hora)—the precise age of whose stone structure has, however, not been established; at any rate, it does not seem that this was the site of the original citadel.

To be sure, in Novgorod, too, the Detinets was apparently not the original core section of the city. It is now mostly assumed, in accordance with Valentin Lavrent'yevich Yanin's hypothesis, that the unified city on the Volkhov emerged as a result of the fusion of three original settlements (or townships): Slavno (later Slavenskiy konets, or Slavno End) on the right (eastern) bank of the river, originally settled by the Slovene (or Il'men' Slavs, somewhat controversial as to their precise place among Slavic tribes; cf. below), and Nerev (later Nerevskiy konets, or Nerev End) to the north, and to the south, Lyudin (Lyudin konets, Lyudin End—or possibly People's or Common Folks' End, though this interpretation may be based on a folk etymology, subsequently also known as Goncharskiy konets, or Potters' End). The last two were situated on the left (western) river bank, with a Finnic tribe of slightly controversial identity as the original settlers of Nerev and a presumably Slavic, or mixed Balto-Slavic, group—usually believed to be the Krivichi—as the earliest inhabitants of Lyudin (though possibly they replaced or absorbed yet another indigenous Finnic tribe in that district; for details, see below). The two additional boroughs—Plotnitskiy konets (Carpenter's End) north of Slavno, on the right bank, and Zagorod'ye (later Zagorodskiy konets, literally Suburban, or more accurately, Trans-Citadel End), filling the void between Nerev and Lyudin west of the Detinets, or *gorod* proper—were added or incorporated only later, the former in 1168 and the latter toward the end of the thirteenth century. It should also be pointed out that at least the three original boroughs of the city were surrounded by ramparts even after they had already formed part of the larger municipality, while a regular wall enclosing all of the city was erected only considerably later. The tract of the Detinets, at first merely an uninhabited protective haven for the population of the region, was in prehistoric and earliest historical times probably the ground for common worship—pagan and, subsequently, Christian—and joint public assemblies of the three as yet separate but obviously cooperating settlements and trading posts. It was not until it was perceived as the heart of the emerging new town (Old Russian *novŭ gorodŭ* > Novgorod; cf., Newton, Naples, Carthage) that the Detinets became its central administrative and ecclesiastic district.

The townspeoples' political and religious lives thus were centered largely on the left bank, or Sophia Side, where the majority of the mighty boyar clans also had their dwellings. To be exact, these were fenced town estates in Nerev and along Prussian Street, separating Lyudin and Zagorod'ye—the imposing Novgorodian *usad'by* on which, however, dependent craftsmen also were allowed to settle. By contrast, most of the commercial deals transacted in the city were made on the opposite Market Side where both the Market Square (Torg, crowded with several churches) and foreign trade stations were situated. Several of the defensible and relatively fireproof stone churches in Market Square incidentally fulfilled an additional, secondary function, related to the commerce centered there, serving as warehouses or meeting places for certain public affairs (cf. below). Just south of Market Square was the architectural complex known as Yaroslav's Court (Yaroslavovo dvorishche), at one time presumably the town residence of Prince Yaroslav and his successors until the assumed permanent banishment, in 1136, of the Novgorod prince (or his lieutenant) to his out-of-town residential quarters at Gorodishche south of the city. Already prior to that, in 1113, Yaroslav's Court had become the site of the Cathedral of St. Nicholas, rivaling St. Sophia in some respects and for some time serving as the court church of the prince. The open space of the court was occasionally also used as the meeting place for the general assembly, otherwise held outside the city's main cathedral in the Detinets. It should be noted further that Yaroslav's Court and possibly as well some adjacent quarters to its north and south (Market Square, Gotland Yard), where the piers for foreign-trade vessels stretched into the river and the Great Bridge spanning the river reached the eastern bank, initially were not legally part of Slavno End but enjoyed extraterritorial status and were included in that borough only later. It was also here that the temporary Varangian garrison (cf. below) was housed. The craftsmen of Novgorod apparently had their quarters all over the city—including, in particular, Lyudin or Potters' End and Carpenters' End, to judge by their names.[21]

In Kiev, the commercial activities of trade and crafts seem (as indicated) to have been concentrated primarily, but not exclusively, in the large district by the river between Vladimir's Town, Castle Hill, and the adjoining elevation known as Shchekovitsa (now Shchekavytsa), on the one hand, and the Dnieper, on the other. This district was called Podol (now Podil) and included the central Market Square. In addition, economic life flourished in a second, western district named Kopyrev (Ukrainian Kopyriv) konets. There is reason to believe that the major trade route leading west began (or ended) here.

In Moscow, the Kremlin, with its oldest portion near the confluence of the Moskva River and the brook Neglinnaya, seems to have been the original core section of the settlement. This therefore suggests the city initially functioned as a military fort rather than a trading post. Developing gradually, the district adjacent to the Kremlin was known at first as Zagorod'ye (cf. also Novgorod) but was subsequently referred to as Posad or more often as Velikiy posad. (Posad is the designation for the commercial quarter or suburb of an Old Russian town; cf. the title *posadnik*, "mayor," in use especially in Novgorod and thus at least originally denoting the appointed, later elected, head of the town's common people.) Subsequently, this district assumed the name *Kitay-gorod* (literally, Chinatown), attested as of 1534 and alluding to the Old Moscow commercial district's far-flung trading operations, rather than implying the presence of any Chinese ethnic group residing in the Russian capital, of course.

Between the Kremlin and the Velikiy posad was the Market Square, opening to the Moskva River and roughly coinciding with a portion of today's Red Square.

Suburban districts were Zaneglimen'ye (across the Neglinnaya), Zayauz'ye (on the other side of the rivulet Yauza, entering the Moskva about a mile east of the Neglinnaya), and Zarech'ye or Zamoskvorech'ye (south of the Moskva River). Of these, Zaneglimen'ye was incorporated relatively early into the large district extending all the way around the Kremlin and the Velikiy posad; it was known as Bely gorod (White Town) because of the whitewashed walls surrounding it (cf. the analogous name of the city subsequently to become the Serbian capital). This semicircular region thus reached the northern bank of the Moskva River at two places, spread out as it was on both sides of the Neglinnaya and, in the east, coming close but not quite up to the Yauza. A broad suburban area in the shape of an outer belt, extending in a half-circle beyond Bely gorod, later was called Zemlyanoy gorod (Earth Town, alluding to the earthwork marking its perimeter).[22]

In addition to the great number of churches characteristic in particular of the cityscape of Novgorod and Moscow, two kinds of elements left their specific imprint not only on the urban scene, but even more so on the environs of the three medieval Russian cities. These were the monasteries and the particular settlements known as *slobody*. Yet, although present in all three metropolitan centers and on their outskirts (with the possible exception of early Kiev as far as any attested *slobody* are concerned), these two characteristic components of urban and suburban life differed considerably from one place to another.

In Kiev there was the large St. Michael's Monastery (mistakenly thought by some scholars to have been originally dedicated to St. Demetrios). This monastic architectural complex with several churches took up most of the relatively small district named after St. Michael (and known also as Izyaslav's Town) in the immediate proximity of Vladimir's and Yaroslav's Towns, overlooking the Dnieper. Other monasteries inside Old Kiev were the St. Theodore Monastery and the Convent of St. Andrew (occasionally also referred to as the Yanchin Convent after its first abbess, Yanka) in Vladimir's Town, St. George's Monastery and St. Irene's Convent next to St. Sophia's Cathedral in Yaroslav's Town, and the St. Simeon Monastery in Kopyrev End. In the city's vicinity there was, above all, the previously mentioned, important Caves Monastery near the river about two and a half miles to the southeast. Another cloister, the Monastery of the Mother of God of Blachernae at Klov, halfway between Yaroslav's Town and the Caves Monastery and two more monasteries, St. Cyril, about two and a half miles northwest of Podol, and St. Michael at Vydubichi, approximately two miles south of the Caves Monastery, also belonged to Old Kiev's greater monastic community.

While some religious establishments were located within the city limits of Novgorod—for example, the Monastery of the Nativity at Desyatin and the Monastery of the Holy Trinity at Klopsk(o), both in Lyudin End, or the Convent of the Nativity of the Mother of God in Mikhalitsa Street in Carpenters' End—most of the major monasteries were in the environs of the Volkhov city. Thus, there were two monasteries just outside the northern ramparts (later, city wall) of Nerev End, namely, the Monastery of the Holy Spirit and the Convent of the Intercession (Pokrovskiy) at Zverinets (therefore also known as Zverinskiy). On the opposite side, only a little farther down the river, was the oldest known monastery of the region, the Monastery of the Mother of God, founded at the beginning of the twelfth century by a wealthy merchant, Anthony (possibly of western origin), whence also referred to as Anthony's (Antoniev) Monastery. Its cathedral, built in 1117–19 and dedicated to the Nativity of the Mother of God, was among the early large stone churches of the Novgorod area. A few miles south of the city, on the left bank of the Volkhov, was the grandiose St. George's (Yur'yev) Monastery, from the early thirteenth century on the residence of the head of Novgorod's entire monastic community, the archimandrite. Its large cathedral, dedicated to the same saint, was constructed in 1119–30, undoubtedly, conceived in more than merely symbolic competition with St. Sophia.

Several other mostly fortified monasteries virtually encircled the Volkhov metropolis, thus providing an "early warning system" against approaching enemy forces. Among them were the Monastery of the Transfiguration of Khutyn, founded by Varlaam, the Moses (Moiseyev) Monastery, and the Monastery of the Resurrection (Voskresenskiy) at Derevyanitsa north and northeast of Novgorod. To the east and southeast of the city were St. Cyril's Monastery, the monasteries at Sitno and Skorovodka, as well as the Monastery of the Savior at Nereditsa (Spasa Preobrazheniya na Nereditse); and south of St. George's Monastery was the skete at Peryn, once the site of a pagan sanctuary; yet another monastery, that of the Dormition (Uspenskiy), founded in 1153 by a cleric, Arkadiy, and thus later known as Arkazhi, was southwest of the city. Two further monastic establishments, the Syrkov and Vyazhishchi Monasteries, were situated at some distance, northwest of Novgorod.[23]

Perhaps the oldest of Moscow's monastic houses was the St. Daniel Monastery, founded in the 1290s by the first Muscovite ruler, Prince Daniil, son of Alexander Nevskiy. It was located several miles south of Old Moscow, on the Moskva River. The title of archimandrite, originally bestowed upon its abbot (*igumen*), was shifted in 1330 by Daniil's son Ivan Kalita to the head of the Monastery of the Savior (Spasskiy na Boru) in the heart of the Kremlin; later that monastery was transferred and became known as the Novospasskiy Monastery. Ivan III moved the monks of this religious establishment once again, this time to the suburban village of Krutitsy, where previously the Monastery of the Dormition (Uspenskiy), founded around 1300, was situated. At the end of the thirteenth century Prince Daniil also established the Theophany (Bogoyavlenskiy) Monastery in the Zagorod'ye (Posad) district, while the nearby (Old) Savior-on-the-Sands (Spasskiy na Peskakh) Monastery, though mentioned in the sources for the first time only in the year 1624 and possibly identical with, or directly adjoining, the Monastery of St. Nicholas the Old, was first attested in 1390 but probably founded at the beginning of the fourteenth century. In the late 1350s and early '60s Metropolitan Aleksey established a number of monasteries. Of these, one—the Monastery of the Miracle at Chonae (Chudov)—was in the heart of the old city between the Kremlin and the Velikiy posad (now within the perimeter of the Kremlin);

it subsequently became the Moscow Court Monastery. Others were outside Old Moscow: the Andronik (Andronikov) Monastery across the Yauza, the Monastery of the Dormition (Uspenskiy) at Simonovo, several miles down the Moskva River (with a minor change of location after 1377), and the Convent of the Conception of the Mother of God, moved to the Chertol'ye district a mile or two southwest of the Kremlin in the second half of the sixteenth century. The St. Peter Monastery at Vysoko, a village on the outskirts of the city (at present at the upper end of Petrovka Street), was founded in the reign of Dmitriy Donskoy and is first mentioned in 1377. The Nativity (Rozhdestvenskiy) Monastery at Staroye Simonovo, just southwest of the Dormition Monastery at Simonovo, dates back to circa 1370, while the Convent of the Ascension (Voznesenskiy), next to the Chudov Monastery, established by Dmitriy's wife, Yevdokiya, and the Nativity-on-the-Moat Monastery (Rozhdestvenskiy na Rvu, also known as the Mother-of-God-on-the-Pipe, Bogoroditskiy na Trube) on the left (eastern) bank of the Neglinnaya, less than a mile north of the Velikiy posad, both date from the 1380s. Also the Monastery of the Intercession-in-the-Gardens (Pokrovskiy v Sadekh), on the left bank of the Yauza, farther down the stream than the Andronik Monastery, is first attested by the year 1392.

Other monasteries, among them that of St. John Chrysostom (Zlatoustovskiy), just northeast of the Posad and first mentioned in 1413, of St. John the Forerunner (Baptist), less than a mile south of the Moskva River across from the Posad (recorded in 1415), of St. Elijah at Vorontsovo (east of the old town, earliest attestation 1476), and of Saints Cosmas and Damian, in the Zayauz'ye district (attested since 1498), in terms of their founding all fall into the period of Moscow's rapid development. Southwest of the city, the St. Savva Monastery was established by the Dobrynskiy boyar clan but became soon the property of the Metropolitan of Moscow. In the sixteenth century further monasteries and nunneries were established, for example, the Monastery of the Exaltation-of-the-Cross (Vozdvizhenskiy) and the Monastery of the Resurrection (Voskresenskiy), both in the Zaneglimen'ye district, the Convent of St. John, east of the Velikiy posad, the Monastery of St. Nicholas the Miracle-Worker, a cou-

ple of miles north of town, on the left bank of the Neglinnaya
and first mentioned by the year 1547 but subsequently burned
down. Of major monasteries founded in the environs of Moscow
during the sixteenth century, the New Virgin's (Novodevichiy)
Convent, two and a half miles southwest of Old Moscow on the
left bank of the Moskva River, deserves particular mention. It
was established in 1524 by Grand Prince Vasiliy III to commemorate the return of Smolensk to Russia and, built as a fortress,
to protect the highway leading toward the city and on to Lithuania from which Smolensk had been recaptured. Yet another
large monastic establishment, the Donskoy Monastery, southwest of the Zarech'ye district, was not founded until 1591. Finally, it should be pointed out here that in addition to these and
numerous other monasteries inside and on the fringes of the
city, several of the large monasteries of Muscovite Russia entertained their own "city yards" (*dvory gorodskiye*), serving as
lodgings as well as various economic purposes inside the capital.
This applies, in particular, to the large and important Trinity-
Sergius Monastery (Troitse-Sergieva lavra) in nearby Zagorsk
(founded by St. Sergius of Radonezh in 1337) and the more
distant Monastery of the Dormition, founded in 1397 by Cyril
of the White Lake (and hence better known as Kirillo-Belozer-
skiy, under his secular name) Koz'ma, who was said to have
been an adviser to Dmitriy Donskoy.[24]

   This is not the place for a detailed discussion of the institution
of the *sloboda* (literally, "freedom") in Old Rus'. Suffice it to say
that this term was used to denote a rural or suburban community
whose members were granted certain economic benefits for specific work and services tied to their assigned district of settlement. The benefits could imply tax relief and/or temporary exemption from certain payments and fees, including the tithe, as
well as freedom from socage. The socioeconomic rationale of the
slobody was, of course, to attract and retain a peasant and trade
population engaged in producing consumer goods and providing various services—including, incidentally, military protection (cf. the Streletskiye slobody)—for the upper strata of
society, notably the wealthy institutions, among them the grand-
princely court and the Church. The Old Russian *sloboda* had its

close counterparts not only in Poland (cf. *wola*) but also else-where in Central Europe, especially Germany.

Typically, such *slobody* would be established in the country-side, where they were usually not placed adjacent to other vil-lages. Increasingly, they were also located on the outskirts of larger towns and cities. These settlements with a special status, attested since the second half of the twelfth century, seem to have become more widespread in Rus' only from the thirteenth century on. Little, if anything, is therefore known about any *slobody* in or around pre-Mongol Kiev. By the same token, a number of them, especially rural ones, are attested in the ter-ritories controlled by Novgorod where, in particular, they ful-filled the function of opening up, cultivating, and managing newly acquired farmlands. Thus, for example, the Novgorodian boyars, when inviting some of the princes of Tver' simulta-neously to assume the mostly only honorific title of prince of Novgorod, stipulated that these rulers not establish any *slobody* of their own in Novgorodian territory since this would have infringed on the rights and property of the local feudal lords. While we know of at least some *slobody* also in the vicinity of Novgorod, the type of suburban *sloboda* took on particular sig-nificance in and around Moscow. Thus, a number of *slobody* on the outskirts of Old Moscow are recorded from the fourteenth and fifteenth century. Among them are Goncharnaya (Potters') and Zayauzskaya slobody in the Zayauz'ye district, Simonova sloboda further down the river, on the same (eastern) bank of the Moskva, Golutvina and Novaya slobody on the southwestern fringe of the Zarech'ye district where, in the fourteenth and early fifteenth century, Prince Yur'yev's sloboda also was located. On the eastern side of the city just across the brook Rachka, was Konyushennaya (Grooms') and Il'inskaya slobody, and a little farther out Romodanovskaya sloboda. Straight north of the city, on the right bank of the Neglinnaya, was the location of Pe-trovskaya sloboda.

Toward the end of the sixteenth century and particularly throughout the seventeenth century a great number more of such *slobody* were added on the outskirts of the capital, among them also the famous (Novo-)Nemetskaya (New German) sloboda, a northeastern suburban district on the river Yauza of foreign, primarily German, craftsmen and traders established by Tsar Aleksey Mikhaylovich in 1652, which had not only a commercial but also a considerable cultural impact on Muscovite life. By the end of the seventeenth century, this well-designed suburb with a strikingly European look, sharply contrasting with the urban scene of Old Moscow, was about one-fifth the size of the Russian capital. The original foreign (German) colony, or *sloboda*, made up mostly of Protestant immigrants, was founded by Ivan IV in the Bely gorod region but was scattered during the Time of Troubles. In 1613, after the accession of the first Romanov, Tsar Mikhail Fedorovich, foreigners again began flocking to the Russian capital. Already earlier, however, there had been fairly large foreign enclaves in the Muscovite urban scene and suburban landscape. Poles (and Lithuanians) had settled in the Panskaya (or Staropanskaya) sloboda; a second Panskaya sloboda was subsequently established in the suburban Zarech'ye district where, in addition, also a Tatar sloboda of the Muslim faith was located. A Greek colony was closely associated with the Theophany (Bogoyavlenskiy) Monastery in the Posad not far from the Kremlin and with the Metropolitan See, especially in the times of Metropolitan Theognostos (Feognost, fl. 1328–53), a native of Constantinople. Later, in the seventeenth century, the Greek community grew large enough to occupy its own sloboda, now located in the Zayauz'ye district.[25]

Italians also settled in Moscow, only a part coming directly from Italy (as the invited architects of the last Rurikid tsars and their dependents and servants residing inside the Kremlin had done), but more often arriving from the Genoese colonies in the Crimea and the other regions on the northern shores of the Black Sea, notably from the formerly Greek commerical center of Sugdeia (Soldaia), in Old Russian Surozh (now Sudak), in the Crimea. Still, these Italians (often referred to as Surozhane) and other Romance people, indiscriminately called "Franks" (Fryazi), never were present in Moscow in sufficient numbers to form their own compact settlement, or *sloboda;* also, they and their descendants usually became Russianized within a generation or two and thus melted into the general population of the capital.

Further West European groups residing in Moscow included Englishmen (who had their own trade station in Kitay-gorod), Scots, Swedes, and others.

V

While the *slobody* had their own administrative structure, headed by a *starosta* (elder), the form of government and day-to-day administration of the three cities themselves also deserve at least a brief comment here. Obviously, a certain parallelism can be found in the forms of self-government of the three Old Russian cities. However, it was only in Novgorod that the pertinent instruments of government and administration took on major and literally far-reaching political significance as they came to extend beyond the mere limits of the city, making their authority felt throughout the vast territories of the north Russian city-state. Moreover, while the scales in the balance of power between the prince and the organs of self-government in Novgorod soon were tipped decisively in favor of the autonomous ruling bodies, and only the precise timing and extent of this process remain in need of further clarification, the opposite was the case both in Kiev and in Moscow where the authority of the grand prince over the city as well as the state of which it was the capital unequivocally prevailed over any initial political influence of the citizenry and its elected representatives.

In Kiev, a general town assembly, or *veche*, seems to have existed and functioned at least from the middle of the eleventh century.[26] It comprised representatives of both the upper classes (*muzhi*) and the common people (*lyudi*) of Kievan society. Though legally conceived as a contracting partner of the sovereign in sharing the power with him, the Kiev *veche* rarely seems to have been able to make its voice heard and assert any decision-making influence. This occurred mostly in times of dynastic crisis only, in particular in 1146–1147, when two lines of the Yaroslavichi, the Monomakhovichi and the Ol'govichi (of Chernigov), were competing for the succession to the Kievan throne. Here, the role of the Kiev *veche* was echoed in the account of the Kiev

Chronicle (forming part of the Hypatian Codex), while the Suzdal' Chronicle (contained in the Laurentian Codex) offers a somewhat different version. After 1147 the Kiev *veche* is mentioned in the annals only twice, once in the entry for 1149–1150 and the second time *sub anno* 1176—in the latter instance, moreover, in a general retrospective fashion without reference to any particular event or action involving the *veche*. Thus, whatever its initial role, the Kiev popular assembly's significance was limited and gradually fading away in the Dnieper metropolis.

By contrast, the Novgorod *veche* was and remained the supreme policy-making body of the north Russian city and its territories. At issue here was, to begin with, the problem of adopting the model of shared power between the representatives of the people and the prince as this division of authority applied in other principalities of Old Rus'. The release of Novgorod from the overlordship of the grand principality of Kiev strengthened the free right of the Novgorodians to select their own prince rather than rendering the city as the patrimony (*otchina/votchina*) of any particular line of the Rurik dynasty. Thus the supremacy of one of the original contracting parties, the *veche*, was achieved. The year 1136, when Prince Vsevolod was expelled from the city and took refuge in Pskov, has until recently been considered a turning point in the precarious balance of power between the prince and the citizenry of Novgorod. Yet research of the last decades (especially by V. L. Yanin) now suggests that the significance of that date was previously exaggerated: the rights of the prince had been severely circumscribed even before that year and, by the same token, his power did not cease altogether after 1136. What remains controversial, however, is the actual composition of the *veche*.

While originally representing all of the city's free men, that is, including the lower strata consisting mostly of craftsmen and street traders (*chernye lyudi*)—thus, everyone save the serfs— the *veche* increasingly, especially from the 1250s, seems to have grown into a policy-making body controlled by, if not entirely made up of members of the prosperous boyar class only. Beginning with the 1290s or thereabout, a special delegated organ of the *veche*, the Council of Lords (*Sovet gospod*), took on the function of the de facto cabinet or rather, perhaps, senate of the city-state. It was presided over by the archbishop (*vladyka*) and wielded most of the executive power. Meeting in the Archbishop's Palace (and after 1433, in the adjoining Chamber of the Facets, constructed by German architects and Russian masons at the behest of Archbishop Yevfimiy II), the council, in addition to the archbishop himself, consisted of the highest town officials (*posadnik* and *tysyatskiy*), present and past, as well as the elders (*starosty*) or, later, mayors (*posadniki*) of the five boroughs (*kontsy*). As the office of the chief lord mayor (*stepenny posadnik*) turned into a collectively held office (*posadnichestvo*) with an ever increasing number of members representing constituent districts but with shorter and shorter terms of office for its incumbent head, some of the executive powers of the Council of Lords seem to have been shifted to that organ in the fourteenth and especially the fifteenth century. When it comes to these various decision-making bodies and executive institutions in Novgorod, a comparison readily suggests itself with the political-administrative structure of other city-states, among them in particular that of Dubrovnik and its three councils, the *Concilium maius, Concilium minus,* and *Concilium rogatorum.* It should be mentioned further here that while the nonaristocratic segment of the affluent Novgorod merchants, the *zhit'i lyudi,* may not have had a say in the affairs of the state, at least in the last two centuries or so of the Novgorod Republic's existence, they still exerted considerable influence by dint of their economic clout. Yet at most only some rudimentary forms of a regular merchant guild organization seem to have existed in the Volkhov city (cf. the loose association of the *zamorskiye kuptsy,* that is, overseas merchants and, particularly, the famed St. John's Hundred, Ivanskoye sto, headquartered at the Church of St. John the Forerunner at Opoki in Market Square). There is no record, by the same token, of any organized craft corporations in medieval Novgorod since the *sotni* (to be briefly discussed below) do not seem to have constituted such an organizational structure.[27]

Very little is known about the existence of any representation of the people in Moscow. Only once is there a mention in the Moscow Chronicle of a *veche,* in connection with the Tatar siege

of 1382. In a similar situation in 1445, when Moscow was ravaged
by fire while preparing for another Tatar attack, no organized
people's assembly is recorded. *Veche* meetings for a similar purpose as the one in 1382 in Moscow, when the city had been
abandoned by its grand prince, are attested, to be sure, for some
other northeastern Russian towns: Yaroslavl' in 1257, several
urban centers of the principality of Vladimir in 1262, Rostov in
1289. It is very doubtful, however, that these *veche* meetings,
particularly those of 1382 in Moscow, can be considered to have
had any legislative functions comparable to those of early Kiev
and, above all, Novgorod. In Moscow the local executive power
was apparently vested in the two highest city offices, that of the
tysyatskiy (chiliarch) and the *namestnik* (lieutenant or viceroy),
both appointed by the grand prince. The first recorded Mocow
tysyatskiy was a boyar of the early fourteenth century. It should
be noted, further, that the Moscow *tysyatskiy's* functions differed
from those of his counterparts in Kiev (where the chiliarch's
primary task was that of commander of the city's militia) or in
Novgorod (where he soon took on additional functions on behalf
of the common people, especially as arbitrator at the Commercial
Court in Market Square).[28]

When it comes to the organization of the three cities' local
administration, it can be assumed that the various districts (in
Novgorod and partly also in Kiev known as *kontsy*) had their
own representation and elected officials. Thus we know of district assemblies and elders, later also mayors, of these various
districts. In the Novgorod Land the five city boroughs had their
rural, indeed "colonial," counterparts in the five administrative
territories known as *pyatiny* (fifths) extending across the Novgorod possessions (*volosti*) and encompassing all land under the
city's rule. At least in Novgorod an even smaller unit than the
borough or district, namely the street quarter (*ulitsa*) with its
own elder (*ulichanskiy starosta*) was an integral part of the administrative network.

However, in addition to the topographically defined divisions,
there was in all three cities yet another organizational form of
administration which included most of the urban population.
This was the *sotnya* system, based originally, as indicated by its

name (*sotnya* or rather just *sto*, meaning a hundred), on the number of able-bodied men levied for military service. (Here, the established term *sotnya*, instead of the more accurate plain *sto*, is retained for reasons of traditional usage.) There were, when complete, ten such *sotni* each headed by a *sotskiy* or *sotnik* (in English, approximately, centurion), thus supplying a militia of one thousand men, headed by the *tysyatskiy*, or chiliarch. In Novgorod, these urban *sotni* were further supplemented by an ultimately equal number of rural *sotni*, marshaling an additional defense force. The Novgorod armies of much greater numbers battling the Suzdalians or Muscovites had to draw, obviously, on conscripts and mercenaries from both the city itself and the territories (including the several satellite towns, or *prigorody*) under its control. The *sotnya* system, in addition to serving its original function as a base for the military and, no less important, for tax levy, also provided some sort of general organizational network for the three cities' common people. Though the whole scope of functions of the *sotnya* system in these metropolitan centers has not yet been fully elucidated, it seems reasonable to assume that the system served as the administrative framework for activities in more than one sphere of public and professional life pertinent to the majority of the urban population. Thus it is conceivable, or even probable, for example, that public works such as the construction and maintenance of the cities' sewerage system, were the responsibility of the *sotni*.[29]

VI

This then brings us to the ethnic composition of the three cities discussed, with one major shared feature found in all three of them and other, dissimilar characteristics setting them apart. Obviously, the main trait that Kiev, Novgorod, and Moscow had in common in terms of their ethnic makeup is that they all had a predominantly East Slavic population. But there the overall agreement ends, and we can now ask ourselves in what way the three cities differed ethnically among themselves.

As for Kiev, its reemergence as a Ukranian rather than a gen-

erally East Slavic city in the sixteenth century lies outside the
scope of this paper, as does the impact on the city population
of Lithuanian and subsequent Polish rule from the mid-fourteenth century onward. We are also not concerned here with
any possible pre-Slavic presence at or near the location of Kiev
that may have preceded the settlement of the Slavs and, more
specifically, with the arrival of the tribe of the Polyane, particularly since the earliest Slavic presence in the region is now, on
the basis of archaeological finds, usually thought to have occurred as early as the late fifth to sixth century. We are merely
considering early medieval Kiev in the space of time from the
tenth through the early thirteenth century.

If it is obvious, therefore, that the bulk of Kiev's populace
was made up of East Slavs, primarily members of the tribe of
the Polyane, is there reason to assume that other ethnic elements
were permanently residing in Old Kiev as well? The answer to
this question is undoubtedly in the affirmative. For, first of all,
there are grounds to believe that prior to the full Slavicization
of the Varangian element—predominantly Old Swedish—that
constituted most of the retinue and court entourage of the earliest Kievan princes and grand princes down to at least Yaroslav
the Wise (whose spouse was a Swedish princess and who on
several occasions brought in Varangian mercenary troops to
Rus'), there was a sizable Scandinavian or semi-Scandinavian
component in the uppermost layer of Kievan society. A few
hybrid Scando-Slavic lexical items testify, as a matter of fact, to
the existence of such a mixed population group. Cf., for example,
Old Norse *taparyx*, "ax, hatchet," and *pólútasvarf*, "palace plun-
dering" or possibly, according to A. Stender-Petersen, "round,
tour associated with tax-collecting," both tautological, self-trans-
lating items recorded in Snorri's Saga of Harold Hardruler, forming part of the Icelandic writer's history of Norwegian kings
known as *Heimskringla*.[30] Grand Prince Yaroslav is further known
to have had a number of Greek bookmen and scribes settle in
Kiev (cf. above, especially the quotation from the Primary Chronicle for the year 1037), not to speak of the Byzantine architects
and artists invited to assist in the construction and decoration
of the cathedrals and palaces of the grand-princely capital. Some

Greeks, like Varangians, may well have resided in Kiev even prior to Yaroslav's reign, at least since the times of Princess Olga and, in particular, since Vladimir's conversion in 988. The previously mentioned circumstance that most of the Kievan metropolitans were in fact Greek also suggests some further Greek presence among the highest clergy of the Old Russian capital.

Moreover, we know of Jewish merchants and moneylenders living in Kiev in the eleventh and twelfth century. Saint Theodosius (Feodosiy), the first abbot of the Caves Monastery (eleventh century), is recorded as having had religious disputes with local Jews residing in Kiev. And it is further known from the account of the final sections of the Primary Chronicle (as contained in the Hypatian Codex only) that the events in 1113, immediately preceding Vladimir Monomakh's accession to the Kievan throne, also included the ransacking of the city's Jewish quarter, or ghetto. Reference is also made to the Jewish quarter in the Kievan Chronicle (included in the Hypatian Codex) in the entry for the year 1124, when a fire ravaged the (Old Kiev) "Mount" and all its monasteries, as well as "the Jews" (where the ethnonym, as is often the case in early Slavic sources, stands for the toponym, i.e., the Jewish quarter), just eleven years after the first recorded pogrom in Russian history. It should further be noted that a Jewish Gate is mentioned in the same chronicle in the entries for 1146 and 1151. This gate apparently connected Yaroslav's Town with Kopyrev End, the city's western commercial district; it later became known as the L'vov Gate. However, this can only have been sometime after the second half of the thirteenth century as the city of L'vov (L'viv) is mentioned in the sources for the first time in 1256; probably, though, the name L'vov Gate did not become common before the fifteenth century. The main entrance to the city, known as Golden Gate (echoing the designation of Constantinople's famous entrance) at the southern end of the western city wall and opening to the south from Yaroslav's Town, is mentioned in the Primary Chronicle as having been constructed in 1037, during the reign of Yaroslav. There is reason to believe that both the Jewish Gate and the Polish Gate (Lyadskiye vorota), the latter pointing to the southeast, were erected at about the same time as the Golden

Gate. It also can be assumed that the designation Jewish Gate somehow is associated with the location of the residential quarter of the Kievan Jews. This district therefore was probably in the western section of Yaroslav's Town, inside the Jewish Gate or, though less likely, in the southern part of Kopyrev End, just outside the gate.

What this approximate localization of the Jewish quarter can shed hardly any light on, however, is where the Jews who first settled in Kiev might have come from. Some scholars believe that they arrived from the West, either along the western trade route (with its western terminus in Regensburg; cf. above) or from Poland, for the first time perhaps in connection with the brief seizure of the Dnieper city by Polish troops under King Boleslas the Brave (Bolesław Chrobry) in the 1010s, when the Polish sovereign was an ally of his son-in-law, Yaroslav's rival and adversary, Svyatopolk. Yet against this latter hypothesis speaks the fact that any massive influx of Jews to Poland took place only considerably later, during the reign of the last Piast, King Casimir the Great, in the fourteenth century. It appears somewhat more likely, therefore, that the first Jewish settlers came to Kiev from another region, namely, from the shores of the Black and Caspian Seas and from areas perhaps even farther away, presumably from the realm of the Khazars who had partly been converted to Judaism, and possibly also from some of the flourishing trade centers in the Crimea (cf. also the story about the visiting Khazar Jews at the court of Vladimir prior to his conversion to Christianity reported in the Primary Chronicle). The early—eleventh-century—translations into Slavic of such writings as Josephus Flavius' *History of the Jewish War* and *Josippon* (a collection of medieval tales based on Josephus' *Antiquities*) as well as certain stipulations regarding Jews (and Muslims!) in the legal document known as the Church Charter (*Ustav*) of Yaroslav the Wise that date from the late twelfth or early thirteenth century, further bear out the hypothesis of the existence of a Jewish community in early medieval Kiev.[31]

In addition to the non-Slavic groups just mentioned, other groups, among them Khazars, Cumans (Polovtsians), and perhaps some further Altaic tribes of the nearby steppe region, may well have settled, if only in small numbers and for a limited time, in or around the Dnieper metropolis.

Whereas there is little doubt, in principle at least, as to the ethnic identity of the East Slav population of Kiev, things are less clear when it comes to the Slavic inhabitants of Novgorod. The North Russian city was located in the territory of the Slovenes (or Il'men' Slavs) who also seem to have settled one of the original townships—Slavno—subsequently forming a constituent part of the city. While until not long ago it was rather generally thought that this Slavic tribe belonged, along with others, to the East Slavic branch—in fact forming its northernmost portion—recent scholarship has advanced the hypothesis that the Slovenes originated not from among the East Slavs, but that they were rather immigrants from West Slavic territory, to be precise, from the Pomeranian southern shores of the Baltic Sea. Thus the earliest Slavic population of Novgorod would also have been of original West Slavic stock—specifically, Lekhitic (i.e., Polish-Pomeranian-Polabian). This view does not seem to be sufficiently well corroborated, however, and I submit (as I have done elsewhere in some detail) that any sharp ethnolinguistic division into East and West Slavic for these prehistoric and early historical times—say, the seventh to ninth centuries—is, indeed, not realistic. For in that period these subgroups within the Slavic ethnic entity as a whole were only just emerging and crystallizing. Still, I would maintain that the Slovenes probably had migrated overland while in the process of developing their ethnolinguistic identity for some appreciable period of time during the epoch of the Slavic expansion from the more narrowly defined area of the original Slavic homeland, wherever its precise location, prior to reaching the shores of Lake Il'men' and the banks of the Volkhov.

By the same token, there can be little doubt that Novgorod's Slavic population was to some extent increased by the subsequent arrival of Slavs coming, as a matter of fact, from the southern shores of the Baltic in the twelfth century, particularly following the forceful Christianization of the Baltic Slavs at the hands of the Saxons in 1128. In fact, the legendary tradition of a Pomeranian provenance of the Novgorod Slavs, enhanced also by early commercial contacts between the Volkhov city and the West Slavic towns on the south Baltic seaboard—the fabulously opulent, allegedly submerged Vineta, shrouded in mystery, among them—may well have its roots in this wave of relatively newly arrived immigrants.

As for Lyudin End, while it is possible that its Slavic inhabitants had assimilated and largely replaced a previous Finnic settlement there (cf. the Veps self-designation *l'üdin-/lüüdin'*), it is usually assumed that it was the East Slavic tribe of the Krivichi, otherwise occupying a region at some distance from Novgorod and forming a far-flung half-circle around it as it were, that first settled in that district. For this ethnic group, too, a West Slavic origin has been suggested by some scholars (notably by V. L. Yanin). In my view, such a provenience can, again, not really be proven but can at most be considered a qualified possibility. It is conceivable, incidentally, that the Krivichi were not originally a purely Slavic tribe but that they included some unassimiliated or only partly assimilated Baltic elements as well.

As for a genuinely Baltic component in Novgorod's ethnic makeup, it is quite possible that some Prussians, dislodged by the Teutonic Knights from their homeland between the Lower Vistula and the Neman' (Nemunas) River, arrived in the Novgorod region in the thirteenth and fourteenth century; some may even have settled in Novgorod in the late twelfth century. Not only does the name of one of Novgorod's main thoroughfares, Prussian Street (Prusskaya ulitsa), cutting through the southwestern section of town, possibly echo such an ethnic origin (though it is equally possible that the street name merely indicated the general direction in which the highway pointed), but it has also been proposed, albeit on rather weak grounds, that an older designation of Lyudin was in fact *Prus(s)y* (literally, "Prussians," with the ethnonym used in lieu of the toponym, as in the case of the Kiev "Jews"). The same name, or derivations of it, also occurs in a widespread area outside the original territory of the Baltic settlement, particularly clustered in a region between Lakes Peipus (Pskov) and Il'men'. These may well be vestiges of an earlier settlement of Prussians outside Old Prussia proper.

In addition to its earliest, controversial Slavic and, perhaps, Baltic population, medieval Novgorod is believed to have had a Finnic component at the dawn of its recorded history and for several centuries thereafter. Other than the presumed first Finnic settlers of Lyudin just mentioned, Nerev was undoubtedly a Finnic settlement at first. Its precise ethnic identity—whether Cheremis-Mari (Meryan), Norova-Estonian, Norova-Veps, or Norova-Vote—remains a matter of some controversy, however. Also, there are some other potential reminders of a Finnic population in and around Novgorod (e.g., Chudintseva ulitsa, or Chud' Street, in Zagorod'ye, though it is, again, not clear whether this may not be merely an indication of the street's general direction pointing toward Estonia; *Votskaya pyatina*, or Vote Fifth, the name of the northern administrative territory extending from the city limits deep into and beyond Carelia). In this context it must also be remembered that Novgorod as a whole lies in an area once populated by various Finnic tribes prior to their conquest by the advancing Slavs.

Moreover, there was yet another group which early became a more or less permanent fixture in the urban scene and which was in evidence there in much greater force than in Kiev. I am referring to the Northmen, or Varangians. Whereas the earliest tradesmen, arriving from Gotland, off the east coast of central Sweden, the Åland archipelago, and the Swedish settlements on both sides of the Gulf of Finland, probably usually did not stay for more than half a year at a time, the distinction between what was known as summer travelers and winter travelers applied equally to voyages to the east as to travelers going west in the Viking age. Novgorod, from the time of Vladimir's rule in the city (before c. 980), and certainly in the early eleventh century (1014–1036), served as a Scandinavian stronghold, Yaroslav having established a permanent Varangian garrison in the city. The episode of 1015, recorded with some distortion both in the Primary Chronicle and the First Novgorodian Chronicle, was highly embarrassing for Yaroslav. Idle Varangian mercenaries, housed in the *Poromon' dvor* on the eastern bank of the Volkhov (the Russian name possibly being an echo of Old Norse *farmannagarðr*, i.e., yard of foreign traders, though other etymologies have also been proposed), turned to rioting and raping, only to be massacred by the angered Novgorodians (an act in turn avenged by Yaroslav). Obviously, though, the annalists' earlier statements—based, to be sure, on the rather generally accepted identification of the name Rus' with the Northmen (cf. the Swedish region of Roslagen northeast of Stockholm)—to the effect that "the Novgorodian people are of Varangian stock to this very day" (First Novgorodian Chronicle, *sub anno* 854), or that "the present inhabitants of Novgorod are descended from the Varangian race, but aforetime they were Slavs (Slovene)" (Primary Chronicle, *sub anno*, 863), are gross exaggerations at best.

With time, the Scandinavian element of the North Russian urban community was assimilated and the Varangian mercenaries withdrawn, soon to be replaced by another Germanic—now Low German—component. For not only was the Gotland Yard, the first foreign trade station in Novgorod, perhaps from the outset manned either entirely or to a substantial degree by German merchants from Visby, but the German Hansa towns, especially Lübeck, also played an increasingly dominant role in Novgorod's western trade (fully substituting for the previous West Slavic trade partners). To this were subsequently added Low German merchants from the Livonian-Estonian Hansa towns of Riga, Dorpat, and Reval. It should be remembered, however, that the German Yard (Peterhof) which had absorbed and virtually replaced the commercial activities of the Gotland Yard, remained an extraterritorial, foreign establishent in the city, ruled by its own charter (*schra*) and never truly or fully integrated into the pulsating street life of the North Russian metropolis. Yet people like Bartholomäus Ghotan and Nicolaus Bülow from Lübeck could play significant roles in the intellectual activities of the learned circle of humanists around Archbishop Gennadiy in the 1490s, after Novgorod's loss of independence (in 1478) and at a time when the Hansa establishment was closed down at the behest of Grand Prince Ivan III (in 1494); cf. n. 5 above.

In this connection it is also worth mentioning that Gennadiy, the former archimandrite of the Moscow Court Monastery of the Miracle (Chudov), was a prelate comparable in political shrewdness and cultural involvement to his great predecessor as Novgorod *vladyka*, Archbishop Yevfimiy II (fl. 1429–1458). It should be remembered further that Lord Novgorod the Great, as its proud citizens liked to refer to it, had never, not even at the peak of the Hansa's dealings there, turned into a full-fledged Hanseatic town of the kind that certain other only partly German cities, such as Riga, Reval, Visby, or Bergen, had become. Curiously, western intellectual influence in Novgorod reached its all-time zenith shortly after the incorporation of the city and its territories into the Muscovite state, exactly at the time of the activity of the Gennadiy circle. Thus, for example, it was in 1491 that the Dominican monk Benjamin (Venyamin), a refugee from the Turkish threat to and partial occupation of his Croatian homeland, joined this illustrious, erudite group. He was more instrumental than the just-mentioned two Lübeckers in producing the first full Russian Church Slavic Bible translation (known as the Gennadiy Bible of 1499).[32]

Despite Novgorod's character of being a major commercial hub of Europe there is virtually no evidence of any Jewish life in that city. Speculating on the reasons for this, possible explanations could be that they found the northern climate uncongenial or that trade was from the outset firmly in the hand of others, mostly foreigners. It is thus rather doubtful that the early Novgorod bishop Luka (fl. 1036–1060/1061), called Zhidyata (which means either "little Jew," i.e., a Jewish convert, or perhaps a person with Jewish connections) actually was of Jewish descent, notwithstanding the fact that his straightforward sermons are strikingly free from anti-Jewish statements or allusions otherwise not uncommon in the homiletic and hagiographic literature of medieval Rus'. More likely, the name is merely a distortion of the common Novgorod given name Zhidislav. Likewise, there is little to suggest that the late medieval heresy of the so-called Judaizers (*zhidovstvuyushchiye*), a label attached to them by their Orthodox detractors, which flourished and was soon brutally suppressed in Novgorod and Moscow in the late fifteenth and early sixteenth century, was more than a religious movement entirely within the bounds of Christianity, even

though its adherents displayed a particular interest in the Old
Testament and probably relied on native Jewish informants settled in Lithuanian Ruthenia when preparing East Slavic translations in part directly from the Hebrew; at any rate, they certainly were not ethnic or observant Jews. It also seems that the
Pskovian monk Skharia, whom Archbishop Gennadiy claimed
to be a *strigol'nik*, was deliberately mistaken for a Jew. (The
strigol'niki were an earlier, related heterodox movement, widespread in Pskov and Novgorod, but with a different social appeal.) Skharia had allegedly come to Novgorod from Kiev in the
entourage of the visiting Lithuanian Prince Mikhail Olel'kovich
and was, moreover, confused with the feudal lord Zechariah
Skara of the Genoese clan of the Ghisolfis, ruling at one time
over the Taman' region as a vassal of the Genoese-controlled
town of Kaffa in the Crimea; in Moscow he was erroneously
held to be a Jew.[33]

Turning, finally, to Moscow, it is much more difficult to comment meaningfully on the ethnic composition of its population.
Clearly, the vast majority of its inhabitants was Russian, without
much doubt as to the specific origin of the East Slavic urban
masses. Yet it is certain that in addition to its Russian populace,
Moscow also was the home of several other national groups.
Thus it can be assumed that the long period of Moscow's vas-
salage under the Mongols of the Golden Horde resulted in the
influx of some Tatar elements to the northeast Russian metropolis, some of which settled in the previously mentioned Tatar
(Muslim) *sloboda* across the river. It is difficult, if not impossible,
however, to establish exactly when a Tatar ethnic admixture
beyond the *sloboda* may have occurred. It is conceivable, for
example, that it took place essentially only after the conquest of
the Khanates of Kazan' (in 1552) and Astrakhan' (in 1556) by
Ivan IV, at the very end of the period considered here. While
Italian architects visited and temporarily resided in the Moscow
Kremlin during the reigns of Ivan III, Vasiliy III, and Ivan IV,
their presence in the Russian capital did not result in any large-
scale influx of Italians (or other West Europeans) to Moscow. As
indicated above, the more permanent settling of West European,
mostly German, craftsmen in great numbers on the east-north-

eastern outskirts of the city, in the specially established (Novo-) Nemetskaya sloboda (New German Suburb), occurred only in the seventeenth century.

Other foreign elements (Greeks, Poles, Englishmen, etc.) were mentioned above in connection with the expansion of the foreign *slobody*. By and large, though, it can be said that Novgorod's and to some extent even Kiev's multinational makeup at the time of their greatest flourishing was not really matched by a comparable phenomenon in the more purely Russian capital in the period of its rise to prominence as an urban center and its subsequent attainment of metropolitan status. Essentially xenophobic, Moscow was eager, at least in the early period, to assimilate (Russianize) the foreign component of its population. Some historians maintain that this fact alone, or rather its corollary implying Moscow's isolation from the rest of the world, has in a crucial way affected the course of Russian and, indeed, world history.

VII

If, in conclusion, the specifics of the three major cities of Russia in the premodern era were to be symbolized by some of their most salient, though by no means exclusive, accomplishments in the visual arts, it would perhaps be appropriate to recall the bright Byzantine mosaics of the Kiev Sophia, unique for the capital of the earliest East Slavic state; the magnificent frescoes of some of the churches in and around Novgorod, reminiscent at once of the art of Giotto and El Greco, but more closely related to some of the masterful decorations of medieval monastic churches in Serbia; and finally, the marvelous icons of the cathedrals of Moscow. While the extant Kiev mosaics were created by anonymous masters,[34] in Novgorod particularly the well-preserved, imposing murals of Feofan Grek in the Church of the Savior of the Transfiguration in Il'ina Street—including the serene Christ Pantocrator, the ascetic stylites and saints, and the playful cherubim—come readily to mind.[35] On the same high level of artistry are also the anonymous wall paintings of the suburban Churches of the Assumption at Volotovo Pole and of the Savior of the Transfiguration at Nereditsa (both tragically and forever lost in the destruction of World War II), as well as those of the Church of the Savior at Kovalevo (now skillfully being restored thanks to the selfless efforts of A. P. Grekov and his team).[36] The most beautiful icons in Moscow were painted by such eminent artists as Feofan Grek, Andrey Rublev, Daniil Cherny, and Dionisiy, all having produced works which in their harmonious composition and refined palette easily rank with the great masterpieces of a Perugino or a Raphael.[37]

Equally characteristic but less easily visualized in their former appearance are such monuments of ecclesiastic architecture as the lavishly decorated Church of the Tithe in Vladimir's Town, the original Cathedral of St. Sophia in Yaroslav's Town, and the Cathedral of the Archangel Michael in Izyaslav's Town, all three once rising above the bounds of Old Kiev. Similar considerations apply to the virtually intact, austere, yet majestic St. Sophia of Lord Novgorod the Great, with its magnificent Romanesque bronze doors by German and Russian foundry masters. This also holds true for the other stately churches of the city, those of St. Nicholas in Yaroslav's Court and of St. George in the outlying monastery, the two cathedrals representing ultimately unfulfilled aspirations of the prince and the local monastic community. And the same could be said about the splendid Byzantino-Italian Cathedrals of the Assumption, of the Annunciation, and of the Archangel Michael in the Moscow Kremlin, not to speak of the more intricate, indeed overburdened Cathedral of St. Basil the Blessed in Red Square. They all, and many more, bear—or bore—witness to both Byzantine uniformity and regionally conditioned multiplicity that were the hallmark of the social and cultural fabric of early East Slavic urban society as conspicuously manifested in its three great centers.

NOTES

1. Cf. L. N. Langer, *The Medieval Russian Town*, pp. 12–13 and p. 32, with references to work by Tikhomirov, Rappoport, and Sakharov.

2. See M. Yu. Braychevskiy, *Kogda i kak voznik Kiev*, pp. 29–65; Ya. Ye. Borovs'ky, *Pokhozhdennya Kyeva*, pp. 22–25; S. R. Kiliyevich, *Detinets Kiyeva*, pp. 27–35; idem, *Na gore*, pp. 6–15; D. Ya. Telegin, *Tam, gde vyros Kiyev*, pp. 91–92; B. A. Kolchin & V. L. Yanin, eds., *Arkheologicheskoye izucheniye Novgoroda* and *Novgorodskiy sbornik;* H. Birnbaum, *Lord Novgorod*, pp. 13–39; idem, "On the Prehistory."

3. Cf. e.g., W. Knackstedt, *Moskau*, pp. 18–20.

4. Cf. H. Pirenne, *Medieval Cities*, esp. pp. 144–151; M. Weber, *The City*, esp. pp. 80–81; F. Rörig, *The Medieval Town*, esp. pp. 15–29 and 181–187.

5. Cf. H. Birnbaum, *Lord Novgorod*, pp. 49–52; idem, "Die Hanse"; see further also N. A. Kazakova, *Russko-livonskiye;* A. L. Khoroshkevich, *Torgovlya Velikogo Novgoroda;* and Ye A. Rybina, *Inozemnye dvory.*

6. Cf. esp., W. Knackstedt, *Moskau*, pp. 12–32; A. P. Smirnov, ed., *Arkheologicheskiye pamyatniki;* A. G. Veksler, *Moskva v Moskve*, pp. 22–91.

7. See, e.g., L. N. Langer, *The Medieval Russian Town*, p. 11.

8. See C. Goehrke, "Einwohnerzahl," esp. pp. 29–30, 44–47, 49–50, 52.

9. Cf., e.g., H. Birnbaum, *Lord Novgorod*, pp. 71–79 and pp. 125–126 (nn. 14–21, with further references particularly to work by Goehrke and Yanin).

10. See A. Poppe, *Saint Sophia in Kiev;* cf. further esp. O. Powstenko, *The Cathedral of Saint Sophia.*

11. See A. Poppe, *Saint Sophia in Kiev*, pp. 41–42 and 59–60 (n. 94).

12. Cf. D. S. Likhachev, "Byzantine Influence," esp. pp. 18–20.

13. Cf. H. Birnbaum, "Yaroslav's Varangian Connection."

14. Cf. J. Meyendorff, *Byzantium and Russia*, pp. 85–91; G. Podskalsky, *Theologische Literatur*, pp. 282–301.

15. Cf. H. Birnbaum, *Lord Novgorod*, pp. 42–43 and 118–119 (n. 9). Generally on the Church in Novgorod, its chief representatives and administrative organs (including those of the monastic community), see A. S. Khoroshev, *Tserkov'*, focusing on the political, economic, and social aspects.

16. Cf. D. Obolensky, *Byzantine Commonwealth;* regarding Ladoga as the northernmost outpost of Byzantine art, see p. 354.

17. On Old Novgorod's ecclesiastic and monastic architecture, see esp. V. Gippenreyter et al., *Novgorod;* M. K. Karger, *Novgorod;* H. Birnbaum, "Ancient Russian Art"; I. I. Kushnir, *Arkhitektura;* V. N. Lazarev, *Iskusstvo Novgoroda* pp. 52–62, 98–105, 132–137.

18. Cf. H. Birnbaum, "On the Significance."

19. On Old Moscow architecture, see, esp., M. A. Il'in et al., *Moskva. Pamyatniki arkhitektury;* A. Voyce, *Moscow and the Roots.* Specifically on the Cathedral of the Assumption and the Chamber of Facets, cf. further, T. V. Tolstaya, *Uspenskiy Sobor* and A. Nasibova, *The Faceted Chamber.*

20. Cf. S. R. Kiliyevich, *Detinets Kiyeva.*

21. Cf., e.g., H. Birnbaum, *Lord Novgorod,* pp. 37–39, 55–68, 115–116 (nn. 48–52), and pp. 123–124 (nn. 1–12), with further references.

22. Cf., esp., W. Knackstedt, *Moskau,* pp. 33–65.

23. On the monasteries of Old Novgorod and the Novgorod Land see, in particular, K. Onasch, *Gross-Nowgorod,* pp. 102–130 and A. S. Khoroshev, *Tserkov',* passim.

24. On the early Moscow monasteries, see, esp., W. Knackstedt, *Moskau,* pp. 266–268, and passim. Generally on the monasteries of fourteenth- and fifteenth-century Rus', see particularly I. U. Budovnits, *Monastyri na Rusi.*

25. On the Moscow *slobody,* see esp., M. Snegirev, *Moskovskiye slobody,* and W. Knackstedt, *Moskau,* pp. 151–163.

26. Generally on the institution of the *veche,* see esp., K. Zernack, *Die burgstädtischen Volksversammlungen,* and idem, "Fürst und Volk."

27. On the institution of the *posadnichestvo* of Novgorod and Pskov, as well as its relationship to other political bodies in the two North Russian city-states, see now, in particular, L. N. Langer, "The Posadnichestvo." Langer correctly points out, among other things, that the notion is in fact mistaken that there was a greater degree of democracy in independent Pskov than in Novgorod with its increasingly oligarchic form of government.

28. On the Novgorod *veche,* its delegated body (Council of Lords), and elected officials, see, e.g., H. Birnbaum, *Lord Novgorod,* pp. 82–100 and 128–130 (nn. 1–23), with further references, esp. to work by V. L. Yanin. On possible guilds in Novgorod, cf. ibid., pp. 76–77 and 126 (n. 19, with additional literature), and 170 (Addendum). On a possible *veche* institution in Moscow, see W. Knackstedt, *Moskau,* pp. 163–168.

29. On the *sotnya* system in Novgorod, see particularly H. Birnbaum, *Lord Novgorod,* pp. 56, 68–70, 123, (n. 3). On the *sotni* of Old Moscow, cf. esp. W. Knackstedt, *Moskau,* pp. 147–150 and 154–163.

30. Cf. A. Stender-Petersen, "Le mot varègue."

31. On a Jewish presence in early medieval Kiev, see esp. H. Birnbaum, "On Some Evidence."

32. On Gennadiy's personality and his humanist circle, cf., e.g., K. Onasch, *Gross-Nowgorod*, pp. 160–170; on Ghotan and Bülow, see, esp., D. B. Miller, "The Lübeckers."

33. On the ethnic makeup of Old Novgorod and attendant controversies, see the comprehensive treatment in H. Birnbaum, *Lord Novgorod*, pp. 27–37 and 107–115 (nn. 23–47); idem, "On the Prehistory," pp. 154–164.

34. On the Kiev mosaics, see in particular V. N. Lazarev, *Drevnerusskiye mozaiki*, pp. 21–33 and plates 8–63, 131–149; N. B. Sal'ko, *Zhivopis' Drevney Rusi*, pp. 8–16, 76–79, 298–300, and plates 1–27 and 56–79. Cf., further, the reference to A. Poppe in n. 11, above.

35. Cf. esp. G. I. Vzdornov, *Freski Feofana Greka.*

36. On the Volotovo frescoes, see esp. M. Alpatov, *Freski*. Regarding the Kovalevo frescoes and their restoration, cf. H. Birnbaum, "Ancient Russian Art." For a tentative identification of the chief artist to be credited with the Nereditsa fresco cycle, one Olisey Petrovich Grechin, see B. A. Kolchin, A. S. Khoroshev, and V. L. Yanin, *Usad'ba.*

37. From the extensive literature on these artists, cf. in particular V. N. Lazarev, *Theophanes*; M. Alpatov, *Feofan Grek*; idem, *Andrey Rublev*; G. I. Vzdornov, *Troitsa*; V. Bulkin, *Dionysius.*

BIBLIOGRAPHY

(In addition to works directly referred to in the footnotes this list includes titles consulted but not specifically mentioned in the text of this essay.)

Alpatov, M. *Andrey Rublev. Okolo 1370–1430* [Andrey Rublev. C. 1370–1430]. Moscow: Izobrazitel'noye iskusstvo, 1972.

_____. *Feofan Grek/Theophanes the Greek*. Moscow: Izobrazitel'noye iskusstvo, 1979.

_____. *Freski tserkvi Uspeniya na Volotovom Pole/Frescoes of the Church of the Assumption at Volotovo Polye*. Moscow: Iskusstvo, 1977.

Ananich, B. V., V. F. Andreyev, et al., eds. *Novgorodskiy istoricheskiy sbornik* [Novgorod historical collection], 1(11). Leningrad: Nauka, 1982.

Artemenko, I. I. et al., eds. *Drevniy i srednevekovy Kiyev* [Old and Medieval Kiev] *Istoriya Kiyeva* [History of Kiev], Vol. I. Yu. Yu. Kondufor et al., eds. Kiev: Naukova dumka, 1982.

Aseyev, Yu. S. *Arkhitektura drevnego Kiyeva* [The Architecture of Old Kiev]. Kiev: Budivel'nyk, 1982.

Bakhrushin, S. V., A. A. Novosel'skiy et al., eds. *Istoriya Moskvy*, Vol. I: *Period feodalizma XII–XVII vv. (Istoriya Moskvy v šesti tomakh)* [A History of Moscow, Vol. I: The Period of Feudalism, 12th–17th cc. (A History of Moscow in Six Volumes)]. With Appendix: Prilozheniye k pervomu tomu: Plany [Appendix to Volume I: Plans]. Moscow: Izd-vo Akademii Nauk SSSR, 1952.

Beloded, V. D., V. A. Buslinskiy, A. K. Bychko et al. *Filosofskaya mysl' v Kiyeve (istoriko-filosofskiy ocherk)* [Philosophical Thought in Kiev (A Historical-Philosophical Sketch)]. Kiev: Naukova dumka, 1982. Specifically Chapter I: "Filosofskaya mysl' v drevnem Kiyeve" [Philosophical Thought in Old Kiev]. By I. V. Ivan'o, A. K. Bychko, V. S. Gorskiy.

Birnbaum, H. "Ancient Russian Art—Its Destruction and Restoration." In *Essays in Early Slavic Civilization*, pp. 298–304.

———. "Die Hanse in Novgorod." In *Korrespondenzen, Festschrift für Dietrich Gerhardt*, A. Engel-Braunschmidt and A. Schmücker, eds. *Osteuropastudien der Hochschulen des Landes Hessen, 2: Marbuger Abhandlungen zur Geschichte und Kultur Osteuropas*, 14. Giessen: W. Schmitz, 1977, 28–35. Reprinted in *Essays in Early Slavic Civilization*, pp. 207–214.

———. *Essays in Early Slavic Civilization/Studien zur Frühkultur der Slaven.* Munich: Wilhelm Fink, 1981.

———. *Lord Novgorod the Great. Essays in the History and Culture of a Medieval City-State* (UCLA Slavic Studies, 2). Columbus, Ohio: Slavica, 1982.

———. "Lord Novgorod the Great and Its Place in Medieval Culture." *Viator*, 8. Berkeley, Los Angeles, London: 1977, 215–254. Reprinted in *Essays in Early Slavic Civilization*, pp. 167–206.

———. "On Some Evidence of Jewish Life and Anti-Jewish Sentiments in Medieval Russia." *Viator*, 4. Berkeley, Los Angeles, London: 1973, 225–255. With an Addendum and a slightly abridged title reprinted in *Essays in Early Slavic Civilization*, pp. 215–245.

———. "On the Prehistory and Early History of Old Novgorod." In *Essays in Early Slavic Civilization*, pp. 145–166. Abridged version of essay number one in *Lord Novgorod the Great*, pp. 13–19. See above.

cance of the Second South Slavic Influence for
ussian Literary Language." *International Journal
Poetics*, 21. The Hague: 1975, 23–50. Reprinted
Civilization, pp. 305–332.
⌐ of Medieval Russia: Chronology, Regional
⌐ᵢal Links, and External Influences." *Viator*, 15.
⌐ᵧ, Los Angeles, London: 1984, 181–222.

———. "Yaroslav's Varangian Connection." *Scando-Slavica* 24. Copen-
hagen, 1978, 5–25. Reprinted in *Essays in Early Slavic Civilization*, pp.
128–144.

Borovskiy, Ya. Ye. *Mifologicheskiy mir drevnikh kiyevlyan* [The Mytholog-
ical World of the Ancient Kievans]. Kiev: Naukova dumka, 1982.

———. [Borovs'ky, Ya. Ye.] *Pokhozhdennya Kyeva. Istoriohrafichny narys*
[The Origins of Kiev. A Historiographic Sketch]. Kiev: Naukova
dumka, 1981.

Braychevskiy, M. Yu. *Kogda i kak voznik Kiyev* [When and How Kiev
Originated]. Kiev: Naukova dumka, 1964.

Budovnits, I. U. *Monastyri na Rusi i bor'ba s nimi krest'yan v XIV–XV
vekakh* (po "zhitiyam svyatykh") [The Monasteries in Rus' and the
Peasants' Struggle Against Them (According to the 'Lives of Saints')].
Moscow: Nauka, 1966.

Bulkin, V. *Dionysius*. Leningrad: Aurora, 1982.

Dejevsky, N. "The Churches of Novgorod: The Overall Pattern." In
Medieval Russian Culture. H. Birnbaum and M. S. Flier, eds. *California
Slavic Studies* 12. Berkeley, Los Angeles, London: University of Cal-
ifornia Press, 1984, 206–223.

Faensen, H., V. Ivanov. *Early Russian Architecture*. Photographs by K.
G. Beyer. New York: G. P. Putnam's Sons, 1975. East German edition:
Berlin: Union Verlag, 1972.

Froyanov, I. Ya. "K voprosu o gorodakh-gosudarstvakh v Kiyevskoy
Rusi (istoriograficheskiye i istoriko-sotsiologicheskiye predposylki)
[On the Problem of the City-States in Kievan Rus' (Historiographic
and Socio-Historical Conditions)]." In *Gorod i gosudarstvo v drevnikh
obshchestvakh. Mezhvuzovskiy sbornik* [The City and the State in Ancient Societies. A Collection for College Use]. Leningrad: Izdatel'stvo
Leningradskogo universiteta, 1982, pp. 126–140.

Gippenreyter, V., E. Gordiyenko, S. Yamshchikov. *Novgorod*. Moscow:
Planeta, 1976.

Goehrke, C. "Einwohnerzahl und Bevölkerungsdichte altrussischer
Städte—methodische Möglichkeiten und vorläufige Ergebnisse." In

Forschungen zur osteuropäischen Geschichte (Osteuropa-Institi
Freien Universität Berlin. *Historische Veröffentlichungen*, M. L
and W. Philipp, eds., 18). Wiesbaden (Berlin): Otto Harrassu
1973, 25–53.

———. "Die Sozialstruktur des mittelalterlichen Novgorod." In *Unter
suchungen zur gesellschaftlichen Struktur der mittelalterlichen Städte in
Europa*, pp. 357–378. *Reichenau-Vorträge, 1963–1964 (Vorträge und Forschungen*, T. Mayer, ed., 11). Constance and Stuttgart: Jan Thorbecke,
1966, pp. 357–378.

Golobutskiy, V. A., O. K. Kasimenko et al., eds. *Istoriya Kiyeva* [A
History of Kiev], Vol. I. Kiev: Izd-vo Akademii Nauk Ukrainskoy
SSR, 1963.

Gupalo, K. N. *Podol v drevnem Kiyeve* [Podol in Old Kiev]. Kiev: Naukova
dumka, 1982.

Hellman, M., ed. *Handbuch der Geschichte Russlands*. Band 1: *Bis 1613.
Von der Kiever Reichsbildung bis zum Moskauer Zartum*. Stuttgart: Anton
Hiersemann, 1981–.

Il'in, M. A. *Iskusstvo Moskovskoy Rusi epokhi Feofana Greka i Andreya Rub-
leva. Problemy, gipotezy, issledovaniya* [The Art of Muscovite Rus' at
the Time of Theophanes the Greek and Andrey Rublev: Problems,
Hypotheses, Studies]. Moscow: Iskusstvo, 1976.

Il'in, M., A. Aleksandrov, E. Steynert. *Moskva. Pamyatniki arkhitektury
XIV–XVII vekov/Moscow. Monuments of Architecture of the 14th–17th
Centuries*. Moscow: Iskusstvo, 1973.

Karger, M. K. *Drevniy Kiyev. Ocherki po istorii material'noy kul'tury drev-
nerusskogo goroda* [Old Kiev. Essays on the Material Culture of an Old
Russian City]. Vols. I and II. (Vol. II subtitled *Pamyatniki kiyevskogo
zodchestva X–XIII vv.* [Monuments of Kievan Architecture, 10th–13th
Century]). Moscow and Leningrad: Izd-vo Akademii Nauk SSSR,
1958/61.

———. *Novgorod. Architectural Monuments 11th–17th Centuries*. Leningrad: Aurora, 1975.

Kazakova, N. A. *Russko-livonskiye i russko-ganzeyskiye otnosheniya. Konets
XIV–nachalo XVI v.* [Russian-Livonian and Russian-Hanseatic Rela-
tions. From the End of the 14th to the Beginning of the 16th Century].
Leningrad: Nauka, 1975.

Khoroshev, A. S. *Tserkov' v sotsial'no-politicheskoy sisteme Novgorodskoy
feodal'noy respubliki* [The Church in the Sociopolitical System of the
Novgorod Feudal Republic]. Moscow: Izd-vo Moskovskogo universiteta, 1980.

Khoroshkevich, A. L. *Torgovlya Velikogo Novgoroda s Pribaltikoy i Zapadnoy Yevropoy v XIV–XV vekakh* [Novgorod the Great's Trade with the Baltic Region and Western Europe in the 14th and 15th Centuries]. Moscow: Izd-vo Akademii Nauk SSSR, 1963.

Khromov, S. S., A. A. Preobrazhenskiy, et al., eds. *Istoriya Moskvy. Kratkiy ocherk* [A History of Moscow: A Concise Sketch]. Chaps. 1–3, pp. 7–59. 3d ed. Moscow: Nauka, 1978.

Kiliyevich, S. R. *Detinets Kiyeva IX-pervoy poloviny XIII vekov. Po materialam arkheologicheskikh issledovaniy* [The Kiev Citadel, the 9th through the First Half of the 13th Century. On the Basis of Archaeological Data]. Kiev: Naukova dumka, 1982.

———. *Na gore Starokievskoy* [*On the Old Kiev Mount*]. Kiev: Naukova dumka, 1982.

Knackstedt, W. *Moskau. Studien zur Geschichte einer mittelalterlichen Stadt. Quellen und Studien zur Geschichte des östlichen Europa,* M. Hellmann, ed., 8. Wiesbaden: Franz Steiner, 1975.

Kolchin, B. A., A. S. Khoroshev, V. L. Yanin. *Usad'ba novgorodskogo khudozhnika XII v.* [*The Mansion of a Novgorod Artist of the 12th Century*]. Moscow: Nauka, 1981.

Kolchin, B. A., V. L. Yanin, eds. *Arkheologicheskoye izucheniye Novgoroda* [*The Archeological Study of Novgorod*]. Moscow: Nauka, 1978.

———. *Novgorodskiy sbornik. 50 let raskopok Novgoroda* [A Novgorod Collection: 50 Years of Excavation in Novgorod]. Moscow: Nauka, 1982.

Kowalenko, W., G. Labuda, et al. *Słownik starożytności słowiańskich.* [Encyclopedia of Slavic Antiquities]. *Wrocław: Ossolineum.* Specifically, the entries "Kijów" by W. Molè, II; 2 (1965), pp. 406–413; "Moskwa" by H. Łowmiański, III: 1 (1967), pp. 303–305; and "Nowogród Wielki" by W. Molè, III: 2 (1968), pp. 421–432.

Kudryts'ky, A. V. et al., eds. *Kyiv. Istorychny ohlyad.* Karty, ilyustratsiyi, dokumenty [Kiev: A Historical Survey (Maps, Illustrations, Documents)]. Kiev: Holovna redaktsiya Ukrayins'koyi radyans'koyi entsyklopediyi, 1982.

Kushnir, I. I. *Arkhitektura Novgoroda* [Novgorod's Architecture]. Leningrad: Lenizdat, 1982. Chap. 1, pp. 3–30.

Langer, L. N. "The Medieval Russian Town." In *The City in Russian History,* M. F. Hamm, ed. Lexington: The University Press of Kentucky, 1976, pp. 11–33.

———. "The *Posadnichestvo* of Pskov: Some Aspects of Urban Administration in Medieval Russia." *Slavic Review,* 43. Stanford, 1984, 46–62.

Lazarev, V. N. *Drevnerusskiye mozaiki i freski XI–XV vv.* [Old Russian Mosaics and Frescoes, 11th–15th Centuries]. Moscow: Iskusstvo, 1973.

———. *Iskusstvo Novgoroda* [*The Art of Novgorod.*] Moscow and Leningrad: Iskusstvo, 1947.

Leuschner, J. *Novgorod. Untersuchungen zu einigen Fragen seiner Verfassungs- und Bevölkerungsstruktur. Giessener Abhandlungen zur Agrar- und Wirtschaftsforschung des europäischen Ostens*, 107. Berlin: Duncker & Humblot, 1980.

Likhachev, D. S. "The Type and Character of the Byzantine Influence on Old Russian Literature." *Oxford Slavonic Papers*, 13. Oxford, 1967, 14–32.

Meyendorff, J. *Byzantium and the Rise of Russia: A Study of Byzantino-Russian Relations in the Fourteenth Century.* Cambridge: Cambridge University Press, 1981.

Miller, D. B. "The Lübeckers Bartholomäus Ghotan and Nicolaus Bülow in Novgorod and Moscow and the Problem of Early Western Influences on Russian Culture." *Viator*, 9. Berkeley, Los Angeles, London: 1978, 395–412.

Nasibova, A. *The Faceted Chamber in the Moscow Kremlin.* Leningrad: Aurora, 1978.

Novgorod. *Novgorod: Art Treasures and Architectural Monuments. 11th–18th Centuries. Architecture, Frescoes, Archeological Artefacts, Minor Arts, Icons, Illuminated MSS.* Leningrad: Aurora, 1984.

Obolensky, D. *The Byzantine Commonwealth. Eastern Europe, 500–1453.* New York: Praeger, 1971.

Onasch, K. *Gross-Novgorod. Aufstieg und Niedergang einer russischen Stadtrepublik.* Vienna and Munich: Anton Schroll & Co., 1969. (East German ed., Leipzig: Koehler & Amelang, 1969).

Pamyatniki. *Pamyatniki arkhitektury Moskvy. Kreml', Kitay-gorod, Tsentral'nye ploshchadi* [Moscow's Architectural Monuments. The Kremlin, Chinatown, the Central Squares]. Moscow: Iskusstvo, 1982. Volume I of a 4-volume set, *Pamyatniki arkhitektury Moskvy* [Moscow's Architectural Monuments], M. V. Posokhin et al., eds.; Volumes II–IV, in preparation, will include: *Bely gorod, Zemlyanoy gorod; Moskva v granitsakh XVIII veka; Okrestnosti staroy Moskvy* [The White Town, the Earthwork Town; Moscow in its 18th-Century Limits; The Environs of Old Moscow].

Pirenne, H. *Medieval Cities.* Trans. F. Halsey. New York: Doubleday & Anchor, 1956.

Podskalsky, G. *Christentum und theologische Literatur in der Kiever Rus'* *(988–1237)*. Munich: C. H. Beck, 1982.

Popov, G. V. *Zhivopis' i miniatyura Moskvy serediny XV-nachala XVI veka* [Painting and Book Illumination in Moscow from the Mid-15th to the Early 16th Century]. Moscow: Iskusstvo, 1975.

Popova, O. S. *Iskusstvo Novgoroda i Moskvy pervoy poloviny chetyrnadtsatogo veka. Yego svyazi s Vizantiyey* [The Art of Novgorod and Moscow During the First Half of the Fourteenth Century. Its Ties with Byzantium]. Moscow: Iskusstvo, 1980.

Poppe, A. "The Building of the Church of St. Sophia in Kiev," *Journal of Medieval History*, 7. Amsterdam, 1981, 15–66. Reprinted in *The Rise of Christian Russia*, chap. IV. London: Variorum Reprints, 1982.

Powstenko, O. "The Cathedral of St. Sophia in Kiev," *Annals of the Ukrainian Academy of Arts and Sciences in the U.S.*, 3/4. New York, 1954, 9–162.

Rabinovich, M. G. *O drevney Moskve. Ocherki material'noy kul'tury i byta gorozhan v XI–XVI vv.* [On Old Moscow. Essays on the Material Culture and Life Style of the Townspeople in the 11th–16th Centuries]. Moscow: Nauka, 1964.

————. *Ocherki etnografii russkogo feodal'nogo goroda. Gorozhane, ikh obshchestvenny i domashniy byt* [Essays on the Ethnography of the Russian Feudal Town. The Townspeople, Their Public and Private Life Style]. Moscow: Nauka, 1978.

Riasanovsky, N. V. *A History of Russia*. 4th ed. New York: Oxford University Press, 1984.

Rörig, F. *The Medieval Town*. Berkeley and Los Angeles: University of California Press, 1967.

Rybakov, B. A. *Kiyevskaya Rus' i russkiye knyazhestva XII–XIII vv.* [Kievan Rus' and the Russian Principalities of the 12th–13th Centuries]. Moscow: Nauka, 1982.

————. *Remeslo Drevney Rusi* [The Crafts of Old Rus']. Moscow: Izd-vo Akademii Nauk SSSR, 1948.

Rybina, Ye. A. *Inozemnye dvory v Novgorode, XII–XVII vv.* [Foreign Yards in Novgorod, 12th–17th Centuries]. Moscow: Izd-vo Moskovskogo universiteta, 1986.

Sagaydak, M. A. *Velikiy gorod Yaroslava* [The Great Town of Yaroslav]. Kiev: Naukova dumka, 1982.

Sal'ko, N. B. *Zhivopis' Drevney Rusi XI–nachala XIII veka. Mozaiki, Freski, Ikony/Early Russian Painting: 11th to Early 13th Century. Mosaics, Frescoes, Icons*. Leningrad: Khudozhnik RSFSR, 1982.

Salmina, M. A. *Povesti o nachale Moskvy. Issledovaniya i podgotovka tekstov* [Tales about Moscow's Beginnings. Studies and Text Editions]. Moscow and Leningrad: Nauka, 1964.

Smirnov, A. P., ed. *Arkheologicheskiye pamyatniki Moskvy i Podmoskov'ya. Sbornik statey (Trudy Muzeya istorii i rekonstruktsii Moskvy, 5)* [Moscow's and the Moscow Area's Archeological Monuments. A Collection of Essays (Studies of the Museum of the History and Reconstruction of Moscow, 5)]. Moscow: Gos. izd-vo kul'turno-prosvetitel'noy literatury, 1954.

Smirnova, E. S. *Zhivopis' Velikogo Novgoroda. Seredina XIII-nachalo XV veka* [Painting in Novgorod the Great: From the Mid-13th to the Early 15th Century]. Moscow: Nauka, 1976.

Smirnova, E. S., V. K. Laurina, E. A. Gordiyenko. *Zhivopis' Velikogo Novgoroda. XV vek* [Painting in Novgorod the Great: The 15th Century]. Moscow: Nauka, 1982.

Snegirev, M. *Moskovskiye slobody* [The Moscow Slobodas]. Moscow: Moskovskiy rabochiy, 1947.

Stender-Petersen, A. "Le mot varègue polutasvarf." In *Varangica.* Aarhus [no publisher]: 1953, pp. 151–164.

Sytin, P. *Proshloye Moskvy v nazvaniyakh ulits* [Moscow's Past in the Names of Its Streets]. 2d ed. Moscow: Moskovskiy rabochiy, 1948.

Telegin, D. Ya. *Tam, gde vyros Kiyev* [Where Kiev Emerged]. Kiev: Naukova dumka, 1982.

Tikhomirov, M. N. *Drevnerusskiye goroda* [Old Russian Towns]. 2d ed. Moscow: Gos. izd-vo politicheskoy literatury, 1956.

_____. *Srednevekovaya Moskva v XIV–XV vekakh* [Medieval Moscow in the 14th–15th Centuries]. Moscow: Izd-vo Moskovskogo universiteta, 1957.

Tolochko, P. P. *Drevniy Kiyev* [Old Kiev]. Kiev: Naukova dumka, 1983.

_____. *Istorychna topohrafiya starodavn'oho Kyeva* [The Historical Topography of Old Kiev]. Kiev: Naukova dumka, 1970.

_____. *Kiyev i Kiyevskaya zemlya v epokhu feodal'noy razdroblennosti XII–XIII vekov* [Kiev and the Kievan Land During the Period of Feudal Disintegration in the 12th–13th Centuries]. Kiev: Naukova dumka, 1980.

_____. "Veche i narodnye dvizheniya v Kiyeve [The Town Assembly and Popular Movements in Kiev]." *Issledovaniya po istorii slavyanskikh i balkanskikh narodov. Epokha srednevekov'ya. Kiyevskaya Rus' i yeye slavyanskiye sosedi* [Studies in the History of the Slavic and Balkan Peoples. The Medieval Period. Kievan Rus' and Its Slavic Neighbors]. V. D. Korolyuk et al., eds. Moscow: Nauka, 1972, pp. 125–143.

NOVGOROD in the 15th century [after Orlov and Goehrke]

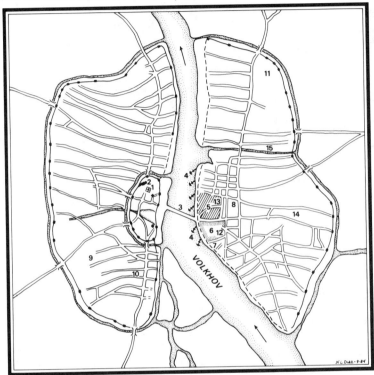

LEGEND

1 St. Sophia Cathedral
2 Archbishop's Palace (with Palace of Facets)
3 Great Bridge
4 Piers
5 Market Square (Torg)
6 Yaroslav's Court (Yaroslavovo dvorishche)
7 Gotland Yard (Gotskiy dvor)
8 Presumed site of St. Peter's or German (Hansa) Yard
   (Nemetskiy dvor, St. Petershof)

9 Monastery of the Nativity of the Mother of God
10 Monastery of the Holy Trinity
11 Convent of the Nativity of the Mother of God
12 St. Nicholas Cathedral in Yaroslav's Court
13 Church of St. John the Baptist in Opoki
14 Church of Our Savior in Il'ina (Elijah) Street
15 Church of St. Theodore Stratilates on the Brook

MOSCOW in the 15th-16th centuries

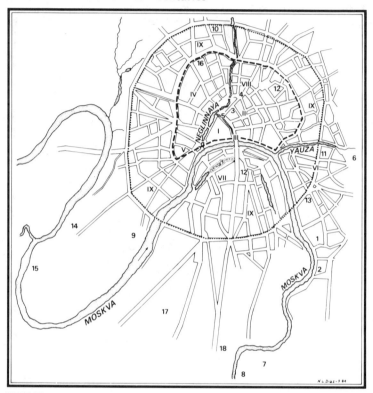

LEGEND

DISTRICTS:
  I   Kremlin
 II   Velikiy posad (or Zagorod'ye, subsequently Kitay-gorod)
III   Market Square (Torg)
 IV   Zaneglimen'ye
  V   Chertol'ye
 VI   Zayauz'ye
VII   Zarech'ye (Zamoskvorech'ye)
VIII Bely gorod
 IX   Zemlyanoy gorod

PRINCIPAL MONASTERIES (CONVENTS)
 1. New Savior's (Novospasskiy) Monastery
 2. Dormition (Uspenskiy) Monastery at Krutitsy
 3. Theophany (Bogoyavlenskiy) Monastery
 4. St. Nicholas-the-Old Monastery
 5. Miracle (Chudov) Monastery
 6. Andronik Monastery
 7. Dormition (Uspenskiy) Monastery at Simonovo
 8. Nativity (Rozhdestvenskiy) Monastery
       at Staroye Simonovo
 9. Conception-of-the-Mother-of-God Convent
10. St. Peter Monastery at Vysoko
11. Intercession-in-the-Gardens Monastery
12. St. John Chrysostom (Zlatousty) Monastery
13. Sts. Cosmas-and-Damian Monastery
14. St. Savva Monastery
15. New Virgin's Convent
16. Resurrection (Voskresensky) Monastery
17. Donskoy Monastery
18. St. Daniel Monastery

2

The Urban Development of Medieval Poland, with Particular Reference to Kraków

Paul W. Knoll

INTRODUCTION

Urban development in Poland began in prehistoric times. At the moment in the tenth century when Poland emerged into the consciousness of written records of West, there were already important settlements in each of the regions which came to constitute the medieval Polish state. Gniezno and Poznań in Great Poland, Płock in Mazovia, Gdańsk and Szczecin in both Pomorzes, Wrocław and Opole in Silesia, and Kraków in Little Poland, among others, all had urban roots that lie hidden in the shadows of the distant and unwritten past. Even the accumulating data of archaeological investigations have been unable to provide us with a complete picture.

Our records are, however, sufficiently full and unambiguous to enable us to speak directly to two frequently disputed historiographical issues connected with the history of towns in Europe and in Poland. On the one hand, it is clear that Polish towns were not the continuation of earlier Roman settlements. The lands of the Oder, Warta, and Vistula river basins had effectively lain outside the limits of Roman influence; and whatever urban development may be observed, they cannot have come as the result of Roman foundations. On the other hand, the fact that these settlements may be traced to Polish prehistory means that a colonial theory of the origins of Polish towns can no longer be defended. Such a theory argues that there was no urban life in Poland before the legal establishment of towns under German law in the period of location (late twelfth century and after).

Though the foregoing indicates what may be disregarded from the debates in previous scholarship, it leaves open other more difficult issues. Three in particular are of importance: (1) the question of the nature of urban development in Poland prior to the period of location; (2) the question of whether town development in Germany had any influence upon the development of settlements in the Polish lands; and (3) the question of what the process of location was and its impact in Poland upon both preexisting towns and the social and urban milieu of new towns founded in this period.

The present study bears upon each of these issues. It does so by focusing, first, upon a description of the general structure and pattern of urban development in Poland, though without trying to be exhaustive or dealing in detail with the individual histories of all Polish cities. I draw here upon the very substantial scholarly literature that has appeared in recent decades. Second, this study concentrates upon the development of a particular Polish city, Kraków, because it emerged early as a royal capital and became the most important commercial center in the kingdom. In addition, other Polish cities followed divergent paths of political allegiance in the generations following the middle of the twelfth century. As a result, by the end of the middle ages, Kraków was not only the most important city of Poland, it was the *urbs celeberrima regni Poloniae* ("the most famous city in the Kingdom of Poland") in the eyes of such foreigners as Aeneas Sylvius de Piccolomini (1405–1464), later Pope Pius II.[1] Within the structure of this study, therefore, one can see more clearly the form of one variant of the urban society of Eastern Europe in premodern times.

THE GENERAL PICTURE

The Early Period

The beginnings of town formation in Poland may be observed in the early centuries of the first millenium A.D. For example, the geographer Ptolemy makes reference in about 150 to καλισία, that is, the city of Kalisz[2]. There are additional archaeological data which confirm other such settlements.[3] During the first, second and third centuries the Slavonic populations of the Oder, Warta, and Vistula river valleys enjoyed a relatively high degree of material prosperity and their culture reflected a relatively sophisticated political and social organization. While there were yet no towns in the formal sense of units having an existence in law, there were certainly organized centers where the population was involved in occupations other than agriculture. During the next three centuries, however, conditions deteriorated. These people both participated in, and were subject to, the great *Völkerwanderungen* whose impact upon the Roman Empire was so great. From time-to-time these Slavonic peoples were subject, in greater or lesser degree, to such powerful groups as the Huns and the Avars. It was only after about 700 that this proto-Polish population could begin its recovery from this time of troubles.[4] By the end of the prehistoric period, evidence of town nuclei, and what Witold Hensel has called "incipient towns,"[5] is widespread. Many of these settlements were of the types known as fortress towns, that is, they were found either within fortified centers or in close conjunction to them. Among the most striking examples of these are Gniezno, Poznań, Wrocław, and, as we shall see, Kraków. Their rise to predominance is closely connected to important transformations in the larger society.

Previously, society had been organized around the tribal assembly of freemen (the *wiec*) presided over by the elders. This group discussed all problems, decided issues by consensus, and chose military leaders who were given limited authority to rule. In the eighth, ninth, and tenth centuries, however, the military leaders (Latin *dux,* Polish *knędz,* later *książę*) sought to transform their tenuous political control into something more substantial, attempting to secure wealth and office for themselves and their heirs. They and their families established fortified settlements (Latin, *castrum;* Polish, *gród*) which enabled them to extend their authority over the surrounding territory. They were supported in this by military retainers similar to the Germanic war band (Latin, *comitatus;* Polish, *drużyna*). Gradually, through generations of protracted conflict, the earlier, more democratic tribal structure was replaced by one dominated by a new political aristocracy which was able to reduce some of the peasantry to servitude and to obtain tribute from the remainder of the free population. These new leaders were thus able to exercise administrative control over their regions and, throughout what would eventually become Polish lands, there emerged a number of small-scale territorial organizations.[6] At least five were located in Silesia in the upper Oder valley; the most important center among several in central Poland was that of the duke of the Polanie tribe (Polanes) in the vicinity of Gniezno; and in the south, the Wiślanie (Vislanes) controlled the region around Kraków. These tribal states under the leadership of the dukes waged war on one another in an effort to consolidate even larger areas of control. Eventually the whole region was dominated by the state of the Polanes, whose ruling family took its name from that of its legendary founder, the wheelwright Piast.[7]

Although there are individual variations among the fortress towns that emerged in these centuries, their general similarity is clear.[8] They were established, sometimes upon the sites of previous settlements, in places of both military and commercial importance. The fortifications associated with them provided a guarantee of safety from external threats and internal opposition. In most such towns there was a stronghold that served as the residence of the duke or his agents who came eventually to be known as castellans. It was to this place that tribute, income, and taxes were sent from the jurisdiction claimed by the duke.

It was here also that the military retainers and other officials of the duke resided.

But this ducal stronghold was only one of three components of the fortress town. In addition there was a fortified *suburbium,* either separate from or, more commonly, adjoining, where those who served the ruler's needs lived. Servants, craftsmen, and the rank and file of knights were settled here. It was they who provided the necessary support structure that enabled the political, economic, and social controls of the duke or his lieutenants to function. Of particular importance in this group were those who fashioned weapons and served military needs directly.

The third part of the town was the suburban market settlement.[9] Perhaps there had been a market site in the place before the fortification or, more commonly, open settlements that formed early around these complexes. They were inhabited by craftsmen, by those who did some farming and stockbreeding, and by merchants. This market met the needs of both travelers and residents of the town. Sometimes market settlements were themselves important enough to be enclosed within walls; in other instances, particularly in the earlier stages of development, they remained open. Ducal authority extended over these communities—which were in no sense autonomous at this point—and his officials watched over affairs here closely. The population of this area eventually came to include members of the local nobility, and as the market settlement evolved it became a second focus for the life of the community.

Many of the features outlined above had taken shape by the middle of the tenth century. But this same period also saw the beginnings of the Christianization of Poland, and this had an important impact upon both the physical form of these early towns and the society resident therein.

The first historical ruler of Poland was Duke Mieszko I (d. 992), who had successfully united the lands of central Poland under his control.[10] (Perhaps he had only maintained successfully a position that had been achieved by one or more of his predecessors, but this cannot be determined with surety from written sources). Eventually he also subdued the region around Kraków. By virtue of having come into contact in 963 with Saxon rule to the west, Mieszko was confronted with the problem of how best to cope with the expanded world of Poland's experience. He soon recognized the cultural and political importance of conversion to Christianity,[11] and in 966 he and his court retinue were baptized.[12] In subsequent generations, with some setbacks, the conversion of Polish society was accomplished, first under a missionary bishop, then—after the Congress of Gniezno in 1000—led by an organized Polish church with Gniezno as its archiepiscopal head.[13]

The importance of this for Poland's development cannot be overemphasized. Poland was henceforth a participant, and not an outsider, in the emerging civilization of the Latin and Germanic west. Poland was able to assimilate the cultural achievements of the more advanced centers with which it now came in contact and, having done so, was able to produce its own distinctive culture. Moreover, the Christianization of Poland provided religious sanction for the authority of the duke (and, later, for Polish kings). By providing organizational models and trained officials, the church helped Polish rulers extend their authority and consolidate their internal administration. Finally, the process of conversion and the organization of the church in Poland was implemented in such a way as to ensure Mieszko's and Poland's religious independence from its neighbors. This in turn helped ensure political independence, for Mieszko and his successors were able to avoid the dependency which elsewhere accompanied the extension of the imperial German church with its proprietary character.[14]

With Christianization came church buildings. Because the duke had been the instrument by which the new religion was introduced, it is not surprising that the very earliest churches are often associated with the ruler's seat in the fortress town.[15] If there was not a chapel within the residence itself (and there frequently was), a church building was certain to be found in the fortified *suburbium*. Where the town was the seat of an archbishop (Gniezno) or a bishop (Wrocław, Kraków, Płock, etc.), such a structure might be very impressive and dominate all the other physical features of the town except, possibly, the residence of the ruler. The close association of the fortified seat of political authority with the religious at this time is reflected in the etymological derivation of the Polish word *kościół* (church) from the Latin *castellum* or *castrum* (fortress).[16] Even in fortified towns which were merely the seat of the duke's castellans and which were not episcopal sees, there were church buildings within the fortified areas. In addition, in the suburban market settlements there came to be an even greater incidence of church buildings. Parish and collegiate churches, religious foundations for both men and women, and, eventually, the houses and churches of the great urban religious orders of the thirteenth century all proliferated. Even though the city population was predominantly defined by its political or economic function, a significant minority segment of society was composed of either secular or regular clergy.

Before moving to a discussion of the social and economic transformations of the High Middle Ages, particularly in the thirteenth century, it is appropriate to summarize briefly the foregoing discussion. Archaeological evidence and written sources provide us with an understanding of the earliest urban settlements of historical Poland. We see a pattern of (1) stronghold, (2) fortified service *suburbium*, (3) suburban market settlement, and (4) ecclesiastical foundations. The emergence of this pattern over time is particularly well reflected in the reconstructions by Kazimierz Żurowski of the three-stage development of the fortress town of Gniezno from the end of the eighth century to the twelfth century.[17] This general pattern characterized Polish towns of this type for more than two centuries. By the end of the twelfth century there were probably about 250 urban centers in Poland, the most important of which were the fortress towns described here. None of these settlements had a very substantial population—a town of over 3,000 was a large settlement—and few of them extended over more than five hectares.[18]

The Period of Location

Many early scholars who dealt with the history of Polish towns
were unwilling to grant that such a phenomenon had existed
prior to the thirteenth century.[19] They used a narrow legal approach which defined a town as an autonomous legal and political unit having a charter of foundation. The most they would
have concluded about the kinds of phenomena we have discussed to this point was that the areas were urban settlements
or handicraft and trade centers. Scholarship in the twentieth
century, however, derived in part from the influence of such
figures as Max Weber, has adopted a very different approach.[20]
As Witold Hensel has written:

> We can now attempt to outline a general theory of the genesis of
> towns in . . . [Poland] . . ., accepting a definition of the town as a
> settlement possessing the following characteristics: (a) a separate
> economy, (b) consistent space structure, (c) a defensive character,
> (d) a distinct position in the country's military and administrative
> system, and (e) an existence in law. . . . A basic distinguishing factor
> for the earlier years must be the economic status of a center, and we
> might then accept, as the essential feature of urbanism, the nature
> of the employment of the population, for this distinguished the town
> from neighbouring rural communities.[21]

Some of these criteria were fulfilled in the centuries prior to
the era known as "the period of location." Especially since the
seminal research and publication of Kazimierz Tymieniecki and
Karol Buczek there has emerged a picture of early Polish town
history very different from the legalistic approach noted above.
A brief description of the contributions of these scholars is appropriate here before we move to a consideration of the transformations that occurred in the "period of location."
     Tymieniecki was the first to apply economic criteria to a def-
inition of Polish town development, thus breaking with the traditions of legal historians.[22] (The constitutional and legal approach to all questions of Polish history, not only social and
economic issues, has always been particularly strong in Polish
historiography.)[23] Central to his conclusions was the thesis that

the town as an economic center was capable of developing even if it did not have the twin hallmarks required by previous scholarship, that is, autonomy and separate municipal law. Although he recognized the importance of the phenomenon of location (i.e., foundation under some form of law, usually German and hence foreign—see below), he nevertheless was convinced that town law need not necessarily have been something conferred from some external source. Town law, he argued, could have evolved out of actual market institutions.

This last point was taken up in depth by Buczek.[24] He carefully analyzed the problem of markets and towns under Polish law and determined that there was indeed such a phenomenon. But where previous Polish scholarship had seen evidence of this as part of the emergence of town autonomy (i.e., prior to, or at least independent of, the granting of charters in German law),[25] Buczek showed clearly that the institutions of market law and the emergence of the *forum liberum* or *libertas fori* did not imply self-government with separate municipal institutions and a system of town planning and development. The thrust of these two scholars' work has been to cast the discussion over the significance of the period of location into an entirely different light. Instead of the legal approach, the social and economic are our avenues of understanding. Conversely, instead of de-emphasizing the importance of location, we can see now how profound were the transformations it wrought—social, spatial, legal, and cultural.

The word "location" (from Latin *locatio*) has a number of meanings. How one understands the word influences one's perception of the phenomenon being described. One loose though incorrect usage has been to make the word interchangeable with "foundation" (*fundatio*) and to interpret location simply as the beginning of a settlement and/or the establishment of its urban character. Another possible meaning was one proposed by Tymieniecki.[26] Basing his arguments in Roman law, he suggested that *locatio* was synonymous with a lease and that a *locator* was the party who leased out the land. But Benedykt Zientara has shown that the transplantation to central Europe and to Poland of the institutions of Roman law was a much later phenomenon;

it long postdated the process of location we are here describing and cannot, therefore, be used as an interpretive key to that process.[27]

Expanding upon and refining the etymological analysis of Richard Koebner,[28] Zientara has shown that "location" (from *locare*) "became a technical term of colonization and found its way from the chancelleries of Magdeburg archbishops and other German rulers in the region between the Elbe and Odra [i.e., Oder] into documents issued by Polish dukes." The term as used in Poland had three different meanings. One denotes the founding *de novo* of a settlement. This meaning is, for example, reflected in Bishop Thomas I of Wrocław's grant in 1237 to Peter of Nysa regarding establishment of new villages in the Nysa region.[29] In such a case a colonial population would have to come to the village, either from the locality or from abroad. The colonial population would have been composed in large part of individuals in the emigrant pool established by the approximately 2,000 persons a year who left German lands west of the Elbe in the twelfth and thirteenth centuries to resettle east of the Oder. It has been estimated that in the thirteenth and fourteenth centuries, 250,000 Germans settled in a Poland whose indigenous population probably did not exceed 1,500,000.[30] This settlement was, of course, uneven, with the densest concentrations in parts of Silesia, along the Baltic littoral, and in the major towns.[31]

A second meaning referred to the way in which the physical, or spatial, organization of an existing settlement was to be changed. Characteristically, the new physical form regularized the pattern of settlement and the routes of contact and traffic within the town. This form was in most instances derived from models that had previously evolved in towns lying between the Elbe and the Oder rivers.[32] (The extent to which these, in turn, had been influenced by the Roman *civitas* of late antiquity remains in dispute.) The third meaning of location referred to the legal process by which a settlement was separated from the administration of the grantor (usually a duke) and placed under the jurisdiction of some other law, typically German law of some kind.[33] It is important to note that such a grant of location was made to the headman of the village or settlement (Latin *scultetus* = German *Schultheiss* or *Schulze* and Polish *sołtys;* or Latin *advocatus* = German *Vogt* and Polish *wójt*). Although the charters of location sometimes spoke of the political system of the town or the liberties of the town, these were defined—especially in the thirteenth and fourteenth centuries—within the controls the headman had over the town. We do not, therefore, have to deal at this stage with legal autonomy or any kind of communal freedom. It is simply that the system of jurisdiction governing the town was being changed: from ducal to German law.

Ultimately, of course, many Polish towns did become autonomous (though for reasons associated with other distinctive features of Polish history, they nowhere came to assume the kind of powerful political role in the national or regional scene that they did, for example, in Italy and the Lowlands).[34] The achievement of autonomy was neither sudden nor revolutionary. It was rather a gradual, evolutionary process, marked at some points by moments of high drama. This process was accomplished during the period of location and was in many instances due to the particular course that location followed. It is possible to distinguish roughly two features in this. Though they were symbiotically related, we shall here treat them separately.

The first feature was the process by which the legal principle of autonomy was established. Though some scholars have seen this as central to, and having been accomplished by, the grants of location which the dukes issued, the actual case was more complex for some of the legal reasons noted above. The germ of municipal autonomy lay in several elements. In addition to whatever explicit guarantees of autonomy may have been contained in the charter (and it should be emphasized again that there are not many examples of this) one element was the way in which the market judge (*iudex fori*), who had been a representative of the interests of the duke in the period prior to location, gradually became the specialist on market affairs with a separate sphere of interest and jurisdiction under the *advocatus* or *scultetus* after location. Even though the headman had been freed from ducal jurisdiction after location, he continued to represent many of the economic interests of the duke (with regard to rents and fees, for example). The specialized responsibilities of the market judge often caused him to defend his prerogatives against those in authority over him.[35] Particularly as a money economy developed in Poland and the importance of the markets increased was this true.

A second, and even more important, element was constituted by the grants of autonomy to foreign merchants, many of whom were German. When these individuals came to Poland they had the status of being under the special jurisdiction and protection of the duke.[36] When they were present in sufficient numbers in individual towns, they tended to unite to defend their common interests against all outsiders, be it the duke, his official representatives, or even the local population. We see such autonomous groups in Szczecin, Wrocław, and Kraków by the beginning of the thirteenth century.[37] The transformation of their legal status into representatives of municipal autonomy would not have been possible without the second feature of the process—the physical aspect of location—to be discussed below. For convenience, however, it can be noted here that throughout the thirteenth and fourteenth centuries the governing bodies of these merchant groups strove to reduce both direct ducal intervention in town affairs and indirect ducal controls through the headman.

This they did by the expensive process of buying up most of the municipal properties they did not control, by buying out the right of the duke to town incomes and/or by converting the duke's right to income from resources within the city (the aforementioned rents, fees, and the like) into an obligation on the part of the town to pay a fixed tax to the ruler. Ultimately, of course, these municipal bodies sought to control the office of *advocatus* or *scultetus* by buying the right to it or by seeking to have it abolished completely.[38] They were not always successful in this. All these things combined to create an urban political policy which facilitated increased growth of trade and handicrafts. These, in turn, promoted merchant interests through the organs of town government and, to a certain extent, formed an effective political force which exerted pressure upon the duke and other groups in society (i.e., the landed nobility).

The second feature was the physical, or spatial, aspect of location, together with some legal aspects which have not yet been mentioned. The grant of location, when given to a previously existing urban complex, typically contained certain jurisdictional considerations. One of the most important of these defined and delimited the located town, often including only a part of the previous complex. In most instances, the duke or grantor transferred jurisdiction over only the market settlement. In order for the town headman actually to administer this new legal unit, he had to be the dominant owner of the municipal land. This often meant buying out claims of the landed aristocracy. This was expensive and so, where conditions allowed it, the site of the town was actually moved at the time of the grant. The located town arose beyond the area of the prelocated town. Thus we have, in Łęczyca, for example, the old town (*stare miasto*) and the new town (*nowe miasto*); there is Stary Sącz and Nowy Sącz, and, more simply, there is Nowy Targ (literally "new market").[39] (It is interesting to note that in these centuries the Polish word *miasto* [from *miejsce*, place] came to replace *gród*, fortress as the name for a town.)[40]

The alternative of a move was not always possible. Older centers with well-established traditions, where some fortifications already existed and where the ducal stronghold and ecclesiastical centers were crucial to the rest of the town settlement, could not be re-sited. Even in such cases, however, the grant of location included only part of the prelocation settlement complex. The shape given to the located town was quite different from what had obtained before.[41] Where necessary, existing buildings, houses, gardens, and the like were razed or destroyed. Only well-established stone buildings were left in place. An effort was made to employ a town plan based upon models from towns in the lands between the Elbe and the Oder. A checkerboard or grid plan was implemented, with streets intersecting at right angles, although the shape of located towns—both the older, established ones and those founded *de novo*—tended to be rectangular rather than square.[42] Some kind of central market was always provided. (Szczecin, where particular problems of long settlement and of drainage prevented this, was an exception; it has no real market square.[43]) Existing networks of roads had either to be adapted to this plan or the rectilinear approach had to be modified.

Residences on the market square were designed to give the maximum number of units frontage on the square, and these tended to be held by the wealthiest merchants. The remainder of the general pattern, particularly in the larger centers, has been nicely summarized by Zientara:

> Additional market squares for special markets, i.e., horse, vegetable, and hay markets, were created. Craftsmen settled on streets often bearing the name of their handicraft specialty, while Jews were set-tled in peripheral areas. Baths and hospitals were constructed on the edge of town or outside the town wall. Tanners, not generally welcomed in the centre of town due to the smells emitted from their workshops, also often settled in outlying areas. Mills, bleacheries, cutlery workshops and fulling mills were also constructed beyond the town wall on a river or moat. These outlying handicraft concen-trations constituted the beginnings of development of the suburbs.[44]

There was a twofold impact resulting from location. One was that towns became much more compactly settled, particularly as they were enclosed—either totally or partially—by fortifica-tions. The second was that over time the landed nobility tended to disappear from urban residence. They were either bought out by the new, largely German patriciate or they were forced to liquidate their holdings. Increasingly, the towns developed an urban population with an urban outlook, and increasingly these towns were socially and ethnically differentiated into identifiable strata. The period of location, therefore, had a major impact upon the form and character of urban society in Poland.

The Late Middle Ages

In the fourteenth and fifteenth centuries the process of urban-ization continued. Older Polish towns took on their final physical forms as fortifications were completed and interior space was exploited. New towns continued to be founded as foreign trade grew and the Polish economy matured, and the social and political differentiation in the towns became more pronounced. By the end of the fifteenth century there were approximately 600 urban centers in Poland (excluding Lithuania, which had been joined to the *regnum* by a personal, dynastic union in 1385).[45] Of these, only a few exceeded 10,000 in population. Gdańsk was the largest with about 30,000, while Kraków had about 17,000 to 18,000. Wrocław, whose population at this point was at least equal to Kraków's (if it did not exceed it), was no longer part of the Polish kingdom. The city of Warsaw, which had received a charter of location in the fourteenth century and which was to become the royal capital by the end of the sixteenth century, had a population of only about 5,000 to 6,000. As an indication of the general weakness of urban settlement at this point, it should be noted that less than 15 percent of the total population lived in cities.[46]

In contrast to the very extensive research that has been devoted to the period of location, the late medieval period has been less systematically studied. It is clear that these centuries saw the beginnings of craft and lesser merchant guilds, and that their development was in general a less tumultuous and violent one than their western counterparts'. But, apart from studies devoted to individual guilds or to individual cities, the guild movement as a whole has received little attention. Despite our lack of a general picture, there are isolated instances which suggest that there was opposition to the political monopoly enjoyed in the cities by the patriciate of the wealthiest merchants. The weavers' rising in Wrocław in 1333 and the bakers' riots in Kraków in 1375 are particularly good examples of this. The relationship of this unrest to ethnic considerations remains yet to be examined.[47]

This is of particular importance for an understanding of the rise of national consciousness in this period. While there is clear evidence of a simple *Heimatgefühl* and of a more sophisticated *Landespatriotismus* in Poland in earlier years, this had generally been associated with the nobility and the lesser knights, and not with the town dwellers. For a fully developed national consciousness of the late medieval variety to emerge (as indeed it did in fifteenth-century Bohemia), not only must there be a segment of society to articulate this ideology (most typically the clergy), but there must also be an ethnically and nationally conscious urban population.[48] Whether Poland had this national consciousness at this point is a topic that deserves closer attention. In addition, the important social tensions in the fifteenth century need to be studied with regard to religious factors. It is clear that there was hostility between townsmen and the clergy based on ecclesiastical exemptions from the jurisdiction of town law and municipal taxation. Whether or not this anticlerical sentiment was in any way related to the Hussite movement, whose influences may be observed elsewhere in Polish society in the early fifteenth century, must be more closely studied than heretofore.[49]

The emergence of town social consciousness in this period is a related issue. Urban dwellers have different values from rural inhabitants; merchants and artisans have different ways of expressing their interests from those who till the soil for a living. Thus the outlook of the patriciate and of the rest of the town dwellers (who may not yet in Poland, at least, be called bourgeoisie) deserves close attention.[50] Only a start has been made in this respect. Finally, the general effects of warfare and weather upon economic and social conditions in the cities is a subject of importance. While these twin factors have begun to receive attention, especially for the Duchy of Wrocław, much remains yet to be done.[51]

Against this general background of towns in medieval Poland, the particular history of Kraków stands out. In some ways it reflects the overall pattern. In other ways, Kraków was unique.[52]

KRAKÓW IN THE MIDDLE AGES

The Prelocation Period

The beginnings of the city of Kraków are to be found in the dim mists of prehistory. On the upper course of the Vistula River the limestone acropolis which came to be known as Wawel hill dominates the countryside. It rises some twenty-five meters above the surrounding *stożek prądnika*, the Pradnik terrace, a tongue of land which extends south from the Little Poland highlands into the postglacial valley bed of the Vistula.[53] This rocky outcropping turns the course of the river south and east around it. Because it was easily fortified and defended, it early came to constitute an important settlement site. Long before Poland became a part of the western tradition in the tenth century, the leaders of the Wiślanie tribe had begun to organize the surrounding region under their control, using this military stronghold as their base. [54] This process, whose details are probably lost to us forever, was of great importance, for it assured that Kraków would be both an important urban and a political center. Could we recreate these details, however, we would undoubtedly—and unfortunately—find them a good deal more prosaic than the medieval legends about the eponymous hero Krak and the dragon of Wawel (the *smok Wawelski*) which he conquered, thereby receiving in marriage the daughter of the previous ruler and, in consequence, establishing his own rule.[55]

By the end of the tenth century, Wawel was well-settled, though it was just one zone of what eventually came to be the incorporated medieval city of Kraków. When Duke Mieszko of Great Poland joined the region of Little Poland to the newly unified state under his rule, there was, atop the hill at the eastern end of Wawel, a wooden palisade that enclosed this part of the acropolis.[56] Within the palisade was a wooden fortress with at least one stone tower; this constituted the ducal residence. In addition, there were other wooden structures which housed the retinue of the ruler. There was also a small stone church in the form of a rotunda. Dedicated to Saint Mary (and in later years rededicated to Saints Felix and Adauctus), this was one of the earliest churches of Kraków. Its very form—a compact fortress— and its probable function as the duke's chapel remind us of the close association between the ruler and the religion at this time. Other buildings which were probably located atop Wawel hill at this time, included a second, recently discovered, rotunda (the so-called "Church B")[57] and a rectangular stone building with an elongated, enclosed corridor. Some have suggested that this latter structure may have served after 1000 as an episcopal residence.[58] The extent of this settlement, plus additional urban development on the terrace below to which we shall turn shortly, reflects the accuracy of the comment made by Ibrahim-ibn-Jakub in the tenth century to the effect that Kraków was an important trading point on the commercial route running from Kiev through Prague to Ratisbon.[59] Among the goods carried on this route were salt, slaves, and amber.

Events in the eleventh and twelfth centuries stimulated further urban development and building on Wawel. On the western part of the hill, quarters for individuals attached to either secular or ecclesiastical leaders were considerably expanded. This section was eventually included within the rampart erected around the whole crest of Wawel. Parts of this remained earthen, with a timber palisade; other parts, however, were replaced by stone construction. The most impressive buildings on the hill were ecclesiastical. Apparently during the lifetime of Duke Bolesław Chrobry (the Brave), who became king of Poland in 1025, a cathedral building was begun. Dedicated to the memory of the martyred Duke Václav of Bohemia (d. 929), it was constructed chiefly of sandstone. The basilican structure was an ambitious building, consisting of three naves, a transept, a closed apse, and a crypt which measured some 7.5 meters by 5 meters. We do not know whether it was ever completed; even if it was, it did not long survive. There is evidence that it stood in ruins by the last quarter of the eleventh century.[60] The remains of what is known as Cathedral I lie today within the western wing of the Renaissance castle built by the Jagiellonian kings of a later time.

During the lifetime of Saint Stanisław, the most famous early medieval bishop of Kraków (d. 1079), construction was begun (perhaps under his patronage) on a second cathedral, slightly to the west of the first. It was not to be completed until the following century. Like its predecessor, it was an ambitious three-nave structure, though probably without a transept.[61] This Romanesque-style Cathedral II, the so-called cathedral of Władysław Hermann which contains the famous crypt of St. Leonard, was later incorporated into the Gothic cathedral which stands today. One other ecclesiastical building dating from this time, though no longer extant, should be noted here. This is the small collegiate church of St. Michael, whose early Romanesque foundations mark it as one of the earliest structures on Wawel. (The Gothic elements identified in archaeological investigations were, of course, added later.) This building lay to the south and slightly to the southeast of the site of Cathedral II.[62] Thus by the end of the twelfth century, Wawel had emerged as one of the important settlement zones of Kraków. But there were others, to which we now turn.

Lying at the northeast foot of Wawel and extending north nearly to the area of the later Franciscan and Dominican churches, was the *suburbium* proper of medieval Kraków, the district known as Okół. Until recently it was thought that this area was not settled until the twelfth century or even later. Recent archaeological investigations have shown, however, that continuous development of this zone began as early as the mid-ninth century.[63] Prior to about the year 1000 this community, whose area of 8.5 hectares (20.1 acres) ranged in measurement from some 180 to 275 meters across and some 450 meters long, was apparently defended on at least the east side by a wooden palisade. In the following century this was replaced by a timber-earth-stone rampart that may have surrounded the entire site. On the northern boundary, one of the numerous waterways of the Kraków area served as an effective moat. Most of the buildings in Okół were wooden and were concentrated along one of the two thoroughfares within the district.[64] One of these ran roughly where the southern part of Canon's Street (ul. Kanonicza) lies today. This route exited in the southwest to the ford on the Vistula and, on the north, along a road which is today represented by Carpenter's Street (ul. Stolarska). From there it ran to the eastern reaches of Ruthenia. Another route, roughly equivalent to the present-day Castle Street (ul. Grodzka), came to be known later as the "salt road." These two routes crossed near the center of Okół; and where they did, the market grew up. Numerous references in contemporary and later documents identify this *forum mercatorum*,[65] but its exact location is difficult to determine. Some evidence suggests it lay in the vicinity of the present-day Wit Stwosz Square (pl. Wita Stwosza)[66]

The most important ecclesiastical building in medieval Okół

was the Church of St. Andrew.[67] The construction of this monumental Romanesque church, with its characteristic westwork,
was begun by Bishop Lambert of Kraków (d. 1101). Archaeological investigation into the early architectural history of Okół
does not enable us to say much about what ecclesiastical building
had been constructed in this zone prior to the end of the eleventh
century. Two factors suggest that evidence has yet to be uncovered of a church structure at St. Andrew's that predates the
structure begun by Lambert. One is the general development of
Okół prior to this point. It is reasonable to expect that there
would have been some ecclesiastical development to comple-
ment the other urban development. The second factor is the
pattern, replicated in numerous Polish sites, of constructing a
newer and larger church upon the site of the foundation of a
previous building. Additional investigation may yet tell us something of the prior history of Okół.

In addition to Wawel and Okół, there was a third zone of
settlement in medieval Kraków. It encompassed roughly the area
which was included in the municipal charter of 1257. But of this
area, only the southern part was very extensively developed by
the end of the twelfth century. Archaeological evidence shows
that the earliest development was around three nuclei: (a) the
site of the later episcopal palace; (b) the approximate location of
the later Dominican monastery; and (c) the site of St. Wojciech's
(Adalbert's) church. By the end of the tenth century these had
gradually coalesced into a single urban area.[68] The total area was
probably about 7.5 hectares (about 18.5 acres), making it slightly
smaller than Okół. Early foundries were located in the western
section of this settlement, while precious metals were worked
in the vicinity of St. Wojciech's church. In addition, the chief
market area of this settlement zone seems to have developed
near this church. One reconstruction of the early thoroughfares
suggests that a division in the north to south trade and com-
munication route at this point contributed to this development.
While there may have been additional settlement north of the
present town square (the Rynek) it probably was not far advanced at this point. The urban focus of the zone remained on
the southern half of the area chartered in 1257.

The most important ecclesiastical building in this third zone was the church dedicated to the tenth-century martyr, Wojciech/ Adalbert, whose personal history was so closely intertwined with the early development of Piast Poland, Přemyslid Bohemia, and Árpád Hungary. The limestone building which now stands rests upon remnants of a structure built in the late eleventh or early twelfth century. This in turn had incorporated parts of two earlier wooden structures whose remains have only recently been identified.[69] The older of these is nearly contemporary with the death of Wojciech (d. 997); the more recent dates to the mid-eleventh century. The presence of these early buildings antedating the construction of the stone Romanesque building, reflects the close involvement of the church with the other aspects of urban development.

Four other settlement sites in the general area of Kraków should be noted here, even though they lay outside the chief zones mentioned so far. One was the so-called Gródek (i.e., little fortress) which in the Middle Ages was a self-contained fortified settlement, surrounded eventually by a moat.[70] Its autonomous status was not ended until the fourteenth century during the reign of Władysław Łokietek—the Short (d. 1333), who incorporated it into the municipal fortifications and placed it under princely control. During the prelocation period this area was inhabited (and perhaps had been so since the end of the ninth century), but there was apparently no church building there. Recent archaeological excavations near Gródek have uncovered a burial site from the late tenth or early eleventh century.[71] It is apparently the only such site not associated with a church in this general area. A second settlement whose existence can be traced to this period lay in the district eventually known as Stradom.[72] Its low level (actually in the normal flood basin of the Vistula) prevented extensive urban development, though its proximity to Wawel made it the occasional site of weaponsmakers. A third settlement, dating to prehistory, lay about one and one-half kilometers west of Wawel, up the Vistula. After the coming of Christianity, the church of the Holy Savior (Salwator) was built in this area atop what came to be known as St. Bronisława's hill. Remnants of two early stages of stone construction long antedate the first written mention, in 1148, of the construction of the present building.

Archaeologists variously date these two earlier forms—one of which contained a semicircular apse, the other a rotunda— to the second half of the tenth century or the early eleventh century.[73] Though now part of the city of Kraków, Salwator remained separate from the city proper throughout the Middle Ages and was, apparently, never fortified. Finally, there is the area of settlement on the Skałka hill, another limestone outcropping with steep sides and a relatively level top, which lies half a kilometer south of Wawel. Fragmentary archaeological evidence confirms habitation here as early as the ninth and tenth centuries.[74] It was in connection with this settlement that the church constructed a small rotunda on Skałka (*na Skałce*). Johannes Długosz, the fifteenth-century historian, reported that this building was of white stone, circular in shape, and had been erected near a pond where pagan Poles had earlier made sacrifices to their gods.[75] When this rotunda (whose remains can be seen in some late medieval and early modern iconographic evidence[76]) was incorporated into a large Gothic structure, and when that building was in turn replaced by the baroque church that now stands there, most traces of earlier settlement upon the hill were disturbed and lost. Thus, regarding Skałka we know only that according to later testimony[77] it was there that the bishop of Kraków, Stanisław of Szczepanów, found a martyr's death in 1079.

The ecclesiastical and architectural development of Kraków in the period before location was complemented by a political evolution which must be treated briefly.[78] The early Piast state under Mieszko I and Bolesław Chrobry had been centered upon the region of Great Poland, with the cities of Gniezno and Poznań as two of its major focuses. Kraków's importance had been merely regional. In the course of the eleventh century, however, great changes had taken place. Internal weaknesses within the Polish monarchy had allowed foreigners and local princes to range at will within the country. The depredations of the Bohemians were particularly devastating. Duke Břetislav attacked Poland in the 1030s and sacked Kraków and Gniezno. In the former city, he may have destroyed the new cathedral building begun under Bolesław Chrobry, in the latter city, he carried off many valuable treasures and relics, including the remains of Saint Wojciech. In religious matters there was also change. The veneer of Christian culture and ecclesiastical organization, which had been the heritage of the tenth century, did not survive the eleventh century untouched. A so-called "pagan reaction" swept the land and completely disrupted the life of the church, bringing to naught the ecclesiastical polity which had been established at the Congress of Gniezno in 1000. Both politically and religiously it was necessary to begin anew.

The work of King Kazimierz Odnowiciel (the Restorer) (1034–1058) was particularly decisive. He rebuilt towns and churches, reorganized and invigorated the Polish clergy, and revived monastic life. But not all the ecclesiastical problems were solved in his lifetime. For example, the issues of where the Polish metropolitan was to be and the ecclesiastical status of Kraków in relation to Gniezno were not resolved in Gniezno's favor until the twelfth century. One of the most significant acts of King Kazimierz was that he transferred the residence of the Polish ruler from Great Poland to Kraków, thus establishing this city as the capital. This promoted what had been merely a town, albeit an important one, into a royal metropolis. Henceforth Kraków was, as later writers put it, "the city and seat of the king," and the place "where the Polish crown has been since antiquity (*ab antiquo*)."[79]

During the twelfth century the internal tensions between ruler and nobility that had become evident in the early Piast-ruled state eventually broke the country into political fragments. The royal title fell into disuse and various branches of the Piast family became political pawns of the nobility. Duke Bolesław III, called the Wry-mouthed (d. 1138) tried to stabilize the centrifugal forces within the country and to maintain Kraków as, at least, the seat of authority for a senior duke who was to be *primus inter pares*. His effort failed, however, and by the end of the twelfth century Poland was divided into competing duchies, some of which followed political paths that eventually took them out of the sphere of Polish politics proper. Until the early fourteenth century, Po-

land was riven by petty particularism and political fragmentation. To this depressing picture should be added one additional
factor which had a major impact upon Kraków itself: foreign
invasion.

The Tatar attack of 1241 was carried out by a diversionary arm
of the main Mongol army, which struck toward Hungary. But
the devastation left by these fast-riding horsemen on that occasion (and in subsequent attacks) was enormous.[80] When they
came to Kraków they found a settlement with only rudimentary
fortifications. Some stonework was present, but the bulk of the
defense was ineffectually provided by earthworks and a wooden
palisade. Unable to defend the city, the inhabitants retreated to
whatever shelter they could individually find. For many it was
not enough. The Tatar attack left half the population dead and
most wooden structures in ruin. Only stone buildings or those
buildings—such as on Wawel—protected by stone walls survived. This disaster was not, however, the end of Kraków. In
the era of location which followed, a more prosperous and successful city arose, phoenix-like, from the ashes.

The Era of Location

Throughout the Polish lands in the late twelfth- and early thir-
teenth-centuries the phenomenon of "location," described
above, was increasingly common. Provincial rulers sought
means by which the growing commerce and expanding money
economy of the time could be stimulated and turned thereby to
their advantage. They experimented with new foundations, with
the granting of legal privileges to merchant groups, and with
expanded economic relations that would attract new settlers,
more merchants, and greater numbers of handicraft workers and
artisans. Thereby came the thirteenth-century breakthrough that
Benedykt Zientara has termed the *melioratio terrae*.[81]

That Kraków, too, should participate in this pattern was not
surprising. It was already an important economic center. But in
addition, the political influence of Duke Henry I, the Bearded,
of Silesia had been particularly strong in Little Poland and in
Kraków in the early thirteenth century. He had ruled the city

for a time, and it was he who—as we have seen—had been particularly important in setting precedents by his numerous acts of location.[82]

There is evidence that at least some part, or parts, of the urban settlement of Kraków had been granted rights under some kind of German law long before the *locatio* of 1257. There are, for example, traces of a located settlement in the vicinity of the Holy Trinity Church about the year 1220 or shortly thereafter.[83] In 1228, and again in 1230, there is a certain Petrus mentioned in documents as the scultetus of Kraków, that is, the legal head man with rights in German law.[84] In addition, yet another *scultetus* (Salomon by name) is mentioned in 1250.[85] Older scholarship tended to view these individual items as evidence that there had been a first location of Kraków which had been a necessary legal first step to the act of 1257.[86] More recent analyses, however, have tended to suggest that these data reflect successive efforts by competing dukes (Conrad of Mazovia, Władysław Spindleshanks, and—most important—Henry I of Silesia, known as Henry the Bearded) to confirm their control over Kraków.[87] None were successful for a very long time, though Henry and his son Henry II, the Pious, apparently influenced the city's development most profoundly. What they did was to establish the precedent of an urban community possessing rights in German law. Though no documents explicitly confirm the interpretations of Józef Mitkowski and others, their judgment that Henry the Bearded was most probably responsible for the presence of the *scultetus* seems sound.

In the aftermath of the Tatar attack, it was possible for yet another duke to act. On 5 June 1257 Bolesław V, the Chaste, of nearby Sandomir issued a much more comprehensive document.[88] It incorporated under German (i.e., Magdeburg) law the urban community that had lain to the north and northeast of Okół; it defined a much larger physical location than had been occupied previously; it established a new town square to replace the older market area; and it provided for the implementation of a regularized town plan. The economic and political development of the resultant city in the subsequent two and one-half centuries made it one of the most important towns in east-central

Europe. Kraków came to rank with Prague, Wrocław, and Gdańsk as a major center.

The physical plan of the city was laid out within a roughly oval area some 700 meters northwest to southeast and some 800 meters northeast to southwest.[89] The grid of the streets was established with reference to the newly laid-out town square, which measured about 200 meters a side. (By European standards, this was a large town square.) On each side, there were, with the exception of the east side, three streets leading off the square at right angles. On this square were eventually built a cloth hall, the hall of the city government, a municipal scale, and such other buildings as were required to serve the needs of merchants. For the most part, therefore, Kraków was a new city.

But vestiges of the previous urban settlement remained. In the southern part of the city, for example, the rectilinear grid was not fully executed, because previous settlement had already defined the street pattern. In addition, although the parish church of St. Mary's was on the square, it was oriented to it at an angle, reflecting its prior existence. The main route into the square from the northeast came from St. Florian's gate (hence St. Florian's street), but it entered the square at the northeast corner rather than in the center of the northeast side. The route from the square to the castle (Grodzka, castle street) and cathedral on Wawel was not truly part of the grid, for it led directly south out of the southeast corner of the square. These two streets represent the persistence of an older trade route which antedated the location. Finally, with regard to the square, the church of St. Adalbert (Wojciech) which had stood since, perhaps, the eleventh century, was not moved; it remained some meters within the boundary of the square near the southeast corner. To the east of the town square and beyond St. Mary's church, there quickly grew up a second, smaller market place in the second half of the thirteenth century. This *cleyner Iarmarck*[90] (the *mały rynek*) served the functions described above by Zientara (note 44). Elsewhere within the *locus* of Kraków, the fortress of Grodek dominated the central part of the eastern side of town. It eventually became the residence of the *advocatus* who, at first at least, represented ducal interests. Very soon after the location, efforts were begun to enclose the city with stone walls and to limit the points of entrance and exit. Beyond these walls lay slaughter-houses, tanneries, bleaching and fulling mills, and most brew-eries (although some of the beer drunk by Kraków residents was brewed within the city).

In the half-century following the location the economic and urban development of Kraków was rapid. Stone fortifications were completed and a start was made on providing a system of water defense to encircle the city. Eventually the district of Okół was included within the life of the town. Major civic, commercial, ecclesiastical, and private buildings were either completed or begun. A distinct area of Jewish settlement was established in the southwest corner of Kraków.[91] The earliest guilds developed in this period and embryonic organs of municipal self-govern-ment evolved as well. Although Wawel was not legally within the city located in 1257, it, too, developed rapidly in these years: stone fortifications were strengthened and extended, and polit-ical and ecclesiastical buildings on the acropolis were maintained and complemented by new building. Thus the city had begun to take on the form it presented to the wider world of a unified Poland when it reemerged as a royal capital under the last Piasts and the early Jagiellonians.[92]

The Late Middle Ages

In the 1290s and in the early fourteenth century there were attempts made by both native Polish dukes and foreign rulers to reestablish the Polish kingdom. None of them had more than ephemeral success. In the politically confused aftermath of these efforts, Duke Władysław Łokietek of Kujavia (d. 1333) emerged as the single most powerful prince in Poland. After 1306 he held Little Poland, making his capital in Kraków, and in 1320 he was crowned king as Władysław I in Wawel cathedral. Despite some political reverses before his death in 1333, he bequeathed to his son and successor Casimir the Great (Casimir III; d. 1370) a united Polish kingdom.[93] Under these two members of the Piast dynasty and under subsequent rulers from Hungary and Lith-uania (the Anjou and Jagiełło dynasties), Poland prospered and emerged as one of the major political powers of the region. Kraków, too, shared in this ascendancy, and in the final section of this study we turn to the several roles it played in this period. In the fourteenth and fifteenth centuries Kraków was an organized social complex, a commercial center, a royal capital, an urban settlement, and—a factor which made it unusual in the region—a university city. Let us examine in turn each of these roles.

As an organized society and social complex, Kraków's life was divided between two authorities, the *advocatus* and the city council. The power of the former as a ducal or royal representative had originally been very great. Responsible for the defense of the city, the *advocatus* also had jurisdiction over its legal affairs and derived a substantial income from municipal rents, taxes, customs duties and fines levied by the city court over which he presided. But the *advocatus* was not simply a ducal representative, for during the decades of political fragmentation in Poland he had begun to assume an independent role. This development in Kraków came to a climax in 1311, when *advocatus* Albert led a major revolt against the rule of Władysław Łokietek.[94] The situation was compounded by the fact that ethnic hostility played an important role in this revolt: Albert and his followers were German-speaking; Łokietek represented the traditions of native Piast Poland. Besieged on Wawel for a time, the duke had eventually been able to summon reinforcements from elsewhere in Little Poland. By the end of summer 1312 the revolt had been crushed. Those who were suspected of supporting Albert were forced to demonstrate their Polishness by successfully repeating the words *soczewica, koło, miele, młyn;* if they could not, they were assumed to be foreign and were executed.[95] In the aftermath of this suppression, Łokietek sharply circumscribed the powers of the *advocatus*, reducing the income of the office and incorporating the seat of the *advocatus*, the fortress Gródek, into the city fortifications. In the course of the fourteenth and fifteenth centuries the independence of the *advocatus* had been steadily eroded and the city council gradually assumed his powers. In 1475 the last traces of dual governance disappeared when the office was formally purchased by the city and became completely dependent upon the council.[96] Though the title remained, the incumbent was elected by the council from among the citizens of Kraków.

The city council dated from the years immediately following the location. It was theoretically an independent group, based in the merchant community. Under Łokietek and his son Casimir, however, royal authority had been imposed, and the members of the council in the central decades of the fourteenth century were appointed by one of the royal officials. The uncertainties which plagued the Polish monarchy in the wake of the extinction of the Piast dynasty after 1370 changed this. The council came to exercise considerable freedom. By the fifteenth century it was in practice autonomous and self-perpetuating.[97] Originally composed of six members, its size grew over the years to twenty-four. Membership was ostensibly evenly divided between representatives from the craft guilds and the merchant guilds. In reality, the greater merchants tended to dominate and were slow to admit new members to their ranks. Thus one finds a high percentage of *consules seniores* throughout this period, and there are several instances when the membership of the council did not change for several years, despite the fact that appointment was only for a single year.

At the beginning of the fifteenth century opposition to the council developed from the lower strata of Kraków society, which felt their interests, especially in economic matters, were not being represented adequately. They forced the council to accept an advisory group of sixteen which was required to approve taxes, grants, appointments, and the like before they could become effective. This attempt to limit the authority of the council was, however, never very successful. By the end of the century the council was the real master of Kraków. Out of its midst there gradually emerged after 1396 (when some important new laws were passed) the office of mayor (*magister civium* or *proconsul*, Polish *burmistrz* from the German *Bürgermeister*). He was the chairman of the council and was elected by it; he did not therefore have any independent authority or position. As a result the Kraków mayor never developed into the equivalent of the powerful, autonomous figures found in some western towns. Neither was there in Kraków any tradition of conflict between mayor and council to divide and embitter the populace of the city.

Responsibility for the administration of justice in Kraków also lay in different hands at the beginning of the fourteenth century. The *advocatus* had jurisdiction over both civil and criminal issues, while the council in its deliberations and decisions exercised authority over commercial and economic matters. (In addition the clergy, academics, and Jews had their own independent court systems.) But, as with the aforementioned administrative matters, the competency of the council was gradually extended.[98] By the beginning of the fifteenth century almost all legal issues in the city fell under the jurisdiction of its courts.

Within this structure of governance, Kraków society was dominated by its urban patriciate. This group was composed largely of great merchants who had arrived after the location of 1257.[99] They had made great fortunes from the trade and commerce that developed in Kraków. Many were from parts of Germany, more came from Silesia, some traced their geographic origins to Bohemia and Hungary, while others had roots originally in the Lowlands or in Italy. These merchants added a foreign element to Kraków, mainly German-speaking, which was only slowly and incompletely Polonized in the course of the fifteenth century. It is not surprising, therefore, that in the chief parish church of the city, St. Mary's on the town square, preaching was predominantly in German throughout this period. Not all of the patriciate was involved in commerce. Some of its members made their fortunes in real estate; others held lucrative positions in the mint, in the customs office, or even in royal service. In general they were imbued with a sense of responsibility first to themselves and their families and only secondarily to the city and its elements.[100]

Below the patriciate were the craftsmen and lesser merchants of Kraków. These constituted the bulk of society. Although it is difficult to generalize about their ethnic backgrounds, it appears that in the fifteenth century the use of German and Polish was about equal in this group, thus suggesting again a significant foreign element. Some of these individuals made their livings by providing the goods and services basic to all society: they were butchers, bakers, carpenters, coopers, ironmongers, and the like. Others dealt in goods that were more closely related to the court, the council, and the clergy: silver- and goldsmiths, importers of fine cloth from the Lowlands and Italy, bookbinders, and the like. The commercial and industrial life of these groups was organized around the guild. From the city record books of this period some forty different occupations have been identified, although there were apparently fewer than half that many specific guilds.[101] These functioned much like their counterparts in the West, controlling production, establishing standards, and limiting membership.

Finally, within the lay society of Kraków there were the poor and the unskilled, who like their counterparts in all times and urban places lived on the margins of society, without rights and with little hope. Beyond this we know little of their lives, for they appear seldom in the records except when someone excoriates them in a particular instance[102] or when they break one of the many laws set as barriers to keep them apart from the rest of society.

No discussion of the structure of Kraków society would be complete without brief mention of two additional groups, the clergy and the Jews. The city was, in addition to its other characteristics, a religious center. It was the seat of a bishop and many clergy were involved in the ecclesiastical and administrative life of the cathedral on Wawel hill. By the late Middle Ages the residence of the bishop was no longer on Wawel but lay within the city below. Kraków was also the site of a Franciscan and a Dominican monastery, and a Benedictine foundation at Tyniec and a Cistercian house at Mogiło were both in close proximity to the city. In addition, other orders, such as the Bernardine and Clarisian, were located in the city. The numerous secular clergy were involved in the several parish and collegiate churches and in the religious hospitals found in Kraków. The Jews had begun to arrive in Kraków in the thirteenth and fourteenth centuries, when their position in Western Europe deteriorated and they were given grants of protection by a series of Polish dukes and rulers. There was a Jewish area, the *platea*

Judeorum, on the west side of the city and in the recently founded
suburb of Kazimierz there was another Jewish concentration.
Limited by statute and tradition in their participation in urban
life, the Jews were active in small shops serving their own community and in money-lending.[103]

In addition to being a social complex, Kraków was also a
commercial and economic center. In part this role derived from
its location on the crossroads of two major, long-distance trade
routes. The north-south road led out of the northern Balkans
and Hungary through Kraków to the Baltic; the east-west road
ran from southern Germany through Silesia and Wrocław to
Kraków and from there into the vastness of Ruthenia. For the
former route, the increasing importance of the Vistula river as
a waterway since the mid-fourteenth century further facilitated
Kraków's emergence as an important regional center; and after
the conclusion of the Thirteen Years' War with the Teutonic
Knights in 1466, the whole of the river, from Kraków to Toruń
and Gdańsk, lay in Polish hands. In addition to these international routes, local trade between Kraków and Great Poland
(Poznań) and Lithuania further enhanced the capital's importance.[104]

This favorable location enabled the city to achieve three important commercial advantages by the fifteenth century. First,
it gained a monopoly over the storage and processing of Hungarian copper and, eventually, it was able to extend this to all
Hungarian goods. Second, it was able to force all foreign merchants coming from Ruthenia to Great Poland and to the west
into Silesia to use the road through Kraków, to the financial
benefit of the city. Third, it was often able to close the route
from Wrocław to Ruthenia to all foreign merchants, thus giving
Kraków merchants a near-monopoly over the transport of goods
from west to east.[105] As a result the fortunes of the patriciate in
particular were enhanced, and the city benefited by the taxes,
rents, and customs duties it was able to levy.

The most important commercial activity in the city in the early
fifteenth century was the cloth trade. Both raw materials and
finished goods were sold in Kraków. The focus of this activity
was the town square, dominated by the Gothic clothiers' hall.
During the years 1390–1405 an annual average of 16,293 bales

of cloth (each containing between 30 and 44 ells) was registered through the customs office by foreign merchants. Kraków merchants probably were responsible for approximately another 8,000 bales annually.[106] Another important commercial activity was the salt trade. Kraków was located on what had once been the southern shore of the primeval Baltic Sea and, immediately to its south, there were great rock salt mines in Wieliczka and Bochnia. Their control was partly in private hands and partly a royal monopoly. In addition, by the fifteenth century Kraków also handled salt from Ruthenia. As a fundamental commodity in daily life, the salt trade gave rise to numerous conflicts and competitions, and there were many regulations established as to who could sell what kind of salt in Kraków.[107]

Kraków served not only as an emporium and a point of transshipment, it was also a center of production. The present-day pollution problems of the city were foreshadowed in the fifteenth century by the foundry just outside Kraków of the Turzon family, who had come originally from Hungary. There copper, gold, and silver were smelted, and a contemporary remarked that the area "looked like Mt. Etna, with furnaces burning full of . . . [metals] . . . being joined in the fire."[108] In addition there were iron foundries in the area, and the processing of lead was a lucrative business.

One aspect of the economic life of Kraków which deserves closer attention is the important material consideration of the cost of living during this period, that is, prices and wages. The data available for an examination of costs and income are scattered and fragmentary and the picture they present is by no means complete. It is possible, however, to sketch the general outlines. Prices in Kraków were calculated usually with reference to the *grossus Cracoviensis,* which had been introduced into Poland during the reign of Casimir the Great. Forty-eight of these constituted a *marcus,* or mark. The silver *grossus,* known in the vernacular as the *grosz,* had remained generally stable in value in the fourteenth century; in the fifteenth century, however, its value had declined. At the beginning of the century it contained 1.386 grams of silver; in mid-century, this had fallen to .943 grams; and at the end of the 1400s, the silver content of the *grosz* was only .754 grams.[109] This gradual depreciation was counterbalanced in some cases by a general decline in prices, particularly in the second half of the century.

The following examples, incomplete as they are, must suffice for an understanding of the broad picture.[110] Using a Base Index of 100, derived from quite full data for the half-decade 1596–1600, prices of foodstuffs followed this pattern: In the first two decades of the fifteenth century the index was in the mid-forties; it rose to about 65 in the 1420s, then declined to 40 for the 1430s. Thereafter there was a sharp decline; and from the 1460s to the end of the century, the index held relatively steady between the high twenties and the low twenties. A slightly different pattern may be observed with regard to cloth and clothing prices. At the beginning of the century the index stood at 85, then fell in the second and third decades to about 55, sinking even further in the 1430s to 35. Thereafter our data fail us until the 1470s, by which time the index had risen to above 80. It dropped sharply thereafter to about 50, where it remained for the last two decades of the 1400s. Building materials and fuel also showed similar fluctuations. The beginning of the century reflects a price index of about 65, and the last decade shows an index of 50, with prices dropping even further after that.

In between, however, the index reached a high of 70 in the 1410s and a low of 15 in the 1470s. At other times in the century these prices fluctuated between 45 (the 1430s), 57 (the 1460s), and 45 (the 1480s).

Little that is meaningful can be determined from prices in this sector. With regard to the costs of livestock and fowl, however, a more regular pattern emerges from the data. The beginning of the century saw the index at about 55. It declined gradually thereafter (50 in the 1410s, 44 in the 1420s) to just under 35 in the 1430s. The next decade saw a rise to above 45, but by the 1460s the price index had fallen again, this time to less than 30. Thereafter it began a gradual rise, reaching 43 in the 1490s and continuing to rise after that. What these data reflect is a generally stable economic picture in Kraków. Despite fluctuations, there was no prolonged period of economic depression; neither was there anything like the explosion of prices that marked the late sixteenth century, in Poland as well as in Europe as a whole.

This picture of general economic stability is reinforced by the information we have about salaries in the fifteenth century.[111] The annualized salary for several different occupations in the city shows the following patterns: In 1400 a senior notary received an income of 1,600 *grossi*. Thereafter, this salary increased to 1,920 in 1401 and 1402 and rose to 2,278 by 1405. Data for the remainder of the century are more scattered, but in the late 1480s an individual in this occupation still received a salary of about 2,000 *grossi*. A junior notary earned 667 *grossi per annum* at the beginning of the century and this remained much the same thereafter. (The figure of 1,320 *grossi* for a junior notary's salary in 1487 is probably an anomaly.) The fragmentary information regarding other occupations reinforces this picture of reasonable stability. Clockmasters had a salary of between 192 and 240 *grossi per annum* throughout the century, stablemasters consistently earned 624 *grossi,* and carpenters received 864 *grossi.* Such incomes would, of course, have been small in comparison with those of the secular and ecclesiastical magnates of the city,[112] but that they were stable in relation to prices suggests that Kraków in this period was not beset by economic crises and the kind of potential for social strife which, for example, plagued some western European cities in the same period.

In addition to the two roles Kraków played that have been mentioned to this point, the city was also a royal capital.[113] This lent a particular character to the city, for although the royal residence at Wawel and the town proper were two separate entities, in practice they were closely connected and interrelated. As one Polish scholar commented, "Nothing that happened in the castle was uninteresting to the citizens of Kraków, and the residents of Wawel were in no way indifferent to the daily affairs and problems of the citizens."[114]

The modern concept of a capital as the permanent residence of the ruler was generally unknown in the Middle Ages. The medieval monarchy was largely an itinerant institution, for, as another Polish scholar has remarked, "The presence of the ruler in his lands was made necessary by the demands of internal politics . . . The king traveled *pacem firmando, legem faciendo.*"[115] Thus we find the Polish kings of the fifteenth century spending relatively little time in Kraków. Particularly after the death in 1399 of his child-bride Jadwiga of Anjou, Władysław II Jagiełło traditionally spent the winter in Lithuania, coming to Kraków for Lent, then touring Great Poland and Kujavia. He returned to Kraków in early summer, but left in mid-August for an autumn progress through Ruthenia, usually ending on the Feast of Saint Martin (11 November) near Kraków in Niepołomice. From here, or from the capital if he spent some time there, he went to Grodno or Vilno in Lithuania for Christmas.[116] Unlike his father Jagiełło, Władysław Warneńczyk (1434–1444) did not travel widely in his kingdom.[117] During the first six years of his reign, he spent most of the time in Kraków, never going to Great Poland or Lithuania (which was ruled by his younger brother and eventual successor as king). This was in some respects due to the concentration of power during this period in the hands of the Little Poland nobility, led by Bishop Zbigniew Oleśnicki of Kraków. The young king left Poland in 1440 to pursue his claims to the Hungarian throne and perished four years later in the disastrous crusade of Varna, from which his Polish sobriquet derives.

Casimir IV, the Jagiellonian (ruled 1447–1492), returned to the pattern of his father, except that he also spent long periods wholly in Lithuania, totaling nearly one-third of his reign. During the period between 1480 and 1492 he was only in Kraków four brief times. The interests of the multi-national Polish-Lithuanian state clearly required his presence elsewhere.[118] His son and successor, John Albert (*reg.* 1492–1501), spent the whole of his reign in the kingdom proper. Although he toured widely there, he also resided for the great majority of the decade in Kraków itself.[119] This fifteenth-century pattern of residence and travel meant that for long periods Kraków was a capital without a ruler. Without the presence of the king, the city was able to pursue its own interests, and its municipal autonomy was considerably strengthened in this period.

Nevertheless, there were times when the monarchy was resident at Wawel and the impact upon Kraków was substantial. The royal character of the city is nowhere so well illustrated as by the following two events. In 1364 Kraków was the site of the most glittering international congress of the fourteenth century.[120] To Poland came King Peter Lusignan of Cyprus, Emperor Charles IV of the Holy Roman Empire, King Václav (Wenceslaus) of Bohemia, King Louis of Hungary, and King Waldemar of Denmark. In addition, Dukes Otto of Bavaria, Bolko of Świdnica, Władysław of Opole, Ziemowit of Mazovia, and Bogusław of Pomorze-Wołogoszcz were in attendance, along with large retinues and many lesser princes and nobles. The rulers were King Casimir's guests in the royal castle on Wawel, while the others found lodgings in the city. The festivities connected with the congress were magnificent. Casimir distributed gifts liberally to his guests, numerous tourneys and games were held, and Mikołaj Wierzynek, a municipal councillor and reputedly the richest man in Kraków, sumptuously entertained the whole congress in his private quarters on the central market square. It was in conjunction with this congress that Casimir was able to announce the foundation of the University of Kraków, the first such *studium* in Poland and only the second (after Prague) east of the Rhine and north of the Alps. It is not surprising that the contemporary chronicler and Casimir's royal vice-chancellor, Janko of Czarnków, should have remarked:

> It is not possible to describe the extent of delight, magnificence, glory, and abundance that there was in this "convivium," not even if it were given to everyone to report as much as they wished. The kings and princes promised and affirmed great friendship for one another, and were given many gifts for themselves by King Casimir of Poland.[121]

Sixty years later Kraków was again the center of royal social attention. At the coronation of King Władysław Jagiełło's new wife, Sonia, in 1424, the city and the court together celebrated the festivities. On this occasion one of the most famous knights of the time, Zawisza the Black of Garbów, feted all the guests in a lavish dinner in his private home. Those assembled included the emperor (who was also king of Hungary and claimed the title in Bohemia), the king of Denmark, the apostolic cardinal-legate to Poland, and numerous other secular and ecclesiastical princes from the region.[122]

Whatever the relation between Wawel and the city, the two were seldom out of one another's consciousness. From the city the acropolis dominated the view. Conversely, from the royal height it was possible for all to look down on Kraków and see it not only as a royal capital, but as a planned urban settlement. This was the fourth role Kraków played.

We have already seen the fundamental way in which the *locatio* of 1257 changed the spatial organization of Kraków. But the planning implemented after the location extended even to the water courses that surrounded the city. The Vistula and the Rudawa rivers (the latter a smaller tributary to the former) were the chief elements utilized to give the city protection by water and, at the same time, to furnish power for the several mills about the town.[123] In earlier times the Vistula had spread widely through several channels on the west side of Kraków. By the end of the fourteenth century, however, it had been forced into a single channel there, leaving behind a series of ponds and marshlands. To the south of Wawel the stream split into channels, one flowing east between Kraków and the suburb of Kazimierz, the other flowing around the south of Kazimierz. To the east the two eventually joined again. In the course of the fifteenth century efforts were made to dam the Vistula beneath Skałka hill in Kazimierz, thus draining the southern channel.[124] These generally proved unsuccessful, and in time of high water the river flowed through both beds, often flooding great parts of the district of Stradom. The Rudawa was a less powerful stream. Flowing out of the north toward the Vistula, it was easily diverted. By the end of the thirteenth century it had been channeled along the north and part of the east sides of the city and, by at least 1401,[125] its course had been extended along the west side down to the base of Wawel hill. In the following decades a further segment on the east was constructed. Thus by the end of the fifteenth century Kraków was completely encircled by the Rudawa.[126] Within the circumference of this moat lay the fortifications of the city.

By 1400 Kraków had been completely encircled by walls for more than a century.[127] Averaging ten meters in height, they were constructed largely of relatively scarce native stone. Along their course were placed a series of towers (at least fourteen have been identified) which both strengthened the wall and provided positions for lookout and defense. In case of an attack each of the guilds in Kraków was assigned a specific tower to defend. The city was entered through one of the seven great gates that pierced the wall. These were named predominantly for the streets that ran to them. On the southwest was the Wiślna gate (Vistula), built in 1310; on the west was the Szewska gate (Bootmaker), built in 1313; on the north were the Sławkowska (Famous) and Floriańska (St. Florian) gates, built in 1311 and *ante* 1307 respectively; the east wall was dominated by the Mikołajska gate (St. Nicholas), which dated from the late thirteenth century, and the "New" gate, built in 1328; the southern entrance was through the Grodzka gate (castle), which was the earliest, dating from the late thirteenth century. In a few instances the walls were breached by small private gates that provided access to individual residences. The municipal system of fortifications was completed late in the fifteenth century (1495–1498) by the construction of a brick barbican, completely surrounded by a wide moat and attached by a drawbridge to the Floriańska gate. It was accessible from outside the city walls only by its own drawbridge. As with other walled medieval cities, Kraków closed and locked its gates by night, even in peacetime. The ringing of a bell was the signal for all day visitors to leave and all residents to return. Since the keys to the gates were delivered to the mayor after nightfall, it was extremely unlikely, except in the most urgent circumstances and for someone of considerable importance, that a latecomer would be admitted.

Wawel was a completely separate area.[128] Its original fortifications and those built by the last Piasts were considerably extended during the fifteenth century, eventually enclosing the whole acropolis. In addition, several bastions were built into the walls to strengthen them. Entrance to the hill itself was apparently only from the south side during this period. On the crown of the hill was a complex of many buildings. The royal castle and the cathedral dominated the hill. The latter was rebuilt in the gothic style by the last Piasts, while the former was enlarged slightly by the early Jagiellonians.

Beneath Wawel, the area within the city walls was dominated by the central town square (*circulus,* later *forum;* Polish *rynek* from German *Ring*).[129] On it stood the great rectangular cloth hall (*camerae pannorum*), begun in the time of Casimir the Great and completed in the last decades of the fourteenth century. In it, and in the parallel structure called the "rich men's shop" (*institae opulentae seu crammi*), wealthy merchants handled cloth and other costly goods. Other merchandise was sold in the numerous wooden structures which dotted the open square. Below the cloth hall stood the main city scale and beside it, to the south and west, was the town hall, where the city government—both the council and the judiciary—had its seat. Begun in the late thirteenth century, its upper story and tower were finished in the fifteenth. The square was also the site of the small romanesque Church of St. Wojciech (Adalbert). The most important building fronting on the square was the leading parish church of the city, St. Mary's. Rebuilt of brick in the gothic style between 1320 and 1380, a second tower was added and the earlier tower raised in height during the fifteenth century.[130] From atop one of these, the city watchman was always prepared to sound an alarm by trumpet in case of danger or fire. A cemetery was located on the southeast side of the church, and the small chapel of St. Barbara in it was remodeled late in the fifteenth century into a small gothic church. Preaching in St. Mary's was usually in German; in St. Barbara's it was in Polish. Surrounding the square were the two- and three-story homes of wealthy merchants. Some of these buildings were constructed of stone or brick, but the majority, even at the end of the fifteenth century, were of wood. Thus the cumulative effect of the central *rynek* was of a municipal center on a grand scale, reflecting the prosperity and importance of the city.

For administrative purposes the city of Kraków was divided into four quarters, using the central square as a point of reference.[131] The Grodzki quarter (castle, *castrense*), encompassed approximately the southeast quadrant. The Rzeźniczy quarter (butchers, *laniorum* or *carnificum*), extended through a quarter-arc in the northeast. The chief street of this quarter, on which were numerous stone houses of prosperous citizens, was Floriańska. It constituted part of the old *via regia* from the north, through St. Florian's gate to the *rynek* and south along Grodzka street to Wawel. The Sławkowska (famous, *Slawcoviense*, from Polish *sława*, fame, glory) encompassed the northwest quadrant. This section was the least urbanized in Kraków, and stretches of open land extended to the walls in places. The last quarter of the city, the Garncarski (potters, *figulorum*) was formed by the southwest quadrant. There were numerous stone houses in this section, and it was both prosperous and well built-up. At the beginning of the fifteenth century the Jewish settlement was located here, but in the course of the 1400s this quarter emerged as the chief locus of the university. In addition to the later *Collegium maius*, the chief university structure, other *bursae* and *collegia* were located here.

Within these four quarters the total population of Kraków, if one excludes the university students (who never in most years numbered more than a few hundred), was probably about 12,000 at the beginning of the fifteenth century, perhaps as high as 14,000 at the end.[132] The lives of these residents were often affected by the twin phenomena of epidemics and fires. At no time in the fifteenth century was Kraków so cruelly afflicted by plague as western Europe had been during the mid-fourteenth century with the outbreak of the Black Death. Nevertheless there were several instances of citywide epidemics during this period. Of unknown nature, they swept through the populace at least four times between 1450 and 1482. On such occasions many followed the proverbial advice, "Quickly flee the plague, long avoid the place of infection, return home slowly."[133]

Fires were more destructive of physical property, though it is probable that loss of life was minimal. Despite the boast of a later historian that Casimir the Great, in effect, had "found a Poland of wood and left one of stone,"[134] and despite the general prosperity of the city and the presence of many stone houses and buildings, much of Kraków was still built of wood and fire was a constant threat. The city employed watchmen to guard against the spread of a blaze and one was always positioned on the highest tower in town, the *turris excubiarum* of St. Mary's church on the square. If a fire was spotted, he gave the signal by trumpet, at which all were to assemble in a bucket brigade. According to a municipal statute of 1395 the first to arrive on the scene with water received a prize of twelve *groszy* (a quarter of a mark), the second six *groszy*, the third two *groszy*.[135] Some fires could not be located or contained, however, and spread through whole quarters of the city. Two of the worst serve as examples. In 1462, some members of the Dominican monastery were experimenting late at night with alchemical combinations. These exploded and started a conflagration which eventually swept into the area of the university.[136] An even more serious fire broke out in July 1492. Starting near the Szewska gate it spread south and burned many of the houses in the university quarter, including the *Collegium maius*.[137]

Finally, with regard to Kraków as an urban settlement, it should be noted that it had its own suburbs.[138] To the south, Kazimierz was, strictly speaking, not one of these. It was an independent municipality "located" by Casimir the Great in 1335. By the end of the fourteenth century it was completely enclosed by walls. Within these, the northeast section of the town was the most completely urbanized. The approximately 2,000 inhabitants of the city were predominantly small crafts-workers and merchants, and there was an increasingly important Jewish community settled there. Between Kazimierz and Kraków lay the area of Stradom, which we have noted before. It was largely an agrarian community and its few craft guilds were closely associated with those in Kazimierz. In 1419 King Władysław Jagiełło incorporated Stradom into Kazimierz. East of Kraków was an area, Wesoła, which can scarcely be called a suburb. It was only lightly populated and built up. North of Kraków lay the open settlement of Kleparz. After the middle of the fifteenth century it, along with Kazimierz, competed vigorously for trade with Kraków.[139] This area was also known as Florencia from the name of its leading church, the collegiate foundation of St. Florian. This church was of great importance for the University of Kraków, for the *studium* held six, later nine, and eventually ten well-endowed benefices there. A common sight in the fifteenth century was the processsion of professors from the university to St. Florian's, where they performed their ecclesiastical responsibilities, after which they took the long walk back to the *Collegium maius*.

Mention of these matters is sufficient to bring us to the last role which Kraków played in the late Middle Ages, that of university town. We have mentioned this institution several times in passing. Its presence in Kraków lent a particular character to the city.

The Casimiran foundation of 1364 had not prospered. Too few students, lack of faculty and, most important, the death of the founding Maecenas in 1370 had all combined to render the university merely a paper institution.[140] Although the memory of the *studium* was maintained and a few students may actually have graduated, the school virtually disappeared in the 1380s. It was briefly revived in the early 1390s and permission was obtained in 1397 from the papacy to add a theological faculty. But it was not until 1400 that a new era began. In July of that year, acting to fulfill one of the most passionately held ambitions of his wife Jadwiga, Władysław Jagiełło established the University of Kraków. In the course of the fifteenth century the school came to be the "pearl of powerful learning" that Jagiełło had hoped it would be in his decree of foundation.[141] It was a jewel which not only adorned the *corona* of Poland, but which also embellished the city of Kraków. More than 200 students matriculated in 1400, and by the last decade of the century matriculation neared 500 in some years. All told, more than 18,000 individuals, many of them from foreign lands, enrolled at Kraków in the fifteenth century.[142] Increasingly, as the university prospered it made its presence felt in the city. Nowhere was this more evident than in the growth of the *Collegium maius*.

The history of this building begins before the history of the revived *studium*.[143] Prior to the early fifteenth century, the area that eventually became the university district was a Jewish ghetto. Late in the thirteenth or early in the fourteenth century someone had built a large rectangular stone house there, which, because of its size, was known as the *domus maius* or *lapidea magna*. During the 1390s Jagiełło and Jadwiga had arranged for the acquisition of the house, perhaps because they intended some benefaction connected with education. Whatever the case, in 1400, Jagiełło gave it to the university to house the masters and provide a place for teaching. The original home of the university measured some ten by twenty meters. It was not long before it was apparent these quarters were insufficient. After a difficult first decade, the university began to prosper. New endowments added professors in both the arts and the higher faculties and the numbers of students increased. As a result, efforts were made to enlarge the building. In 1417 the faculty succeeded in purchasing the adjoining two houses and remodeling them into a single unit. Throughout the course of the century this process of acquisition and remodeling continued steadily. By the late 1480s the university had succeeded in gathering houses and land around its original home in such a manner that its properties constituted a block approximately fifty meters square. In the aftermath of the disastrous fire of 1492,[144] the faculty approved a rebuilding and remodeling process which, with one or two significant changes early in the sixteenth century, brought the *Collegium maius* into its final form. This century-long process shaped a physical unity which both contributed to and reflected the commonality of the intellectual and academic endeavor within it.

Just as the city of Kraków was a unity in diversity, so was the university which made it famous throughout the region a corporate unity—both legally and intellectually. It is not surprising therefore that Kraków should be described by the late fifteenth century chronicler Hartmann Schedel as a city "surrounded by high ramparts, . . . whose citizens live in many beautiful and noble houses . . . and where there is a large and glorious gymnasium filled with many famous learned men to teach the liberal arts, rhetoric, poetics, philosophy and physics. In the whole of Germany," he concludes, "one cannot find a more famous school."[145] Kraków had become the "urbs celeberrima" of Poland. All five of the elements we have defined in this study went together to create an urban unity.

NOTES

1. In his *De Europa* (XXV: "De Polonia," 272), Aeneas (Silvius) commented that "Cracovia est praecipua regni civitas, in qua liberalium

artium schola floret," and in a letter to Martin Mayer he described the city as an "urbs litterarum studiis ornata" (*Pii II Commentarii*, 675). For an elaboration of these themes, see Ignacy Zarębski, "Stosunki Eneasza Sylwiusza z Polską i Polakami," *Rozprawy Polskiej Akademii Umiejętności: wydział historyczno-filozoficzny*, ser. 2, XLV (1939), 281–437, especially, in this context, pp. 358 ff.

2. See, Bronisław Biliński, "Dwa świadectwa antyczne: *Kalisia* Ptolemeusza (*Geographia* II: 11, 13), i *Halisii* Tacyta (*Germania* 43, 2)," in *Osiemnaście wieków Kalisza, Studia i materiały do dziejów miasta Kalisza i regionu kaliskiego*, two vols., (Kalisz 1960–1961) II: 7–40.

3. Some of the more important contributions in this regard are discussed in *I Międzynarodowy Kongres Archeologii Słowiańskiej*, VI (Wrocław 1968); Witold Hensel, *Archeologia i prahistoria* (Wrocław 1971); Hensel, *Méthodes et perspectives des recherches sur les centres ruraux et urbains chez les Slaves (VIIe–XIIIe ss.)* (Warsaw 1962); and Hensel and Lech Leciejewicz, "En Pologne médiévale: l'archéologie au service de l'histoire. I: Villes et campagnes," *Annales: Économies–Sociétés–Civilisations* (1962) XVII: 203–222. There are also important, up-to-date contributions under individual rubrics in the "Słownik starożytności słowiańskich, Władisław Kowalenko, Gerard Labuda, et al., eds. (Wrocław 1961—[in progress]).

4. This period is well-treated in the first three volumes of Henryk Łowmiański, *Początki Polski* (Warsaw 1964–1967). See also, the comments of Norman Davies, *God's Playground: A History of Poland*, two vols. (New York 1982) I: 38–52; and, more briefly, my own forthcoming observations in "Poland," in "Dictionary of the Middle Ages," general editor Joseph R. Strayer (New York 1982—[in progress]).

5. Hensel, *Anfänge der Städte bei den Ost- und Westslawen* (Bautzen 1967), p. 29f., and in "The Origins of Western and Eastern European Slav Towns," in *European Towns, Their Archaeology and Early History*, M. W. Barley, ed. (London, New York, and San Francisco 1977), p. 375.

6. There is an enormous literature on this often controversial process. Among the most important recent contributions are the following items: Tadeusz Lalik, "Organizacja grodowo-prowincjonalna w Polsce XI i początków XII w.," *Studia z Dziejów Osadnictwa* V (1967), 5–51; Karol Buczek, "Z badań nad organizacją grodową w Polsce wczesnofeudalnej. Problem terytorialności grodów kasztelańskich," *Kwartalnik Historyczny* LXXVII (1970), 3–29; Buczek, "Gospodarcze funkcje organizacji grodowej w Polsce wczesnofeudalnej (wiek X–XIII)," *Kwartalnik Historyczny* LXXXVI (1979), 363–384; and Karol Modzelewski, *Organizacja gospodarcza państwa piastowskiego. X–XIII wiek* (Wrocław

1975). See also the treatment of this process in Łowmiański, *Początki Polski*, Volumes IV and V. For a convenient guide in English to this problem, compare Modzelewski, "The System of the Ius Ducale and the Idea of Feudalism," *Quaestiones Medii Aevi* I (1977), 71–99; and Tadeusz Wasilewski, "Poland's Administrative Structure in Early Piast Times," *Acta Poloniae Historica* XLIV (1981), 5–31.

7. The historical and legendary elements connected with "Piast" are discussed by Kazimierz Ślaski, *Wątki historyczne w podaniach o początkach Polski* (Poznań 1968), pp. 69–84; Buczek, "Zagadnienie wiarygodności dwóch relacji o początkowych dziejach państwa polskiego," in *Prace z dziejów Polski feudalnej ofiarowane Romanowi Grodeckiemu w 70 rocznicę urodzin* (Warsaw, 1960), pp. 45–70; and Kazimierz Tymieniecki, "Legendy i spór o tradycję historyczną," *Studia Źródłoznawcze* X (1965), 101–108.

8. The characteristics discussed below are analyzed in comparative context by Leciejewicz, "Early Medieval Sociotopographical Transformations in West Slavonic Urban Settlements in the Light of Archaeology," *Acta Poloniae Historica*, XXXIV (1976), 29–56; especially pp. 33–52.

9. Although there has been much significant scholarship in recent years on the development of markets, the following older works have not been superseded: Roman Grodecki, *Targi w Polsce przed kolonizacją na prawie niemieckim* (Kraków 1922); Karol Maleczyński, *Najstarsze targi w Polsce i stosunek ich do miast przed kolonizacją na prawie niemieckim* (Lwów 1926); and Stefan Weymann, *Cła i drogi handlowe w Polsce piastowskiej* (Poznań 1938). As noted below, however, not all of Maleczyński's conclusions may be accepted. For a more recent work, see Lalik's article "Targ," in *Słownik starożytności słowiańskich*, VI.

10. Zygmunt Wojciechowski, *Mieszko I and the Rise of the Polish State* (Toruń and Gdynia, 1936); and Juliusz Bardach, "L'Etat polonais aux Xᶜ et XIᶜ siècles," in *L'Europe aux IXᶜ–XIᶜ siècles*, edited by Tadeusz Manteuffel and Aleksander Gieysztor (Warsaw 1968), pp. 279–319.

11. For the most important recent work on pre-Christian religion among the Slavs in general and the Poles in particular, see Łowmiański, *Religia słowian i jej upadek (w. VI–XII)* (Warsaw, 1979), pp. 202–236 in particular; and Gieysztor, *Mitologia Słowian* (Warsaw 1982).

12. For his baptism, compare Jerzy Dowiat, *Metryka chrztu Mieszka I i jej geneza* (Warsaw 1961), pp. 55–86 especially, with A. P. Vlasto, *The Entry of the Slavs into Christendom* (Cambridge 1970), pp. 113–117.

13. Władysław Abraham, *Organizacja Kościoła w Polsce do połowy wieku XII* (Lwów 1890); Dowiat, *Chrzest Polski* (Warsaw, 1958 and later

editions); Zygmunt Sułowski, "Początki Kościoła polskiego," in *Kościół w Polsce* I: *Średniowiecze* (Kraków 1966), pp. 17–123; and Łowmiański, *Religia słowian*, pp. 302–317.

14. See Gieysztor, "Przemiany ideologiczne w państwie pierwszych Piastów a wyprowadzenie chrześcijaństwa," in *Początki państwa polskiego, Księga tysiąclecie*, two vols. (Poznań 1962). II: 155–170; and Mantueffel, *The Formation of the Polish State, The Period of Ducal Rule, 963–1194* (Detroit, 1982), pp. 47–76.

15. On this point, see the comments of Jan Zachwatowicz, "Architektura," in Michał Walicki, ed., *Sztuka Polska przedromańska i romańska do schyłku XIII wieku*, two vols. (Warsaw 1971), I: 71–90.

16. Via the Old Slavonic *kostelŭ* (and perhaps throught the Czech *kostel*). On this point, see Vlasto, *The Entry of the Slavs into Christendom*, p. 25.

17. His narrative text and reconstructions are in Jerzy Topolski, ed., *Dzieje Gniezna* (Warsaw, 1965), pp. 24–44. A similar reconstruction of the development of Wrocław in this same general period may be found in *Dzieje Wrocławia do roku 1807*, by Wacław Długoborski, Józef Gierowski, and Karol Maleczyński (Warsaw 1958), p. 29.

18. Irena Gieysztorowa, "Badania nad historią zaludnienia Polski," *Kwartalnik Historii Kultury Materialnej* XI (1963) 543f., and, more briefly, by the same author, "Research Into the Demographic History of Poland, A Provisional Summing-up," *Acta Poloniae Historica* XVIII (1968) 10. The number 250 is taken from the estimate given by J. K. Fedorowicz, ed., *A Republic of Nobles, Studies in Polish History to 1864* (Cambridge 1982), p. 135, in his introduction to an article by Maria Bogucka.

19. The classic statement of this position is by Richard Koebner, "Dans les terres de colonisation: Marchés slaves et villes allemandes," *Annales d'Histoire économique et sociale* IX (1937) 547: " . . . [en Pologne] la fondation des villes s'effectua sur une table rasé." See also his comments in "Das Problem der slavischen Burgsiedlung und die Oppelner Ausgrabungen," *Zeitschrift des Vereins für Geschichte Schlesiens*, LXV (1931) 113 ff. His view was by no means the property of a small number of historians; it was, indeed, the majority view of western historians until recent decades.

20. The best example of this trend among Polish scholars is the article by Gieysztor, "From Forum to Civitas: Urban Changes in Poland in the Twelfth and Thirteenth Centuries," in *La Pologne au XIIe Congrès international des sciènces historiques à Vienne* (Warsaw 1965), pp. 7–30. Among Gieysztor's other important contributions in this regard are the following studies: "Le origini della città nella Polonia medievale,"

in *Studi in onore di A. Sapori* (Milan 1957) I: 129–145; "Les origines de la ville slave," in *Settimane di studio,* VI (Spoleto 1959), 279–315; and "Les chartes de franchises urbaines et rurales en Pologne au XIII*ᵉ* siècle," In *Les libertés urbaines et rurales du XI*ᵉ *au XIV*ᵉ *siècle* (Brussels 1968 [*Collection Histoire—Historische Uuitgaven,* no. 19]), pp. 103–125. Each of these summarize more substantial works, by Gieysztor and others, done in Polish. German scholarship has also followed some of the same paths. See the articles by both German and Polish scholars in Walter Schlesinger, ed., *Die Deutsche Ostsiedlung des Mittelalters als Problem der europäischen Geschichte* (Sigmaringen 1975 [*Vorträge und Forschungen,* Vol. XVIII]).

21. Hensel, "Origins of Western and Eastern Slav Towns," p. 375.

22. Tymieniecki, "Zagadnienie początków miast w Polsce," *Przegląd Historyczny* XXI (1918) 319–345, reprinted in his *Pisma wybrana* (Warsaw 1956), pp. 205–228.

23. On this point, see the observations of Bernard Ziffer, *Poland, History and Historians, Three Bibliographical Essays* (New York 1952), pp. 21, 37.

24. Buczek, *Targi i miasta na prawie polskim (okres wczesnośredniowieczny)* (Wrocław 1964).

25. See especially Maleczyński, *Najstarsze targi w Polsce,* pp. 94ff., 104ff.; Gerard Labuda, "Miasta na prawie polskim," in *Studia historica w 35-lecie pracy naukowej Henryka Łowmiańskiego* (Warsaw 1958), pp. 181–197; Zdzisław Kaczmarczyk, "Początki miast polskich, zagadnienia prawne," *Czasopismo Prawno-Historyczne* XIII, ii (1961), 9–45; and Stanisław Pazyra, *Geneza i rozwój miast mazowieckich* (Warsaw 1959), especially pp. 178ff.

26. Tymieniecki, "Prawo czy gospodarstwo?," *Roczniki Dziejów Społecznych i Gospodarczych* VIII (1946), 280ff.

27. Benedykt Zientara, "Socio-Economic and Spatial Transformation of Polish Towns During the Period of Location," *Acta Poloniae Historica* XXXIV (1976), 63f.

28. Koebner, "Locatio. Zur Begriffssprache und Geschichte der deutschen Kolonisation," *Zeitschrift des Vereins für Geschichte Schlesiens* LXIII (1929), 1–32.

29. For this example, see the extremely rich collection of documents, H. Helbig and L. Weinrich, eds., *Urkunden und erzählende Quellen zur deutschen Ostsiedlung im Mittelalter,* two vols. (Darmstadt, 1968–1970); here II, no. 24.

30. See Walter Kuhn, "Die Siedlerzahlen der deutschen Ostsied-

lung," *Studium Sociale, (Mélanges K. V. Müller)* (Cologne and Opladen 1963), pp. 132–136.

31. Gieysztor, "Urban changes in Poland," pp. 20f. Zdzisław Kaczmarczyk, *Kolonizacja niemiecka na wschód od Odry* (Poznań 1945) is the most thorough study. See also Stanisław Trawkowski, "W sprawie roli kolonizacji niemieckiej w przemianach kultury materialnej na ziemiach polskich," *Kwartalnik Historii Kultury Materialnej* VIII (1960) 183–206; and Trawkowski, "Zur Erforschung der deutschen Kolonisation auf polnischem Boden im 13. Jahrhundert," *Acta Poloniae Historica* VII (1962), 78–95.

32. See Zientara's comments in "Zur Geschichte der planmässingen Organisierung des Marktes im Mittelalter," in *Wirtschaftliche und Soziale Strukturen im saekularen Wandel. Festschrift für Wilhelm Abel zum 70. Geburtstag,* two vols. (Hannover 1974), II: 345–365.

33. Zientara, "Socio-Economic and Spatial Transformation of Polish Towns," p. 66f. One of the most important examples of ducal locations was the systematic policy toward foundation and location (the two not being synonymous) of towns in Silesia by Duke Henry I, the Bearded, in the early thirteenth century. His initiative showed the way for later ducal policies in Silesia, Great Poland and Little Poland; while his acts often became precedents which were followed in later foundations. The older studies of his town policy, especially that by Henryk Münch, "Początki średniowiecznego układzie miejskiego w Polsce ze szczególnym uwzględnieniem Śląska," *Kwartalnik Architektury i Urbanistyki* V (1960) 357–375, have now been totally superseded by Zientara, *Henryk Brodaty i jego czasy* (Warsaw 1975), which is, in many ways, one of the finest examples of historical scholarship and writing in recent years.

34. See the brief comments of Fedorowicz, *A Republic of Nobles,* p. 136 f.; and, in somewhat greater length, the observations of Maria Bogucka, "Polish Towns Between the Sixteenth and Eighteenth Centuries," in Fedorowicz, *A Republic of Nobles,* pp. 138–152. There is forthcoming the important volume by Bogucka and Henryk Samsonowicz, "Dzieje miast i mieszczaństwa w Polsce przedrozbiorowej," which will provide a synthesis of much recent work on the general question of the weakness of Polish urban development in the early modern period.

35. Buczek, *Targi i miasta,* pp. 65 ff.

36. Buczek, "O tak zwanym rittermeszig man i o 'gosciu' w najdawniejszym spisie prawa polskiego," *Czasopismo Prawno-Historyczne* XII, i (1960), 141–164.

37. *Dzieje Szczecina wiek X–1805,* Gerard Labuda, ed. (Warsaw 1963), pp. 46–51; *Dzieje Wrocławia,* pp. 62 ff.

38. There is a good summary and analysis of this process in Samsonowicz, "Samorząd miejski w dobie rozdrobnienia feudalnego w Polsce," in Henryk Łowmiański, ed., *Polska w okresie rozdrobnienia feudalnego* (Wrocław 1973), pp. 133–159.

39. See Gieysztor, "Urban Changes in Poland," p. 27 f.; and, with particular reference to Łęczyca, Tadeusz Lalik, "Stare Miasto w Łęczycy. Przemiany w okresie poprzedzającym lokację: schyłek XII i początek XIII wieku," *Kwartalnik Historii Kultury Materialnej* IV (1956), 631–678.

40. On this development, see Herbert Ludat, "Die Bezeichnungen für 'Stadt' im Slawischen," in *Syntagma Friburgense, Festschrift H. Aubin* (Lindau, 1956), pp. 107–124.

41. The views of Henryk Münch in this matter received wide circulation during the 1950s, but recent scholarship, based on both written and archaeological sources (see note 42), has demonstrated them to be in error. Of Münch's many works, two in particular were widely read and cited: *Geneza rozplanowania miast wielkopolskich XIII i XIV w.* (Kraków 1946), and "Über den frühmittelalterlichen und mittelalterlichen Stadtgrundriss in Polen und seine Erforschung," in *L'artisanat et la vie urbaine en Pologne médiévale[Ergon III (1962)]*, pp. 346ff.

42. Tadeusz Zagrodzki, "Regularny plan miasta średniowiecznego a limitacja miernicza," *Studia Wczesnośredniowieczne* V (1962), 1–101, is now the standard work on this subject.

43. Labuda, ed. *Dzieje Szczecina,* p. 72.

44. Zientara, "Socio-Economic and Spatial Transformation of Polish Towns," p. 80.

45. Bogucka, "Polish Towns," p. 138.

46. Data on Wrocław are taken from *Dzieje Wrocławia,* p. 206; other data are summarized by Bogucka, "Polish Towns," p. 138f.

47. Much important monographic work is synthesized by Zientara in "Nationality Conflicts in the German-Slavic Borderland in the 13th–14th Centuries and Their Social Scope," *Acta Poloniae Historica,* XXII (1970) 207–225; and "Foreigners in Poland in the 10th–15th Centuries: Their Role in the Opinion of the Polish Medieval Community," *Acta Poloniae Historica* XXIX (1974), 5–28.

48. To the very large body of Polish scholarship on the question of "national consciousness" (for example, Roman Grodecki, *Powstanie polskiej świadomości narodowej* [Katowice 1946]; and Roman Heck, "Świadomość narodowa i państwowa w Czechach i w Polsce w XV w., *Pa-*

miętnik X Powszechnego Zjazdu Historyków Polskich w Lublinie [Warsaw 1968], I: 126–151), there should now be added the very sophisticated comparative analysis by the Czech scholar in emigration, František Graus, *Die Nationenbildung der Westslawen im Mittelalter* [*Nationes*, 3] (Sigmaringen 1980), pp. 64–73, 116–129, and 182–190 especially.

49. The case for Hussite influence is overstated, in my judgment, in the standard work on this question, Roman Heck and Ewa Maleczyńska, eds., *Ruch husycki w Polsce. Wybór tekstów żródłowych (do r. 1454)* (Wrocław 1953).

50. For the thirteenth century, there is an excellent study by Samsonowicz, "Ideologia mieszczańska w Polsce w XIII w.," in *Sztuka i ideologia* (Wrocław 1974), pp. 153–164. An example of how important the outlook of the bourgeoisie can be is reflected in the useful study by Brygida Kürbisówna, "Mieszczanie na Uniwersytecie Jagiellońskim w XV w. i ich udział w kształtowanie świadomości narodowej," *Studia Staropolskie* V (1957) 5–79.

51. See the work of Richard C. Hoffmann, "Warfare, Weather, and a Rural Economy: The Duchy of Wrocław in the Mid-fifteenth Century," *Viator* IV (1973) 273–305; and "Nazwy i Miejscowości: trzy studia z historii sredniowiecznej okregu Wrocławskiego," *Sobótka* (1974) 1, pp. 1–25. The major contribution of Hoffmann is his "Studies in the Rural Economy of the Duchy of Wrocław, 1200–1530" (unpublished Ph. D. dissertation, Yale University, 1970).

52. By focusing upon Kraków in the remainder of this study, I do not mean to imply that it was the only important and distinctive urban center in Poland. Certainly such cities as Wrocław, Gniezno, and Gdańsk deserve attention; but in a presentation of this scope, arbitrary limitations have had to be made. Nevertheless, the following brief comments may be helpful. All three cities were as old (or nearly so) as Kraków as urban settlements, and each had considerable political importance, either in the ecclesiastical or secular sphere. For most of the late Middle Ages Wrocław and Gdańsk lay outside the polity of the Polish kingdom and, in a number of distinctive ways, both were more directly influenced by foreign elements—German and/or Czech—than was Gniezno (and also Kraków). This factor had implications, not only in the arena of politics, but also in the pattern of economic growth, cultural evolution, and even—to a degree—social differentiation. Wrocław and Gdańsk were also major commercial centers whose regional economic importance equaled and, at times, surpassed Kraków's. Gdańsk, with its maritime site and *longea platea* (*Langmarkt* or *Długi Targ)*; Wrocław, with its distinctive *Ring* and *Rath-*

haus; Gniezno, with its multiple fortified complex; and all three with
their pattern of settlement and development amidst river channels and
islands represent important variations upon the themes to be explored
in Kraków's history in the pages below. To follow the histories of each
city, see respectively the appropriate sections of *Dzieje Wrocławia*, pp.
24–293 especially; Topolski, *Dzieje Gniezna*, pp. 10–256 especially; and
Gdańsk, jego dzieje i kultura [Gdańsk, Its History and Culture] (Warsaw
1969), pp. 11–27, 29–42, 129–135, and 142–149 especially. Each city is
treated within a broader synthetic or comparative context in, among
other places, articles in *Acta Poloniae Historica* XXXIV (1976) by Tadeusz
Rosłanowski, Lech Leciejewicz, Benedykt Zientara, and Tadeusz
Lalik—all of whom provide good bibliographies; in the first volume
of *Miasta polskie w Tysiącleciu* [Polish Cities in the Last Millennium]
(Wrocław 1965); and in the series of articles contained in *Ergon*, III
(1962). A larger context is provided by Hensel, "Origins of Western
and Eastern European Slav Towns," pp. 373–390.

53. The geological and geographical orientation of Kraków given
by Józef Mitkowski, "Dawne warunki geograficzne jako podłoże, na
którym rozwinął się zespół osad Krakowskich," in Jan Dąbrowski, ed.,
Kraków, Studie nad rozwojem miasta (Kraków 1957) pp. 39–64, should
now be supplemented by the following: Maria Borowiejska-Birkenmajerowa, *Kształt średniowiecznego Krakowa* (Kraków 1975), pp. 26–35;
and Kazimierz Radwański, *Kraków przedlokacyjny, rozwój przestrzenny*
(Kraków 1975), pp. 14–43.

54. The fullest treatment of this period, containing much material
derived from his own investigations, is Rudolf Jamka, *Kraków w pradziejach*, in volume I (Wrocław 1963 [Polskie Towarzystwo Archeologiczne, Biblioteka Archeologiczna, vol. XVI]). More briefly, see
Borowiejska-Birkenmajerowa, *Kształt średniowiecznego Krakowa*, pp. 36–
48.

55. The legends were transmitted through the early thirteenth-century chronicle of Bishop Vincent Kadłubek of Kraków. For their historical usefulness, see Slaski, *Wątki historyczne w podaniach o początkach
Polski*, pp. 24–51.

56. A clear presentation on the present state of our knowledge
about Wawel's development is provided by Jan Zachwatowicz, "Architektura," in Walicki, ed., *Sztuka Polska* I: 71–194, passim.; and Radwański, *Kraków przedlokacyjny*, pp. 44–56.

57. Andrzej Żaki, "Odkrycie nowego reliktu przedromańskiego
(tzw. kościół B)," *Sprawozdania z Posiedzeń Kom. Oddz. PAN w Krakowie
za rok 1966* (Kraków 1967), pp. 24–27, and *Sprawozdania . . . za rok 1969*
(Kraków 1969), pp. 46f.

58. Żaki, "Nowoodkryte ruiny budowli przedromańskiej na Wawelu," *Studia do dziejów Wawelu* I (1955) 71–111; and Radwański, *Kraków przedlokacynjy*, p. 49.

59. *Relacja Ibrahima ibn Jakuba z podróży do krajów słowiańskich*, ed. Tadeusz Kowalski, et al., in *Pomniki Dziejowe Polski, Seria II*, I (Kraków 1946).

60. Klementyna Żurowska, "Zagadnienie transeptu I katedry wawelskiej," *Zeszyty Naukowe Uniwersytetu Jagiellońskiego: Prace z historii sztuki* II (1965) 19–94; p. 72 especially. See also Adam Bochnak, "Najstarsze budowle wawelskie," in *Prace z dziejów Polski feudalnej ofiarowane Romanowi Grodeckiemu w 70 rocznicę urodzin* (Warsaw 1960), p. 100.

61. Zachwatowicz, "Architektura," pp. 95–101; Adolf Szyszko-Bohusz, "Studia nad katerdrą wawelską," *Prace Komisji Historii Sztuki* VIII (1939–1946) 107–150.

62. Gabriel Leńczyk, "Badania wykopaliskowe na Wawelu w latach 1948 i 1949," *Studia Wczesnośredniowieczne* II (1953) 83–88; and Żurowska, "Rotunda wawelska. Studium nad centralną architekturą epoki wczesnośredniowiecznej," *Studia do dziejów Wawelu* III (1968) 1–121; p. 88 and note 354 especially.

63. Radwanski, *Kraków przedlokacyjny*, p. 57.

64. The extent and pattern of settlement in Okół is discussed by Borowiejska-Birkenmajerowa in two reports: "Północna rubież krakowskiego okołu," *Sprawozdania z Posiedzeń Kom. Nauk, PAN. Oddział w Krakowie* XIV, ii (1970) 481–484, and "Uwagi o urbanistyce Krakowa w XIII wieku," *Sprawozdania z Posiedzeń Kom. Nauk. PAN. Oddział w Krakowie* XIV, i (1970), 8–10.

65. The sources are summarized and collected by Münch, "Układ urbanistyczny Krakowa do połowy XIII w., *Czasopismo Techniczne* V (1959) 6.

66. See Radwański, *Kraków przedlokacyjny*, pp. 130–141.

67. Aleksander Grygorowicz, "Kościół św. Andrzeja w Krakowie we wczesnym średniowieczu," *Rocznik Krakowski* XXXIX (1968) 5–36.

68. For a convenient summary of this process, and the evidence upon which it is based, see Mitkowski, "Kraków przed lokacją," in Janina Bieniarzówna, ed., *Szkice z dziejów Krakowa* (Kraków 1968), pp. 7–23; Renata Żurkowa, "Kraków wczesnośredniowieczny, (wiek X do połowy XIII)," in Dąbrowski, *Kraków, Studia nad rozwojem miasta*, pp. 98–116; and Borowiejska-Birkenmajerowa, *Kształt średniowiecznego Krakowa*, pp. 61–71.

69. Numerous investigations carried out under the direction of Radwański, and reported in specialized publications, are summarized with regard to St. Wojciech's Church in *Kraków przedlokacyjny*, pp. 169–

190. In addition, see especially his article "Budowle drewniana od-kryte pod poziomami romańskimi kościoła św. Wojciecha w Krakowie," *Materiały Archeologiczne* XI (1970) 7–23.

70. Stefan Swiszczowski, "Gródek krakowski i mury miejskie między Grodkiem a Wawelem," *Rocznik Krakowski* XXXII (1950) 3–41.

71. Helena Zoll-Adamikowa, "Wczesnośredniowieczne cmentarzyska szkieletowe Małopolski," *Prace Komisji Archeologicznej*, XI (1971), 166f.

72. Radwański, *Kraków przedlokacyjny*, p. 244f.

73. Radwański, *Kraków przedlokacyjny*, pp. 247–259.

74. Teresa Lenkiewicz and Radwański, "Wyniki badań archeologicznych prowadzonych na Skałce w Krakowie w latach 1956–1957," *Biuletyn Krakowski* I (1959) 99–133.

75. In *Opera Omnia*, Aleksander Przeździecki, ed. I (Kraków, 1867) 62.

76. In particular, from the Wit Stowosz altar in St. Mary's Church in Kraków and from a triptych in Pławno which dates from about 1520.

77. *Mistrza Wincentego kronika*, in *Monumenta Poloniae Historica*, II, 296f.; *Vita (minor) sancti Stanislai episcopi Cracovienses*, in *Mon. Pol., Hist.* IV: 280–282.

78. Narrative treatment of this period in English is found in Aleksander Gieysztor's text in Stefan Kieniewicz, et al., *History of Poland* (Warsaw 1968), pp. 64–80; Tadeusz Manteuffel, *The Formation of the Polish State: The Period of Ducal Rule 963–1194* (Detroit 1982), pp. 77–118; and Davies, *God's Playground* I: 62–72. A reliable treatment in Polish is given by Jerzy Wyrozumski, *Historia Polski do roku 1505* (Warsaw 1982), pp. 80–115.

79. *Mon. Pol. Hist.*, II: 435; IV: 393.

80. The most vivid medieval account of the Tatar attack is that by Joannes Długosz, *Annales seu Cronicae incliti Regni Poloniae*, edited by Jan Dąbrowski, et al. (Kraków 1964—) IV: 11–32 (Liber septimus, *sub anno* 1241). Długosz was, however, writing more than two centuries after the fact, and his sources need to be checked; see Aleksander Semkowicz, *Krytyczny rozbiór Dziejów Polskich Jana Długosza (do r. 1384)* (Kraków 1887), sub anno 1241 et seqq. The best modern treatment of the attack upon Kraków and the struggle with the Tatars in general is Stefan Krakowski, *Polska w walce z najazdami tatarskimi w XIII w.* (Warsaw 1956).

81. Zientara, "*Melioratio terrae:* The thirteenth-century breakthrough in Polish history," in Fedorowicz, *A Republic of Nobles*, pp. 31–47. These new settlers might come from Polish lands and be either ethnically Polish or foreign; others came directly from the lands of

Germany, or even, in some cases, from lands even further to the west, such as the Lowlands. For the presence of Flemings and Walloons in the migration population and in Slavonic lands, see Zientara, "Walloons in Silesia in the 12th and 13th centuries," *Quaestiones Medii Aevi* (Warsaw) II (1981), 127–150.

82. His grants to merchants at Złotoryja in 1211, and to Środa Śląska (ante 1223) were of particular importance. See Karol Maleczyński's comments in *Historia Śląska* I, 1 (Wrocław 1960) 449.

83. Gieysztor, "Urban Changes in Poland," p. 22.

84. *Zbiór dyplomów klasztoru mogilskiego*, edited by E. Janota and Franciszek Piekosiński, nos. 8 and 11 (Kraków 1865).

85. *Zbiór dyplomów klasztoru mogilskiego*, no. 22.

86. See Stanisław Zachorowski, "Kraków biskupi," *Rocznik Krakowski* VIII (1906) 122ff.; and Marjan Friedberg, *Kultura polska a niemiecka*, two vols. (Poznań 1946) I: 242-244.

87. Mitkowski, "Kraków lokacyjny," in Dąbrowski, *Kraków, Studia nad rozwojem miasta*, pp. 126–132; and (with notes to the more recent literature) Borowiejska-Birkenmajerowa, *Kształt średniowiecznego Krakowa*, pp. 71–83.

88. The Latin text of this *locatio* (which I have not seen) is, I believe, available only in the edition prepared by Polish archivists, *Krakau, Dokumente zur Stadtgeschichte* (Kraków 1942). There is a Polish translation in Adam Kłodziński, *Przywileje lokacyjne Krakowa i Poznania* (Poznań 1947), pp. 17–20.

89. The stages of implementing this plan are analyzed by Mitkowski, "Kraków lokacyjny," pp. 132–139; and, in greater depth (though with some controversial interpretations) by Borowiejska-Birkenmajerowa, *Kształt średniowiecznego Krakowa*, pp. 98–116. Not all will accept the details of her chronology regarding the erection of the city walls.

90. This market area was fully functioning by at least 1310; see the notation in *Najstarsze Księgi i rachunki miasta Krakowa od r. 1300 do 1400*, F. Piekosiński and Józef Szujski, eds., no. 109 (Kraków, 1878).

91. The early background of the Jews in Poland is discussed by Roman Grodecki, *Polska Piastowska* (Warsaw 1969), pp. 595 ff.; while the history of the Jewish settlement in Kraków is the focus of Eugeniusz Müller, *Żydzi w Krakowie w drugiej połowie XIV stulecie* (Kraków 1906 [*Biblioteka Krakowska*, 35], with background on the thirteenth century, pp. 1–5.

92. There is now the excellent survey in English by F. W. Carter, "Cracow's Early Development," *The Slavonic and East European Review*, LXI (1983), 197–225, which covers some of the same material treated

in the preceding paragraphs; see especially Carter's summary comments, p. 224f.

93. For the life and accomplishments of Łokietek, see my study "Władysław Łokietek and the Restoration of the *Regnum Poloniae*," *Medievalia et Humanistica* XVII (1966) 51–78; for the foreign policy of Casimir, see my *The Rise of the Polish Monarchy, Piast Poland in East Central Europe, 1320–1370* (Chicago 1972), pp. 65ff.

94. See Edmund Długopolski, "Bunt wójta Alberta," *Rocznik Krakowski* VII (1905) 135–186.

95. *Rocznik Krasińskich*, in *Mon. Pol. Hist.*, III: 133.

96. *Codex diplomaticus civitatis Cracoviensis*, Franciszek Piekosiński, ed., II, no. 337 (Kraków, 1882) p. 459f.

97. The history of the council is treated in detail by Michał Patkaniowski, *Krakowska rada miejska w średnich wiekach* (Kraków 1934 [*Biblioteka Krakowska*, 82]).

98. Part of this process is reflected in the documents printed by Bartłomiej Groicki, *Porządek sądów i spraw miejskich prawa majdeburskiego w Koronie Polskiej* (Warsaw 1953), pp. 29ff., especially.

99. The Kraków patriciate has been studied by Jan Ptaśnik, "Studya nad patrycyatem Krakowskim wieków średnich," *Rocznik Krakowski* XV (1913) 23–95; and XVI (1914) 1–90.

100. Despite the fact that, in addition to the other roles Kraków played it was also a university city, this stratum of society paid little attention to the patronage of learning. In this regard it compares unfavorably with similar groups in contemporary Italy and Germany.

101. Data on the guilds are gathered by Ptaśnik, ed., *Cracovia artificum 1300–1500* (Kraków 1917). Klemens Bąkowski, *Dawne cechy Krakowskie* (Kraków, 1903 [*Biblioteka Krakowska*, 22]), 20–23, in his survey of Kraków guilds puts the number in the fifteenth century at "about twenty-five."

102. A particularly vehement condemnation of them is cited by Antonina Jelicz, *Życie codzienne w średniowiecznym Krakowie (wiek XIII–XV)* (Warsaw, 1966), p. 40, from MS Krakow Bibl. PAN 1588, 122f.

103. In addition to the material cited above in note 90, see Majer Bałaban, *Historja Żydów w Krakowie i na Kazimierzu 1304–1868*, two volumes (Kraków 1931–1936) I: 24ff.

104. The importance of these routes is stressed by Stanisław Kutrzeba, *Handel Krakowa w wiekach średnich (na tle stosunków handlowych Polski)* (Kraków 1902), pp. 6–16.

105. See Krystyna Pieradzka, "Rozkwit średniowiecznego Krakowa w XIV i XV wieku," in Jan Dąbrowski, *Kraków, Studia nad rozwojem miasta*, p. 152.

106. Kutrzeba, *Handel Krakowa*, p. 118. Data for the latter part of the century are fragmentary, but it is evident that the amount of cloth handled declined considerably in the following decades (see p. 120f.).

107. On the problems of the salt trade in Kraków, see Kutrzeba, *Handel Krakowa*, pp. 131–139.

108. Quoted by Leonard Lepszy, *Thurzonowie w Polsce* (Kraków 1890), p. 7.

109. Information on Polish coinage and the *grossus Cracoviensis* is provided by Ryszard Kiersnowski, *Wstęp do numizmatyki polskiej wieków średnich* (Warsaw, 1964), pp. 128–131.

110. The following data are summarized from the very extensive tables contained in Juljan Pelc, *Ceny w Krakowie w latach 1369–1600* (Lwów 1935), pp. 127–133 especially.

111. These salary data are derived from Pelc, *Ceny w Krakowie*, pp. 79f., 81, 85, 87. To compare some of these salaries with those received by faculty at the University of Kraków, see Gieysztor, "Aspects financiers de l'Université de Cracovie au XVe siècle," in Astrik L. Gabriel, ed., *The Economic and Material Frame of the Medieval University* (Notre Dame, Indiana 1977), pp. 53ff.

112. Bishop Zbigniew Oleśnicki of Kraków (d. 1455) was, for example, estimated to have had an annual income of over 1,000 marks (i.e., 48,000 *grossi*).

113. Two works are particularly useful on the emergence of Kraków as a royal capital. See Franciszek Bujak, "Stolice Polski (Gniezno-Kraków-Warszawa)," in his *Studja Geograficzno-Historyczne* (Warsaw, 1925), 253–292, particularly 259–270; and Horst Jablonowski, "Polens Hauptstädte," *Jahrbuch für Geschichte des Deutschen Ostens*, I (1952) [*Festgabe zum 90. Geburtstag Friedrich Meinecke: Das Hauptstadtproblem in der Geschichte*]), 293–308.

114. Jelicz, *Życie codzienne w Krakowie*, 54.

115. Antoni Gąsiorowski, "Rex Ambulans," *Quaestiones Medii Aevi*, I (1977), 139, quoting the chronicler of the Emperor Conrad, Wipo.

116. See the pattern in Gąsiorowski, *Itinerarium Króla Władysława Jagiełły 1386–1434* (Warsaw, 1972).

117. His itinerary is traced in S. Kwiatkowski, "Itinerarium Władysława (III) Warneńczyka, Króla Polski i Węgier," in *Album uczącej się młodzieży Polskiej poświęcony Józefowi Ignacemu Kraszewskiemu* (Lwów, 1879), 453ff.

118. There is no complete itinerary for the reign of Casimir the Jagiellonian. Data for the period 1480–1492 are provided by Frederick Papee, *Polska i Litwa na przełomie wieków średnich* (Kraków, 1903), I: 381–404.

119. See Papee, *Jan Olbracht*, (Kraków, 1936), 229ff.

120. On this congress, see Grodecki, *Kongres Krakowski w roku 1364* (Warsaw, 1939); and, more briefly, Knoll, *Rise of the Polish Monarchy*, 215–217.

121. Janko of Czarnków, *Chronicon Polonorum*, in *Mon. Pol. Hist.*, II: 631.

122. Joannes Długosz, *Historia Polonica*, 5 vols. (Kraków, 1873–1878 [vols. X–XIV of *Opera Omnia*, ed. Przeździecki]) IV: 320f.

123. On the system of waterways and their changes over the years, see Bąkowski, "Dawne kierunki rzek pod Krakowem," *Rocznik Krakowski*, V (1902) 138–172.

124. Piekosiński, ed. *Codex diplomaticus civitatis Cracovensis*, I, no. 127, p. 336.

125. This extension is first mentioned in *Codex diplomaticus* I, no. 98, p. 138.

126. *Cod. dipl. civ. Crac.* I, no. 232, p. 336.

127. The development of the fortifications of Kraków is best approached through Jarosław Widawski, *Miejskie mury obronne w Państwie Polskim do początku XV wieku* (Warsaw 1973), pp. 192–227 especially. See also Mieczysław Tobiasz, *Fortyfikacje dawnego Krakowa* (Kraków 1973).

128. Both the works cited in the previous note discuss Wawel; in addition, see Szyszko-Bohusz, "Wawel średniowieczny," pp. 17–46.

129. On the *rynek* and the rest of the *śródmieście* (i.e., the central city), the older work by Stanisław Tomkowicz, *Ulice i place Krakowa w ciągu dziejów* (Kraków 1926 [*Biblioteka Krakowska* 63/64]), is still useful; see pp. 14–41 especially.

130. Józef Lepiarczyk, "Fazy budowy kościoła Mariackiego w Krakowie, wieki XIII–XV," *Rocznik Krakowski*, XXXIV (1959), 181–252.

131. The earliest reference to these quarters comes in 1396; see *Libri antiquissimi civitatis Cracoviensis* (Kraków 1878) II: 141. For the discussion which follows, particularly with regard to street names and locations, Tomkowicz, *Ulice i place Krakowa* is most useful.

132. The population of fifteenth-century Kraków is difficult to establish with any precision. Tadeusz Ładogórski, *Studia nad zaludnieniem Polski XIV wieku* (Wrocław 1958), pp. 148, 149, 151, despite some weaknesses in other areas, arrived at the fairly reliable figure of ca. 12,000 for about 1340. This cannot have risen much by the end of the century. For the mid-sixteenth century (1551), Marian Friedberg, "Kraków w dobie Odrodzenia," in Dąbrowski, *Kraków, Studia nad rozwojem miasta*, p. 203, reports a population of ca. 18,000. Much of that increase

came early in the sixteenth century. For some of the problems connected with determining the population of Kraków in this period, see Jan Małecki, *Studia nad rynkiem regionalnym Krakowa w XVI wieku* (Warsaw 1963), p. 2; and Hanna Zaremska, *Bractwa w średniowiecznym Krakowie* (Wrocław 1977), p. 17f.

133. "Cito pestem fugere, longe a loco infecto recedere, tardi reverti domum," cited by Jelicz, *Życia codzienne w Krakowie*, p. 84; see pp. 75–78 for a discussion of medical conditions in Kraków in this period.

134. Długosz, *Annales seu Cronicae* V: 350 (Liber nonus, *sub anno* 1370) and n. 92. The Polish translation of Długosz's history, Jan Długosz, *Roczniki czyli Kroniki sławnego Krolestwa Polskiego [Annals or Chronicles of the Famous Kingdom of Poland]* edited by Jan Dąbrowski, et al. (Warsaw 1961—) V: 443 and note 91, is more explicit than the Latin and provides the Polish proverb quoted in the text: "Polskę zastał drewnianą, a zostawił murowaną."

135. Stanisław Estreicher, ed., *Najstarzy zbiór przywilejów i wilkierzy miasta Krakowa* (Kraków, 1936), p. 24.

136. Długosz, *Historia* V: 342–343.

137. *Mon. Pol. Hist.* V: 908. Another major fire in 1494 is also reported on this page.

138. What follows is based largely on Pieradzka, "Rozkwit średniowiecznego Krakowa," pp. 174–187; and *Studia nad przedmieściami Krakowa* (Kraków, 1938 [*Biblioteka Krakowska*, 94]).

139. See Dabrowski, "Czy Kazimierz i Kleparz założono jako miasta konkurencyjne dla Krakowa," in *Prace z dziejów Polski feudalnej ofiarowane Romanowi Grodeckiemu* (Warsaw 1960), pp. 181–187.

140. For the history of the Casimiran university and its fate, see Knoll, "Casimir the Great and the University of Cracow," *Jahrbücher für Geschichte Osteuropas* XVI (1968) 232–249.

141. "Sitque ibi scienciarum preualencium margaritha . . ." (Wladislai regis Poloniae Studii Generalis Cracoviensis reformatio) in Stanisław Krzyżanowski, "Poselstwo Kazimierza Wielkiego do Awinionu i pierwsze uniwersyteckie przywileje," *Rocznik Krakowski* IV, no. 8 (1900). Jagiełło's document at this point quotes the same phrase from Casimir's document of 1364 (no. 3).

142. For the fifteenth-century history of the university see the chapters by Zofia Kozłowska-Budkowa, Krystyna Pieradzka, Ignacy Zarębski, and Józef Garbacik in Kazimierz Lepszy, ed., *Dzieje Uniwersytetu Jagiellońskiego w latach 1364–1764* (Kraków 1964). I am currently completing an extended story of the history of the *studium* in this century.

122   *Paul W. Knoll*

143. The standard treatment of the history of this building is now
Karol Estreicher, *Collegium Maius—Dzieje Gmachu* (Kraków, 1968). In
English, see his *The Collegium Maius of the Jagiellonian University in Cracow* (Warsaw, 1973), 9–28 especially.
144. In a convocation of the faculty on 1 May 1493, it was resolved
to rebuild the Collegium "in the most beautiful form for both visitors
and for common usage." See *Conclusiones Universitatis Cracoviensis,*
Henryk Barycz, ed. (Kraków, 1933), p. 74f.
145. Hartmann Schedel, *Liber chronicarum* (Nürnberg 1493), p. 267.

BIBLIOGRAPHY

Abraham, Władysław. *Organizacja Kościoła w Polsce do połowy wieku XII*
[The Organization of the Church in Poland to the Middle of the
XIIth Century]. Lwów: Gubrynowicz, 1890.
Bąkowski, Klemens. *Dawne cechy Krakowskie* [The Early Kraków
Guilds]. Kraków: 1903 [*Biblioteka Krakowska* [The Kraków Library,
22].
Bąkowski, Klemens. "Dawne kierunki rzek pod Krakowem" [The Early
River Pattern Around Kraków]. *Rocznik Krakowski* [The Kraków An-
nual] V (1902) 138–172.
Bałaban, Majer. *Historja Żydów w Krakowie i na Kazimierzu 1304–1868*
[History of the Jews in Kraków and Kazimierz 1304–1868]. 2 vols.
Kraków: Nadzieja, 1931–1936.
Bardach, Juliusz. "L'Etat polonais aux X⁰ et XI⁰ siècles" in *L'Europe aux
IX⁰–XI⁰ siècles.* Edited by Tadeusz Manteuffel and Aleksander
Gieysztor. Warsaw: Państwowe Wydawnictwo Naukowe, 1968, pp.
279–319.
Biliński, Bronisław. "Dwa swiadectwa antyczne: *Kalisia* Ptolemeusza
(*Geographia* II: 11, 13) i *Halisii* Tacyta (Germania 43, 2)" [Two An-
tique Testimonies: Ptolemy's *Kalisia* and Tacitus' *Halisius*]. In *Osiem-
naście wieków Kalisza, Studia i materiały do dziejów miasta Kalisza i
regione kaliskiego* [Eighteen Centuries of Kalisz. Studies and Mate-
rials for the History of the City of Kalisz and the Kalisz Region]. 2
vols. Kalisz: Wydawnictwo Poznańskie, 1960–1961, II: 7–40.
Bochnak, Adam. "Najstarsze budowle wawelskie" ["Wawel's Oldest
Buildings"]. In *Prace z dziejów Polski feudalnej ofiarowane Romanowi
Grodeckiemu w 70 rocznicę urodzin* [Works on the History of Feudal
Poland Offered to Roman Grodecki for His 70th Birthday]. (Warsaw: Państwowe Wydawnictwo Naukowe, 1960), pp. 91–106.

Bogucka, Maria. "Polish Towns Between the Sixteenth and Eighteenth Centuries." In J. K. Fedorowicz, ed., *A Republic of Nobles, Studies in Polish History to 1864* (Cambridge: Cambridge University Press, 1982), pp. 138–152.

———. and Henryk Samsonowicz. "Dzieje miast i mieszczaństwa w Polsce przedrozbiorowej." [The History of Cities and Urban Populations in Prepartition Poland] (forthcoming).

Borowiejska-Birkenmajerowa, Maria. *Kształt średniowiecznego Krakowa* [The Shape of Medieval Kraków]. (Kraków: Wydawnictwo Literacki, 1975).

———. "Północna rubież krakowskiego okołu," [The Northern Boundry of Kraków]. In *Sprawozdania z Posiedzeń Kom. Nauk, PAN Oddział w Krakowie*, [Reports of the Sessions of the Scientific Commission, Polish Academy of Sciences Branch in Kraków] XIV, ii (1970) 481–484.

———. "Uwagi o urbanistyce Krakowa w XIII wieku" [Remarks on the Urban Planning of Kraków in the XIIIth Century]. *Sprawozdania z Posiedzeń Kom. Nauk PAN Oddział w Krakowie*, [Reports of the Sessions of the Scientific Commission, Polish Academy of Sciences Branch in Kraków] XIV, i (1970) 8–10.

Buczek, Karol. "Gospodarcze funkcje organizacji grodowej w Polsce wczesnofeudalnej (wiek X–XIII)" [Economic Functions of Castrum Organization in Early Feudal Poland (X–XIII Century)]. *Kwartalnik Historyczny* [Historical Quarterly]. LXXXVI (1979) 363–384.

———. "O tak zwanym rittermeszig man i o 'gościu' w najdawniejszym spisie prawa polskiego," [On the So-Called "Rittermeszig man" and on the "Guest" in the Earliest Register of Polish Law] *Czasopismo Prawno-Historyczne*, [Legal-Historical Journal] XII, i (1960) 141–164.

———. *Targi i miasta na prawie polskim (okres wczesnośredniowieczny)* [Markets and Cities Under Polish Law in the Early Medieval Period] (Wrocław: Ossolineum, 1964).

———. "Zagadnienie wiarygodności dwóch relacji o początkowych dziejach państwa polskiego" [The Problem of the Reliability of Two Accounts of the Early History of the Polish State]. In *Prace z dziejów Polski feudalnej ofiarowane Romanowi Grodeckiemu w 70 rocznicę urodzin* (Warsaw: Państwowe Wydawnictwo Naukowe, 1960), pp. 45–70.

———. "Z badań nad organizacją grodową w Polsce wczesnofeudalnej. Problem terytorialności grodów kasztelańskich" [Research on Castrum Organization in Early Feudal Poland. The Problem of the Territoriality of Castellan Fortresses]. *Kwartalnik Historyczny* LXXVII (1970) 3–29.

Bujak, Franciszek, "Stolice Polski (Gniezno-Kraków-Warszawa)" ["Polish Capitals: Gniezno, Kraków, Warsaw"]. In Bujak, *Studja Geograficzno-Historyczne* [Geographic-Historical Studies]. (Warsaw: Gebethner i Wolff, 1925), pp. 253–292.

Carter, F. W., "Cracow's Early Development." *The Slavonic and East European Review* LXI (1983) 197–225.

Codex diplomaticus civitatis Cracoviensis. Franciszek Piekosiński, ed. 2 vols. (Kraków: Akademia Umiejętności, 1879–1882).

Conclusions Universitatis Cracovensis. Henryk Barycz, ed. (Kraków: Akademia Umiejętności, 1933).

Dąbrowski, Jan, "Czy Kazimierz i Kleparz założono jako miasta konkurencyjne dla Krakowa" [Were Kazimierz and Kleparz (Florentia) Founded As Cities to Compete with Kraków]. In *Prace z dziejów Polski feudalnej ofiarowane Romanowi Grodeckiemu w 70 rocznicę urodzin* (Warsaw: Państwowe Wydawnictwo Naukowe, 1960), pp. 181–187.

Davies, Norman. *God's Playground, A History of Poland.* 2 vols. (New York: Columbia University Press, 1982).

Długoborski. Wacław, Józef Gierowski, and Karol Maleczyński. *Dzieje Wrocławia do roku 1807* [History of Wrocław to the Year 1807]. (Warsaw: Państwowe Wydawnictwo Naukowe, 1958).

Długopolski, Edmund. "Bunt Wojta Alberta," ["The Rebellion of Wójt Albert"]. *Rocznik Krakowski* VII (1905) 135–186.

Długosz, Jan. *Roczniki czyli Kroniki sławnego Królestwa Polskiego* [Annals or Chronicles of the Famous Kingdom of Poland]. Edited by Jan Dąbrowski, et al. (Warsaw: Państwowe Wydawnictwo Naukowe, 1961—[in progress]).

Dowiat, Jerzy. *Chrzest Polski* [The Conversion of Poland] (Warsaw: Wiedza Powszechna, 1958).

Dowiat, Jerzy. *Metryka Chrztu Mieszka I i jej geneza* [The Baptismal Certificate of Mieszko I and Its Origins]. (Warsaw: Państwowe Wydawnictwo Naukowe, 1961).

Dzieje Szczecina wiek X–1805 [History of Szczecin from the Xth Century to 1805]. Edited by Gerard Labuda (Warsaw: Państwowe Wydawnictwo Naukowe, 1963).

Estreicher, Karol. *Collegium Maius—Dzieje Gmachu* [The Collegium Maius—A History of the Structure]. (Kraków: Państwowe Wydawnictwo Naukowe, 1968).

———. *The Collegium Maius of the Jagiellonian University in Cracow.* (Warsaw: Interpress, 1973).

Estreicher, Stanisław. *Najstarszy zbiór przywilejów i wilkierzy miasta Krakowa* [The Earliest Collection of Charters and Legal Decisions of the City of Kraków]. (Kraków: Akademia Umiejętności, 1936).

Fedorowicz, J. K., ed. *A Republic of Nobles, Studies in Polish History to 1864*. (Cambridge: Cambridge University Press, 1982).

Friedberg, Marian, "Kraków w dobie odrodzenia" ["Kraków During the Renaissance"]. In Jan Dąbrowski, ed., *Kraków, Studia nad rozwojem miasta* [Kraków, Studies on the Development of the City]. (Kraków: Wydawnictwo Literackie, 1957), pp. 189–227

Friedberg, Marjan. *Kultura polska a niemiecka*, [Polish and German Culture]. 2 vols. (Poznań: Instytut Zachodni, 1946).

Gąsiorowski, Antoni. *Itinerarium Króla Władysława Jagiełły 1386–1434* [The Itinerary of King Władysław Jagiełło 1386–1434] (Warsaw: Państwowe Wydawnictwo Naukowe, 1972).

_____. "Rex Ambulans," *Quaestiones Medii Aevi* I (1977) 139–162.

Gdańsk, jego dzieje i kultura [Gdańsk, Its History and Culture] (Warsaw: Arkady, 1969).

Gieysztor, Aleksander. "Aspects financiers de l'Université de Cracovie au XVe siècle." In Astrik L. Gabriel, ed. *The Economic and Material Frame of the Medieval University* (Notre Dame, Indiana: University of Notre Dame Press, 1977), pp. 53–65.

_____. "From Forum to Civitas: Urban Changes in Poland in the Twelfth and Thirteenth Centuries," In *La Pologne au XIIe Congrès international des sciences historiques à Vienne* (Warsaw: Państwowe Wydawnictwo Naukowe, 1965), pp. 7–30.

_____. "Le origini della città nella Polonia medievale." In *Studi in onore de A. Sapori* (Milan: Instituto editoriale cisalpino, 1957) I: 129–145.

_____. "Les Chartes de franchises urbaines et rurales en Pologne au XIIIe siècle." In *Les libertés urbaines et rurales du XIe au XIVe siècle* (Brussels: Pro Civitate, 1968 [*Collection Histoire—Historische Uuitgaven*, no. 19]), pp. 103–125.

_____. "Les origines de la ville slave." In *Settimane di studio* VI (Spoleto: Consiglio nazionale della ricerche, 1959), 279–315.

_____. *Mitologia Słowian* [Slavonic Mythology] (Warsaw: Państwowe Wydawnictwo Naukowe, 1982).

_____. "Przemiany ideologiczne w państwie pierwszych Piastów a wyprowadzenie chrześcijaństwa" [Ideological Changes in the State of the First Piasts and the Introduction of Christianity]. In *Początki państwa polskiego, Księga tysiaclecie*, [The Beginning of the Polish State. A Millennium Volume] 2 vols. (Poznań: Państwowe Wydawnictwo Naukowe, 1962) II: 155–170.

Gieysztorowa, Irena. "Badania nad historią zaludnienia Polski" ["Research on the History of Polish Population"]. *Kwartalnik Historii Kultury Materialnej* [Quarterly of the History of Material Culture]. XI (1963) 523–562.

———. "Research Into the Demographic History of Poland, A Provisional Summing-up." *Acta Poloniae Historica* XVIII (1968) 5–17.

Graus, František, *Die Nationenbildung der westslawen im mittelalter* [*Nationes*, 3] (Sigmaringen: Jan Thorbecke Verlag, 1980).

Grodecki, Roman, *Kongres Krakowski w roku 1364* [The Congress of Kraków in 1364] (Warsaw: Gebethner i Wolff, 1939).

———. *Polska Piastowska* [Piast Poland] (Warsaw: Państwowe Wydawnictwo Naukowe, 1969).

———. *Powstanie polskiej świadomości narodowej* [The Rise of Polish National Consciousness] (Katowice: Instytut Śląski, 1946).

———. *Targi w Polsce przed Kolonizacją na prawie niemieckim* [Markets in Poland Prior to Colonization Under German Law] (Kraków: Akademia Umiejętności, 1922).

Groicki, Bartłomiej. *Porządek sądów i spraw miejskich prawa magdeburskiego w Koronie Polskiej* [Legal Order and Municipal Questions Under Magdeburg Law in the Polish Corona] (reprinted Warsaw: Wydawnictwo Prawnicze, 1953).

Grygorowicz, Aleksander. "Kościoł św. Andrzeja w Krakowie we wczesnym średniowieczu," ["The Church of St. Andrew in Kraków in the Early Middle Ages"] *Rocznik Krakowski*, [The Kraków Annual] XXXIX (1968), 5–36.

Heck, Roman. "Świadomość narodowa i państwowa w Czechach i w Polsce w XV w.," ["National and State Consciousness in Bohemia and Poland in the XVth Century"] *Pamiętnik X Powszechnego Zjazdu Historyków Polskich w Lublinie* [Memoir of the Tenth General Conference of Polish Historians in Lublin]. (Warsaw: Polskie Towarzystwo Historyczne, 1968) I: 126–151.

———. and Ewa Maleczyńska, eds. *Ruch husycki w Polsce. Wybór tekstów źródłowych (do r. 1454)* [The Hussite Movement in Poland. A Selection of Primary Texts (to 1454)]. (Wrocław: Ossolineum, 1953).

Helbig, Herbert and Lorenz Weinrich, eds. *Urkunden und erzählende Quellen zur deutschen Ostsiedlung im Mittelalter*. 2 vols. (Darmstadt: Wissenschaftliche Buchgesellschaft, 1968–1970).

Hensel, Witold. *Anfänge der Städte bei den Ost- und Westslawen*. (Bautzen: Domowina, 1967).

———. *Archeologia i prahistoria* [Archaeology and Prehistory] (Wrocław: Ossolineum, 1971).

———. *Méthodes et perspectives des recherches sur les centres ruraux et urbains chez les Slaves (VII*ᵉ*—XIII*ᵉ *ss.)* (Warsaw: Państwowe Wydawnictwo Naukowe, 1962).

———. "The Origins of Western and Eastern European Slav Towns," in M. W. Barley, ed., *European Towns, Their Archaeology and Early*

History (London, New York, and San Francisco: Academic Press, 1977), pp. 373–390.

———. and Lech Leciejewicz, "En Pologne médiévale: l'archéologie au service de l'histoire. I: Villes et campagnes," *Annales: Économies—Sociétés—Civilisations*, XVII (1962), 203–222.

Hoffman, Richard C., "Nazwy i Miejscowości: trzy studia z historii średniowiecznej okręgu wrocławskiego," ["Names and Localities. Three Studies on the Medieval History of the Wrocław Region"] *Sobótka*, XXIX, 1 (1974), 1–25.

Hoffman, Richard C., *Studies in the Rural Economy of the Duchy of Wrocław, 1200–1530* (Unpublished Ph.D. Dissertation, Yale University, 1970).

Hoffman, Richard C., "Warfare, Weather, and a Rural Economy: The Duchy of Wrocław in the mid-fifteenth Century," *Viator*, IV (1973), 273–305.

Jablonowski, Horst. "Polens Hauptstädte." *Jahrbuch für Geschichte des Deutschen Ostens* I (1952 [*Festgabe zum 90. Geburtstag Friedrich Meinecke: Das Hauptstadt-problem in der Geschichte*]) 293–308.

Jamka, Rudolf. *Kraków w pradziejach* [Prehistoric Kraków]. Vol. I (Wrocław 1963 [Polskie Towarzystwo Archeologiczne, Biblioteka Archeologiczna (Polish Archaeological Society, The Archaeological Library) Vol. XVI]).

Janko of Czarnków. *Chronicon Polonorum*, in *Monumenta Poloniae Historica*. II (Lwów, 1872, reprinted Warsaw: Państwowe Wydawnictwo Naukowy, 1960) 601–756.

Jelicz, Antonina. *Życie codzienne w średniowiecznym Krakowie (wiek XIII–XV)* [Daily Life in Medieval Kraków (XIII–XVth Centuries)] (Warsaw: Państwowy Instytut Wydawniczy, 1966).

Joannes Długosz. *Annales seu Cronicae incliti Regni Poloniae*. Jan Dąbrowski, et al., eds. (Warsaw: Państwowe Wydawnictwo Naukowe, 1964—[in Progress]).

Joannis Długossii Senioris Canonici Cracoviensis Opera Omnia. A. Przeździecki, ed. 14 vols. (Kraków: [No publisher listed] 1863–1887).

Johannes Długosz. *Historica Polonica*. 5 vols. (Kraków: [no publisher listed] 1873–1878 [vols. X–XIV of *Opera Omnia*, edited by Przeździecki]).

Kaczmarczyk, Zdzisław. *Kolonizacja niemiecka na wschód od Odry* [German Colonization East of the Oder]. (Poznań: Instytut Zachod", 1945).

Kaczmarczyk, Zdzisław. "Początki miast polskich, zagadnienia prawne" ["The Beginnings of Polish Cities, The Legal Problems"].

Czasopismo Prawno-Historyczne [Legal-Historical Journal] XIII, ii (1961) 9–45.

Kieniewicz, Stefan, et al., *History of Poland* (Warsaw: Państwowe Wydawnictwo Naukowe, 1968).

Kiersnowski, Ryszard. *Wstęp do numizmatyki polskiej wieków średnich* [Introduction to Polish Numismatics in the Middle Ages]. (Warsaw: Państwowe Wydawnictwo Naukowe, 1964).

Kłodziński, Andrzej. *Przywileje lokacyjne Krakowa i Poznania* [The Location Charters of Kraków and Poznań] (Poznań: Biblioteka Źródet Historycznych, 1947).

Knoll, Paul W. "Casimir the Great and the University of Cracow." *Jahrbücher für Geschichte Ostenropas* XVI (1968) 232–249.

_____. "Poland." In *Dictionary of the Middle Ages,* general editor Joseph R. Strayer (New York: Charles Scribner's Sons, 1982—[in progress]), vol. IX [forthcoming].

_____. *The Rise of the Polish Monarchy, Piast Poland in East Central Europe, 1320–1370* (Chicago: University of Chicago Press, 1972).

_____. "Władysław Łokietek and the Restoration of the *Regnum Poloniae*," *Medievalia et Humanistica* XVII (1966) 51–78.

Koebner, Richard, "Dans les terres de colonisation: marchés slaves et villes allemandes," *Annales d'Histoire économique et sociale* IX (1937).

_____. "Locatio. Zur Begriffssprache und Geschichte der deutschen Kolonisation." *Zeitschrift des Vereins für Geschichte Schlesiens* LXIII (1929) 1–32.

_____. "Das Problem der slavischen Burgsiedlung und die Oppelner Ausgrabungen," *Zeitschrift des Vereins für Geschichte Schlesiens* LXV (1931) 90–120.

Krakau, Dokumente zur Stadtgeschichte (Kraków: Stadthauptmann der Stadt Krakau, 1942).

Krakowski, Stefan. *Polska w walce z najazdami tatarskimi w XIII w.* [Poland and the Struggle Against Tatar Attacks in the Thirteenth Century] (Warsaw: Ministerstwo Obrony Narodowej, 1956).

Krzyżanowski, Stanisław. "Poselstwo Kazimierza Wielkiego do Awinionu i pierwsze uniwersyteckie przywileje," [The Deputation of Casimir the Great to Avignon and the First University Charters] *Rocznik Krakowski* IV (1900) 1–101.

Kuhn, Walter. "Die Siedlerzahlen der deutschen Ostsiedlung." *Studium Sociale* (*Mélanges K. V. Müller*) (Cologne and Opladen: West Deutscher Verlag, 1963), pp. 131–154.

Kürbisówna, Brygida. "Mieszczanie na Uniwersytecie Jagiellońskim w

XV w. i ich udział w kształtowanie świadomości narodowej" [Burghers at the Jagiellonian University in the Fifteenth Century and Their Participation in the Formulation of National Consciousness]. *Studia Staropolskie* [Old Polish Studies] V (1957) 5–79.

Kutrzeba, Stanisław. *Handel Krakowa w wiekach średnich (na tle stosunków handlowych Polski)* [Kraków's Trade in the Middle Ages in the Context of Polish Trade Relations] (Kraków: Akademia Umiejętności, 1902).

Kwiatkowski, Saturnin. "Itinerarium Władysława (III) Warneńczyka, Króla Polski i Wegier" ["The Itinerary of Władisław III Warnenczyk, King of Poland and Hungary"]. In *Album uczącej się młodźiezy Polskiej poświęcony Józefowi Ignacemu Kraszewskiemu* [An Album by the Student Youth of Poland Dedicated to Józef Ignacy Kraszewski] (Lwów; [No publisher listed] 1879), pp. 453–483.

Labuda, Gerard. "Miasta na prawie polskim" ["Cities Under Polish Law"]. In *Studia historica w 35-lecie pracy naukowej Henryka Łowmiańskiego* [Historical Studies to Commemorate the Thirty-Fifth Anniversary of Scientific Work by Henryk Łowmiański] (Warsaw: Państwowe Wydawnictwo Naukowe, 1958), pp. 181–197.

_____. ed. *Dzieje Szczecina wiek X–1805* [History of Szczecin from the Xth Century to 1805]. (Warsaw: Pantswowe Wydawnictwo Naukowe)

Lalik, Tadeusz. "Organizacja grodowo-prowincjonalna w Polsce XI i początków XII w." [Castrum-Provincial Organization in Poland in the XIth and early XIIth Century] *Studia z Dziejów Osadnictwa* [Studies on the History of Settlement] V (1967) 5–51.

_____. "Stare Miasto w Łęzycy. Przemiany w okresie poprzedzającym lokacje: schyłek XII i początek XIII wieku" ["The Old Town in Łęczyca. Changes in the Period Preceeding Location: the End of the XIIth and Beginning of the XIIIth Century"]. *Kwartalnik Historii Kultury Materialnej*. IV (1956) 631–678.

Leciejewicz, Lech. "Early Medieval Sociotopographical Tranformations in West Slavonic Urban Settlements in the Light of Archaeology," *Acta Poloniae Historica* XXXIV (1976) 29–56.

Lenczyk, Gabriel. "Badania wykopaliskowe na Wawelu w latach 1948 i 1949," ["Excavation Research on Wawel in the Years 1948 and 1949"] *Studia Wczesnośredniowieczne*, [Early Medieval Studies] II (1953) 83–88.

Lenkiewicz, T. and Kazimierz Radwański. "Wyniki badań archeologicznych prowadzonych na Skałce w Krakowie w latach 1956–1957" ["The Results of Archaeological Research Carried Out on Skałka in

Kraków in the Years 1956–1957"]. *Biuletyn Krakowski* [The Kraków Bulletin] I (1959), 99–133.

Lepiarczyk, Józef, "Fazy budowy Kościoła Mariackiego w Krakowie, wieki XIII–XV" ["Phases in the Construction of the Church of St. Mary in Kraków in the XIII–XVth Centuries"] *Rocznik Krakowski* [The Kraków Annual] XXXIV (1959) 181–252.

Lepszy, Kazimierz, ed. *Dzieje Uniwersytetu Jagiellońskiego w latach 1364–1764* [History of the Jagiellonian University in the Years 1364–1764]. (Kraków: Państwowe Wydawnictwo Naukowe, 1964).

Lepszy, Leonard. *Thurzonowie w Polsce* [The Thurzon Family in Poland]. (Kraków: [Privately printed] 1890).

Libri antiquissimi civitatis Cracoviensis 1300–1400. Franciszek Piekosiński and Józef Szujski, eds. (Kraków: Akademia Umiejętności, 1878).

Ludat, Herbert, "Die Bezeichnungen für 'Stadt' im Slawischen." In *Syntagma Friburgense, Festschrift H. Aubin* (Lindau: Jan Thorbecke Verlag, 1956).

Ładogórski, Tadeusz. *Studia nad zaludnieniem Polski XIV wieku* [Studies on the Population of Poland in the XIVth Century]. (Wrocław: Ossolineum, 1958).

Łowmiański, Henryk, *Początki Polski* [The Beginnings of Poland]. 5 vols. (Warsaw: Państwowe Wydawnictwo Naukowe, 1964–1973).

———. *Religia Słowian i jej upadek (w. VI–XII)* [Slavonic Religion and Its Decline From the VIth to the XIIth Century]. (Warsaw: Państwowe Wydawnictwo Naukowe, 1979).

Małecki, Jan. *Studia nad rynkiem regionalnym Kraków w XVI wieku* [Studies on the Regional Market of Kraków in the XVIth Century] (Warsaw: Państwowe Wydawnictwo Naukowe, 1963).

Maleczyński, Karol. *Najstarsze targi w Polsce i stosunek ich do miast przed kolonizacja na prawie niemieckim* [The Oldest Markets in Poland and Their Relationship to Cities Prior to Colonization Under German Law]. (Lwów: Gubrynowicz, 1926).

———, ed. *Historia Śląska* [History of Silesia]. Vol. I (in 2 parts) (Wrocław: Ossolineum, 1960–1961).

Manteuffel, Tadeusz. *The Formation of the Polish State: The Period of Ducal Rule, 963–1194* (Detroit: Wayne State University Press, 1982).

Miasta polskie w Tysiacleciu [The Polish Cities in the Last Millennium]. Vol. I (Wrocław: Ossolineum, 1965).

Mistrza Wincentego Kronika [*The Chronicle of Master Vincent*] in *Monumenta Poloniae Historica.* Vol. II (Lwów, 1872; reprinted Warsaw: Państwowe Wydawnictwo Naukowe, 1960). 447.

Urban Development of Medieval Poland   131

Mitkowski, Józef. "Dawne warunki geograficzne jako podłoże, na ktorym rozwinął się zespół osad Krakowskich," [The Early Geographic Conditions as the Foundation Upon Which the Settlement of Kraków Developed]. In Jan Dąbrowski, ed., *Kraków Studia nad rozwojem miasta* [Kraków. Studies on the Development of the City] (Kraków: Wydawnictwo Literackie, 1957), pp. 39–64.

———. "Kraków lokacyjny" ["Kraków in the Period of Location"]. In Jan Dąbrowski, ed. *Kraków, Studia nad rozwojem miasta* [Kraków. Studies on the Development of the City] (Kraków: Wydawnictwo Literackie, 1957), pp. 117–139.

———. "Kraków przed lokacją," ["Pre-location Kraków"] in Janina Bieniarzówna, ed., *Szkice z dziejów Krakowa* [Sketches From the History of Kraków] (Kraków: Wydawnictwo Literackie, 1968), pp. 7–23.

Modzelewski, Karol. *Organizacja gospodarcza państwa piastwoskiego. X–XIII wiek* [The Economic Organization of the Piast State from the Xth to the XIIIth Century] (Wrocław: Ossolineum, 1975).

———. "The System of the Ius Ducale and the Idea of Feudalism." *Quaestiones Medii Aevi* I (1977) 71–99.

Monumenta Poloniae Historica. 6 vols. (Lwów and Kraków, 1864–1893 reprinted Warsaw: Państwowe Wydawnictwo Naukowe, 1960–1961).

Müller, Eugeniusz. *Żydzi w Krakowie w drugiej połowie XIV stulecie* [Jews in Kraków in the Second Half of the XIVth Century]. (Kraków, 1906 [*Biblioteka Krakowska (The Kraków Library)* 35].

Münch, Henryk. *Geneza rozplanowania miast wielkopolskich XIII i XIV w.* [Origins and the Planning of Towns in Great Poland in the XIII and XIV Centuries] (Kraków: Akademia Umiejętności, 1946).

———. "Początki średniowiecznego układie miejskiego w Polsce ze szczególnym uwzglednieniem Śląska" ["The Beginnings of Medieval Municipal Systems in Poland, with Particular Reference to Silesia"]. *Kwartalnik Architektury i Urbanistyki*, [Architectural and Urban Planning Quarterly] V (1960) 357–375.

———. "Układ urbanistyczny Krakowa do połowy XIII w.," ["The Urban Planning System in Kraków to the Middle of the Thirteenth Century"]. *Czasopismo Techniczne*, [Technical Journal] V (1959).

———. "Über den frühmittelalterlichen und mittelalterlichen Stadtgrundriss in Polen und seine Erforschung." In *L'artisanat et la vie urbaine en Pologne médiévale* [*Ergon* III (1962)], pp. 346–353.

Najstarsze Księgi i rachunki miasta Krakowa od r. 1300 do 1400 [The Oldest Record Books and Receipts for the City of Kraków from the Year

1300 to 1400]. F. Piekosiński and Józef Szujski, eds. (Kraków: Akademia Umiejętności, 1878).

Papee, Frederick, _Jan Olbracht_ [John Albert] (Kraków: Akademia Umiejętności, 1936).

_____. _Polska i Litwa na przełomie wieków średnich_ [Poland and Lithuania at the End of the Middle Ages]. Vol. I (Kraków: Akademia Umiejętności, 1903).

Patkaniowski, Michał. _Krakowska rada miejska w średnich wiekach_ [The Kraków City Council in the Middle Ages]. (Kraków, 1934 [_Biblioteka Krakowska_ (The Kraków Library) 82]).

Pazyra, Stanisław. _Geneza i rozwój miast mazowieckich_ [The Origin and Development of Mazovian Cities]. (Warsaw: Państwowe Wydawnictwo Naukowe, 1959).

Pelc, Juljan. _Ceny w Krakowie w latach 1369–1600_ [Prices in Kraków in the Years 1369–1600]. (Lwów: Mianowski, 1935).

Pieradzka, Krystyna. "Rozkwit średniowiecznego Krakowa w XIV i XV wieku" ["The Rise of Medieval Kraków in the XIVth and XVth Centuries"]. In Jan Dąbrowski, ed. _Kraków, Studia nad rozwojem miasta_ [Kraków. Studies on the Development of the City]. (Kraków: Wydawnictwo Literackie, 1957).

_____. _Studia nad przedmieściami Krakowa_ [Studies on the Suburbs of Kraków]. (Kraków, 1938 [_Biblioteka Krakowska_, (The Kraków Library) 94]).

_I_ [i.e., _Pierwszy_] _Międzynarodowy Kongres Archeologii Słowiańskiej_, [First International Congress of Slavonic Archaeology] VI (Wrocław: Ossolineum, 1968).

Ptaśnik, Jan. _Cracovia artificum 1300–1500_ (Kraków: Akademia Umiejętności, 1917).

_____. "Studya nad patrycyatem Krakowskim wieków średnich" ["Studies on the Kraków Patriciate in the Middle Ages"]. _Rocznik Krakowski_ [The Kraków Annual] XV (1913) 23–95 and XVI (1914) 1–90.

Radwański, Kazimierz, "Budowle drewniana odkryte pod poziomami romańskimi kościoła św. Wojciecha w Krakowie" ["Wooden Buildings Discovered Under the Romanesque Foundations of the Church of St. Wojciech in Kraków"]. _Materiały Archeologiczne_, [Archeological Materials] XI (1970) 7–23.

_____. _Kraków przedlokacyjny, rozwój przestrzenny_ [Pre-Location Kraków. Its Spatial Development] (Kraków: Polski Towarzystwo Archeologiczne i Numizmatyczne, 1975).

Relacja Ibrahima ibn Jakuba z podróży do Krajów słowiańskich [The Account of Ibrahim-ibn-Jakub of A Journey to the Slavonic Lands]. Tadeusz Kowalski, *et al.*, eds., in *Pomniki Dziejowe Polski, Seria II* [Historical Literary Monuments of Poland, Second Series] I. (Kraków: Akademia Umiejętności, 1946).

Rocznik Krasińskich [The Krasiński Annal] in *Monumenta Poloniae Historica.* III (Lwów, 1878; reprinted Warsaw: Państwowe Wydawnictwo Naukuowe, 1961), 127–133.

Samsonowicz, Henryk. "Ideologia mieszczańska w Polsce w XIII w." ["Burgher Ideology in Thirteenth Century Poland"]. In *Sztuka i ideologia* [Art and Ideology] (Wrocław: Ossolineum, 1974), pp. 153–164.

————. "Samorząd miejski w dobie rozdrobnienia feudalnego w Polsce" [Municipal Autonomy in the Period of Feudal Division in Poland]. In Henryk Łowmiański, ed. *Polska w okresie rozdrobnienia feudalnego* [Poland in the Period of Feudal Division] (Wrocław: Ossolineum, 1973), pp. 133–159.

Schedel, Hartmann. *Liber chronicarum* (Nürnberg, 1493).

Schlesinger, Walter, ed. *Die Deutsche Ostsiedlung des Mittelalters als Problem der europäischen Geschichte.* (Sigmaringen: Jan Thorbecke Verlag, 1975 [*Vorträge und Forschungen*, XVIII]).

Semkowicz, Aleksander. *Krytyczny rozbiór Dziejów Polskich Jana Długosza (do r. 1384)* [A Critical Analysis of the History of Poland by John Długosz (to the Year 1384)]. (Kraków: Akademia Umiejętności, 1887).

Słownik starożytności słowiańskich [Dictionary of Slavonic Antiquities]. Władysław Kowalenko, Gerard Labuda, *et al.*, eds. (Wrocław: Ossolineum, 1961—[in progress]).

Sułowski, Zygmunt. "Początki Kościoła polskiego" ["The Beginnings of the Polish Church"]. In *Kościół w Polsce* [The Church in Poland]. Vol. I: *Średniowiecze* [The Middle Ages] (Kraków: Znak, 1966), pp. 17–123.

Szyszko-Bohusz, Adolf. "Studia nad katedrą wawelską" ["Studies on Wawel Cathedral"]. *Prace Komisji Historii Sztuki* [Works of the Art History Commission] VIII (1939–1946), 107–150.

Ślaski, Kazimierz. *Wątki historyczne w podaniach o początkach Polski* [Historical Elements in the Legends About the Beginnings of Poland]. (Poznań: Poznańskie Towarzystwo Przyjaciół Nauk, 1968).

Swiszczowski, Stefan. "Gródek Krakowski i mury miejskie między Grodkiem a wawelem" ["The Kraków Gródek and the City Walls Between Gródek and Wawel"]. *Rocznik Krakowski* [The Kraków Annual] XXXII (1950), 3–41.

Tobiasz, Mieczysław, *Fortyfikacje dawnego Krakowa* [The Fortifications of Early Kraków]. (Kraków: Wydawnictwo Literackie, 1973).

Tomkowicz, Stanisław, *Ulice i place Krakowa w ciągu dziejów* [The Streets and Squares of Kraków Through the Ages]. (Kraków, 1926 [*Biblioteka Krakowska* (The Kraków Library) 63/64]).

Topolski, Jerzy, ed. *Dzieje Gniezna* [History of Gniezno]. (Warsaw: Państwowe Wydawnictwo Naukowe, 1965).

Trawkowski, Stanisław. "W sprawie roli kolonizacji niemieckiej w przemianach kultury materialnej na ziemiach polskich" ["The Question of the Role of German Colonization in Changes in Material Culture in the Polish Lands"]. *Kwartalnik Historii Kultury Materialnej*, [Quarterly of the History of Material Culture] VIII (1960) 183–206.

––––––. "Zur Erforschung der deutschen Kolonisation auf polnischem Boden im 13. Jahrhundert." *Acta Poloniae Historica* VII (1962) 78–95.

Tymieniecki, Kazimierz, "Legendy i spór o tradycje historyczna," ["Legends and Dispute Over A Historical Tradition"]. *Studia Źródłoznawcze* [Source Studies] X (1965) 101–108.

––––––. "Prawo czy gospodarstwo" [Law or Economy]. *Roczniki Dziejów Społecznych i Gospodarczych* [The Annals of Social and Economic History] VIII (1946), 275–291.

––––––. "Zagadnienie początków miast w Polsce" ["The Problem of the Beginnings of Cities in Poland"]. *Przegląd Historyczny* [Historical Review] XXI (1918), 319–345, and in *Pisma wybrana* [Selected Works] (Warsaw: Państwowe Wydawnictwo Naukowe, 1956).

Vita (minor) sancti Stanislai episcopi Cracoviensis. in Monuments Poloniae Historica Vol. IV (Lwów, 1884 reprinted Warsaw: Państwowe Wydawnictwo Naukowe, 1961), pp. 238–285.

Vlasto, A. P. *The Entry of the Slavs Into Christendom* (Cambridge: Cambridge University Press, 1970).

Wasilewski, Tadeusz. "Poland's Administrative Structure in Early Piast Times." *Acta Poloniae Historica* XLIV (1981) 5–31.

Weymann, Stefan. *Cła i drogi handlowe w Polsce piastowskiej* [Tariffs and Trade Routes in Piast Poland] (Poznań; Poznańskie Towarzystwo Przyjaciół Nauk, 1938).

Widawski, Jarosław. *Miejskie mury obronne w Państwie Polskim do początku XV wieku* [Municipal Defense Walls in the Polish State to the Beginning of the XVth Century]. (Warsaw: Ministerstwo Obrony Narodowej, 1973).

Wojciechowski, Zygmunt. *Mieszko I and the Rise of the Polish State.* (Toruń and Gdynia; Baltic Institute, 1936).

Wyrozumski, Jerzy. *Historia Polski do roku 1505* [A History of Poland to the Year 1505]. (Warsaw: Państwowe Wydawnictwo Naukowe, 1982).

Zachorowski, Stanisław. "Kraków biskupi" ["Episcopal Kraków"]. *Rocznik Krakowski* [The Kraków Annual] VIII (1906), 103–126.

Zachwatowicz, Jan. "Architektura" ["Architecture"]. In Michał Walicki, ed. *Sztuka Polska przedromańska i romańska do schyłku XIII wieku* [Pre-Romanesque and Romanesque Art in Poland to the Close of the XIIIth Century]. 2 vols. (Warsaw: Państwowe Wydawnictwo Naukowe, 1971) I: 71–194.

Zagrodzki, Tadeusz. "Regularny plan miasta średniowiecznego a limitacja miernicza" ["The Regular Plan of a Medieval Town and Measurement Limitation"]. *Studia Wczesnośredniowieczne* [Early Medieval Studies] V (1962) 1–101.

Zarębski, Ignacy. "Stosunki Eneasza Sylwiusza z Polską i Polakami" [Aeneas Sylvius' Relations with Poland and the Poles]. *Rozprawy Polskiej Akademii Umiejętności: wydział historyczno-filozoficzny* [Proceedings of the Polish Academy of Learning: historical-philosophical division]. Series 2, XLV (1939) 281–437.

Zaremska, Hanna. *Bractwa w średniowiecznym Krakowie [Confraternities in Medieval Kraków]. (Wrocław: Ossolineum, 1977).*

Zbiór dyplomów klasztoru mogilskiego [A collection of Diplomas From the Monastery of Mogiło]. Edited by Eugeniusz Janota and Franciszek Piekosiński (Kraków: Krakowskie Towarzystwo Naukowego, 1865).

Zientara, Benedykt. "Foreigners in Poland in the 10th–15th Centuries. Their Role in the Opinion of Polish Medieval Community," *Acta Poloniae Historica* XXIX (1974) 5–28.

_____. *Henryk Brodaty i jego czasy* [Henry the Bearded and His Times]. (Warsaw: Państwowe Wydawnictwo Naukowe, 1975).

_____. "*Melioratio terrae:* the thirteenth-century breakthrough in Polish history," in J. K. Fedorowicz, *A Republic of Nobles, Studies in Polish History to 1864* (Cambridge: Cambridge University Press, 1982), pp. 31–47.

_____. "Nationality Conflicts in the German-Slavic Borderland in the 13th–14th Centuries and Their Social Scope," *Acta Poloniae Historica* XXII (1970), 207–225.

_____. "Socio-Economic and Spatial Transformation of Polish Towns During the Period of Location." *Acta Poloniae Historica* XXXIV (1976) 57–83.

_____. "Walloons in Silesia in the 12th and 13th Centuries," *Quaestiones Medii Aevi* II (1981) 127–150.

————. "Zur Geschichte der planmässingen Organisierung des Marktes im Mittelalter." In *Wirtschaffliche und Soziale Strukturen im saekularen Wandel. Festschrift für Wilhelm Abel zum 70. Geburtstag.* 2 vols. (Hannover: Schaper, 1974) II: 345–365.

Ziffer, Bernard. *Poland, History and Historians; Three Bibliographical Essays.* (New York: Middle European Studies Center, 1952).

Zoll-Adamikowa, Helena. *Wczesnośredniowieczne cmentarzyska szkieletowe Małopolski* [Early Medieval Skeletal Remains from Prehistoric Burial Grounds in Little Poland]. (Kraków; Polska Akademia Nauk, 1971 [*Prace Komisji Archeologicznej* (Works of the Archaeological Commission) XI]).

Żaki, Andrzej. "Nowoodkryte ruiny budowli przedromańskiej na Wawelu" ["Newly Discovered Ruins of Pre-Romanesque Construction on Wawel"]. *Studia do dziejów Wawelu* [Studies on the History of Wawel] I (1955) 71–111.

————. "Odkrycie nowego reliktu przedromańskiego (tzw. kościoł B)" ["The Discovery of New Pre-Romanesque Remains (the So-Called Church B)"]. *Sprawozdania z Posiedzeń Kom. Oddz. PAN w Krakowie za rok 1966.* [Reports from the Commission Session of the Polish Academy of Sciences Branch in Kraków for the Year 1966] (Kraków: 1967), pp. 24–27, and *Sprawozdania . . . za rok 1969* (Kraków: 1969), p. 46f.

————. "Kraków wczesnośredniowieczny (wiek X do połowy XIII)" [Early Medieval Kraków. From the Tenth to the Middle of the Thirteenth Century]. In Jan Dąbrowski, ed., *Kraków. Studia nad rozwojem miasta* [Kraków. Studies on the Development of the City] (Kraków: Wydawnictwo Literackie, 1957), pp. 98–116.

————. "Rotunda wawelska. Studium nad centralną architekturą epoki wczesnośredniowiecznej" ["The Wawel Rotunda. A Study of the Central Architecture of the Early Medieval Period"]. *Studia do dziejów Wawelu* [Studies on the History of Wawel] III (1968), 1–121.

————. "Zagadnienie transeptu I katedry wawelskiej" ["The Problem of the Transept in the First Kraków Cathedral"]. *Zeszyty Naukowe Uniwersytetu Jagiellońskiego: Prace z historii sztuki* [Scientific Notebooks of the Jagiellonian University: Works on Art History] II (1965) 19–94.

3

Buda Between Tatars and Turks

Marianna D. Birnbaum

"Europe has three pearls: Venice on the waters, Buda on
the hills, and Florence on the plains."
Ambrosius Calepinus

When on September 12, 1526, the victorious Suleiman entered
the deserted capital city of Hungary, he was mesmerized by the
beauty of the town and by the splendor of her royal palace. "I
wish I could move this castle to the shores of the Golden Horn,"
he is alleged to have said.[1] He was unable to move the entire
palace, but he did what he could. Laden with the priceless volumes of the Bibliotheca Corviniana, which not so long before
Naldo Naldi called the "sanctuary of wisdom," and with the
detachable treasures his soldiers hoarded on board, Suleiman's
galleys made several trips from Buda to Constantinople. He had
the bronze statues, the silver candelabra, and also the cannons
and the bells of the palace moved. Soon the fabulous capital
became but a skeleton of its previous self, and descriptions about
its past were increasingly used in comparison to the sorry state
Buda had been relegated to in the ensuing centuries. The flowering of Buda lasted for precisely 300-years, from 1241 to 1541,
the latter date marking its final fall to the Turkish army. During
those 300-years, however, the only foreigners within her walls
were travelers, guests and traders.

The pearl on the hill was a small one, less than a mile in
length, and the hills were about five-hundred feet tall altogether.

South of the castle hill, Mount St. Gellért was taller, yet it was rejected in favor of the present site. The numerous caves and caverns of the castle hill provided protection and served as water reservoirs for the medieval population. (Actually they were used not just during the Turkish attacks but much later, in World War II, about 15,000 people found shelter there, during the siege of Buda.) Although settled for about 50,000 years (cf. the Vértes-szöllős excavations), Buda gained import in Hungary's history after 1241 when it was decided to turn it into a fortified capital city against a possible new Tatar attack. At that time, Esztergom, Óbuda and Pest were more important, but Buda was planned to become a link in the chain of resistance along the Danube.

The city's Hungarian name is shrouded in mystery. Folklore ascribed it to Attila's brother (indeed in the Völsung saga, in addition to Attila, Etzel or Atli, and Krimhilde, there is also a Budli). Its German name is easily identifiable: The young city had not only a borrowed name but also a borrowed population. In 1244, the predominantly German citizens of Pest moved to Buda in fear of the Tatars.[2] Pest (meaning oven, furnace in a number of Slavic languages) also had a German name, *Ofen,* which moved with burghers who were seeking protection on the hilly side of the Danube. During the same time began the moving of Zagreb's population to the "castrum in monte Grech iuxta Zagrabiam," but there the protection of the townspeople was required against attacks coming from the west. Their move was completed by 1266.

In the beginning Germans made up Buda's majority. In 1250 the new capital was bi-ethnic, a settlement with two peoples and two separate parish churches. In addition to the Germans and Hungarians, soon many more nationalities arrived. Of the religious orders the Cistercians were—naturally—mainly French. Of the Crusaders stationed in Hungary many were French or Italian. After the extinction of the House of Árpád (1301), the Anjou rulers moved even more Italians to the capital. Most mendicant friars were Italian (an exception to this was the indigenous Paulist order, founded in 1250 by Blessed Eusebius of Esztergom). The capital retained its multiethnic character until 1541.

Prior to Buda, Székesfehérvár and Esztergom were the nation's capitals. It seems that Buda, the "umbilicus regni," became the sole capital only by the fourteenth century. Charles I refers to it "in Budensem civitatem nostram principalem (1308)" In 1233 Andrew II still calls Székesfehérvár "Medium Regni."[3] In 1249 Esztergom is one of the two capitals, and as late as 1253, Óbuda is still called that. Nonetheless, after the 1250s', royal and civilian settlement, "civitas et castrum," were sharing Buda, their administration remaining undivided until the fourteenth century.

According to some scholars (among them László Zolnay), the royal residence was located in the eastern part of the town proper beginning with 1249–1255 to the mid-fourteenth century. In the fourteenth, however, with the building of Stephen's Tower (named after the younger brother of Louis of Anjou), the royal residence was moved, and further developed on the southern slopes of the hill. Arguing for a shared residence of king and people, Zolnay pointed out that until the mid-fourteenth century the rector and royal captain, in the same person ("rector capitaneusque"), administered the town which therefore must have had the royal castle and residence on its territory. Later a "iudex" was appointed—this was when the administration of town and the residence became separated. While in other free towns the community was entitled to elect its own judges and parish priests, in the case of Buda, such privileges were granted only after the separation in the mid-fourteenth century.

The privileges (in nineteen statutes) were still granted to the hospites of Pest. They contained the following main statutes: In case of war the town was expected to provide the king with ten armed soldiers. The citizens were free of customs payments within the country, except for the *tricesima,* a tax for the queen, and customs to the Óbuda Cathedral Chapter. They were exempt from having to lodge royal servants. Their property rights were protected; no one but a Buda citizen was permitted to purchase property, and the properties of those who had died without heirs were to be turned over to the city. The judges were to be elected freely and had to be introduced to the king only after the election. The lieutenant-palatine was not permitted to stay in the city overnight, nor was he allowed to sit in judgment.

Boats, ships and ferries were obliged to stop at Pest at the daily market. Customs of the Buda market were granted by Béla IV to the Dominican nuns of Rabbit Island,[4] a deed which caused permanent friction between them and the town. The nuns became the strongest and wealthiest group of the entire region; the island a veritable kingdom within the realm. Their interests and the interests of the Óbuda Chapter permanently collided with the aims of the burghers, who also had to fight the economic interests of Esztergom, the previous capital.

By the new role of Buda, Esztergom lost its 300-years standing as capital and demanded to retain its staple rights. By the end of the thirteenth century the Dominican nuns, the Óbuda Cathedral Chapter, and Esztergom formed an alliance against Buda and undertook to paralyze its economic growth. The citizens of Buda did not take the clerical interference in their business lightly. It has been recorded that officers of the Óbuda Chapter and tax collectors of the Island's order were frequently dipped in the ice-cold water of the Danube or beaten up in one of the many dark alleys. Buda came out winning: Pest, Óbuda, and Esztergom began to deteriorate in the following centuries, their importance overshadowed by the speedily rising star of Buda. The outraged church made a few more attempts to regain its power; for instance, at one point the rector (Werner) and the citizenry of Buda were excommunicated for having denied Esztergom its staple rights. Excommunication soon became a customary punishment: During the thirteenth century the citizens of Buda were excommunicated at least six times in addition to judicial interdiction. The town was pronounced heretical and a veritable crusade was organized against it by the Curia and the rest of the Hungarian clergy. By the time Buda became the capital, the borders between royal and episcopal lands were firmly established, the levies clearly defined. Later, during the reigns of Sigismund and Matthias, the sources of support for the royal castle and its dominions were radically reorganized. Yet, by 1301 Buda's *civitas* had significant political clout which it also used in the internal turmoil immediately preceding the Anjous.

After the extinction of the House of Árpád, the Hungarian throne had two pretenders. One was the Czech, Wenceslas III, the other Caroberto of Anjou. Both were underage and related to Béla IV on the cognate line. Buda wanted Wenceslas, but Caroberto arrived in 1301. Devastating the countryside, especially the vineyards of the Buda hills, the protégé of Pope Boniface VIII succeeded in taking the capital. Meanwhile, the stubborn citizens of Buda were again excommunicated for having opposed the candidate of the pope. This time however, in response, the priests of Buda anathemized the pope in public. The synod of Óbuda declared Buda in 1307 a heretic town. The events were eternalized in the *Chronicon Hungariae Pictum,* a Hungarian work of 1360–1370.[5] One of the illustrations depicts the pope kneeling. Standing above him, two priests excommunicate him, solemnly. It should be mentioned that Caroberto (Charles I, on the Hungarian throne) always hated the city that antagonized him, and never made it his residence. His court resided first in Temesvár (today Roumania), then in Visegrád. Finally he moved out of the immediate area of the Castle Hill town. From then on the *hospites* of Buda regained their right to elect their own judges.

There is no complete record of the legal system of Buda: its constitution can be culled from the sole extant legal source, the *Ofner Stadtrecht,* a German document (incompletely preserved), from the mid-fifteenth century. Yet it reveals a lot about the daily lives of the people, their duties and privileges. We even learn such details from it as that the citizens of Buda were expected to greet the king upon his return to the capital in front of the city walls. This habit remained functional for a long time. It has been recorded that Matthias, and much later Louis II, upon reaching Buda were greeted by the citizenry led by their judges. Before crossing the gate they were to promise to respect the city's various social and economic rights and not to abolish privileges decreed by law or tradition. The recital of the *Te Deum,* the celebration of royal weddings, coronations, holidays, public mourning upon the death of royalty, were all codified in the *Ofner Stradtrecht.* The kinds and degrees of official contacts between the city and the archbishop of Esztergom, as well as with the *ispan* of the mint, were equally stated in that document. Until 1439 the rights of the German majority were clearly reflected by their representation: of the twelve members of the city council nine were German and only three Hungarian. From 1439 on, however, a parity of 6–6 was established, and the nationality of the judges was to alternate. Yet, there was a stipulation according to which only a person who was a citizen of the town and could prove he had four German grandparents could be a judge in Buda.

The daily life of the city was governed by regulations that also provided for the well-being and peace of its citizens. Buda kept its own guards, militia and hangman. Also a city trash collector was employed who had the elegant title *Mistgraf*.[6] All gates, towers, and moats had guards, including fire guards. The flowering of Buda brought more and more people wishing to become its burghers. By the fifteenth century the cemeteries were removed to the slopes and recent diggings show five to six layered burials. The streets and squares became narrower. Post-WW II excavations—some simply in the course of cleaning up the ruins—exposed many proofs of these changes in city architecture and planning. Buda's gates were closed for the night and only the king's messengers or the magistrates were allowed to move about. By that time the suburbs formed an outer chain of protection. Still, there were arms, later primarily cannons, for defense. During the time of the bow and arrow, the height of the walls was of little import (therefore the height of Mount St. Gellért was disregarded at the time of settlement), but the walls surrounding the city were raised by six to seven feet between the thirteenth and fourteenth centuries, making them more secure against artillery fire. Buda ground its own gunpowder, and since there are records of bell foundries from even before the Tatar invasion, there is every reason to believe that its twin profession, cannon making, was also practiced there.

It is important to mention that there was constant remodeling of private and public buildings during the medieval period. Romanesque Buda disappeared after the Tatar devastation, the rebuilding of the town was done in the gothic style. Only some churches and monasteries using remnants of the earlier romanesque architecture had those incorporated in their new structures. By the end of the Middle Ages there was no house in Buda which lived to see the new times in its original shape.[7]

Buildings were made higher, the second floor connected by elevated, covered bridges. Some houses became parts of the wall system. This kind of *casa forte* was meant to contribute to the defense of the city. Owing to the wealth of natural resources, from the beginning on, the houses of Buda were built of stone, brick and wood. Sandstone carvings or red marble decorated the more elegant dwellings, pillars of limestone, the portals. This sophisticated architecture began earlier than 1241. Otto of Freising—no friend of the Hungarians—while traveling in the country in 1147, commented on its stone houses in surprise.

In medieval Buda, the gothic houses of the patricians—with a few exceptions—go back to one chief type. The main front of the house faced the street, while the main axis ran parallel with it. There was a wide doorway on both sides of which there were one or two rooms. These were used as shops or for storage. The windows, mostly rectangular, opened outward. No staircase has remained intact—only remnants survived (in addition to the general decay during the Turkish occupation, an explosion destroyed much of the buildings on the Castle Hill. The Turks made the Friss Palace of Sigismund into a gunpowder magazine which exploded after having been hit by lightning during a storm in 1578. The 1686 siege then completed the destruction.)[8]

Though the second floors often changed shape beyond recognition, it can be stated that the kitchens were built downstairs, while the dining rooms were generally placed on the upper floors. Most houses had cellars (often rented out as wine cellars) which were reachable by a frontal chute. Architecture was affected by direct and indirect influence of French and German regional styles. Frequently vaults replaced the flammable wooden ceilings. Many houses had tile roofs—the most elegant ones painted, some even in gold. These and the golden globes decorating the Royal Palace made Evlyia Čelebi call the city *Kizil elma*, golden apple. Outhouses were in the back, where also the animals were kept. Excavations show that in addition to domestic animals some rich households kept wild beasts—even a monkey's skeleton was found in one of the yards. There were no bathrooms: wash-kitchens and the river were used for bathing. Water was supplied from the many springs and kept in the caves (Evlyia Čelebi wrote that he had counted over 200 wells in the town).[9]

Matthias of course had a bathroom, actually even a sauna. Heating, mostly by stoves, later also by tile-stoves, was no luxury. Even subterranean heating was used (in the Dominican cloister). Only during the rule of Matthias did the Italian-type fireplace become popular. Sigismund had brought water up to Buda, using clay and lead pipes, and Matthias had the famous architect Chimenti Camicia of Florence design a new system of canals. The architect lived twenty years in Buda (1474–1494) and was also buried there. In terms of water and health care it was, of course, of paramount importance that the city was provided with clean springs and natural hot springs. (The latter were further developed during the Turkish occupation which also acquainted the Hungarians with the sponge. Soap they had known before.)

Infant mortality, puerperal fever, and epidemic marked the Middle Ages everywhere. Actually Hungary had fewer epidemics than, for instance, Italy; yet by the sixteenth century, even syphilis was known, although not how it was transmitted. The doctors, as in most Christian countries, were first priests until in 1279 when the synod prohibited priests to treat the human body surgically. There were a number of secular doctors active in Buda whose names have survived. One was Gerhard of Croatia; another the Jew, Moises de Hungaria. After protests against his Jewish doctor, Louis of Anjou hired a gentile one by the name of Conversino da Ravenna. Medical men were held in high esteem. For example, Sigismund's dentist was enobled, his coat of arms proudly bearing three of the emperor's wisdom teeth. The *Ofner Stadtrecht* made it mandatory that the magistrates pay weekly visits to the city's hospitals which were supported by donation and by begging.

The city was proud of its standards and jealously guarded them. At one time Matthias called upon remiss home-owners and allowed them one year to make the necessary renovations in keeping with these high standards or threatened—and actually lived up to his threat—to confiscate their properties. A functional settling codetermined the profile of the town. Guilds and members of the same profession lived and traded in the same area. Thus butchers, spice shops, pharmacists and doctors had their separate sections in Buda. In addition to this, nationalities preferred to live together: French Street, Italian Street, and the like testify to this. This was based on preference, while Jews were forcibly moved to one particular section (which had been changed several times, depending on the location of the royal residence).[10]

The Jews reappeared in Hungary in 1250. They were expelled in 1222 (cf. the anti-Jewish legislation in the Golden Bull of Andrew II). There were Jews in Hungary even before the Hungarians, especially during Roman times. Later, a part of the Khabar tribes which entered the Carpathian basin with the Magyars were alleged to have been of the Jewish faith. Having been called back after the Tatar devastation, they received special privileges from Béla IV (see, "Golden freedom" statute of 1251). One of them, Henel, became the head of Béla's mint and received the title *comes camerae*. Jewish gravestones have been found from the thirteenth century and a synagogue from 1307. Jews were forced to wear pointed hats and were not allowed to sell on market days (once a week they were permitted to sell the items unclaimed in their pawnshops), but otherwise they lived in relative peace until 1515. Henel, for example, became so rich that for 800 pieces of silver he bought the fort of Komarom and the surrounding lands. Similarly, Mendel, the prefect of Jews during Matthias' time, erected a large synagogue (with two aisles) in Buda. This was excavated in 1960, and can be visited.[11] It should be mentioned here that the Jews of Buda survived the Turkish occupation—actually flourishing during Turkish rule—but were massacred in 1686 by the Austrian-Hungarian liberating armies. The eyewitness report of Isac Schulhof, *Budai krónika* (Buda Chronicle) provides us with a detailed description of the events.[12]

Jews were not the only "exotic" inhabitants of medieval Buda and Pest. Abu Hamid al Garnati, who had visited his son in Pest in about 1150, talked about a sizable Muslim population. He also counted Hungary among those countries where prosperity was the greatest. In connection with this he claimed that one could get a beautiful slave girl for ten dinars, and during times of war the same was available for three.[13] Slavery was practiced at least until the first half of the thirteenth century, since in the anti-Jewish legislation of the Golden Bull it is stated that Jews are not permitted to keep Christian slaves.

There were also gypsies in Hungary, although their number was quite small during the Middle Ages. Their first group crossed the southern borders of Hungary in 1415, escaping the Turks. Sigismund permitted them to settle in Hungary. They seemed to have been popular. Beatrix, the wife of Matthias, had gypsies perform in the intermissions of her famed Csepel horse races. Both her bookkeeping records and the 1525 records of Louis II mention payments for gypsy musicians.

The population mixed freely and met regularly at the biweekly markets or the country fairs. It is known from bookkeeping records, bills, and from the *Ofner Stadtrecht* that by the end of the thirteenth century Hungary's trade expanded beyond Vienna, Brasow and Bratislava and reached Venice, Silesia and Little Poland. By the Renaissance, foreign merchant houses established veritable colonies in Hungary. Local trade took place on both sides of the Danube which was at that time the most frequently used trade route of the Middle Ages. North and south, wine and salt were shipped on large freight boats. The ferrymen who carried merchandise and people across were members of the first guild, owning their own ferries and boats. There was no bridge across the Danube until the Turkish period. In winter, the frozen surface of the river was used. The region was rich in forests and limestone, and the surrounding meadows satisfied the agricultural needs of the Buda population and provided for ample grazing land. In 1433 Bertrandon de la Broquière, the head stableman of the duke of Burgundy, noted that Pest had the world's largest horse fair, where one could buy 2,000 horses in a single day.[14] Horses and cattle were also exported to the Balkans and Italy, and to the market towns of Germany all the time. Trade was made easy by the network of roads developed and left by the Romans. The same road system still governs the direction of trade in today's Transdanubia. The Buda fair grounds also doubled for tournaments. At the fairs Special regulations controlled cleanliness and the freshness of merchandise. The butchers had to slaughter every day and, to prove this, had to hang the fresh hide each day in front of their shops. Wine sales were controlled—nothing was to be sold before mass was over. Wednesday belonged to the German, Friday to the Hungarian sellers. Bears, puppets, games—especially dice—animated the atmosphere.

Not just the marketplace, but every walk of life was regulated by the city's charter. The *Ofner Stadtrecht* states that the judge may pass a death sentence, while it is only the king who may grant pardon. Public order—influenced by German law—was of paramount importance. Whoever offended against it was severely punished. The churches were places of asylum but it is not known whether the Buda parishes ever practiced this. Of the crimes, murder and rape were the most harshly punished. There was a clear definition separating premeditated murder from accidental manslaughter. Rape was especially severely dealt with when the victim was a married woman. All burghers—Jews excluded—were permitted to bear arms (the only exception being on election day). Altogether, the principle of a tooth for a tooth prevailed; only later was it mellowed into monetary restitution. Arsonists died at the stake as did counterfeiters. Prostitution, if not tolerated was, however, relatively lightly punished. Executions were by public hanging and also by drowning in the Danube. (Mothers who taught their daughters immoral behavior were sentenced to be drowned.[15] There is no mention of fathers). There were no prison sentences; the defendant spent time in jail only until his trial date came up.

It is edifying to investigate the actual cultural level of Buda's medieval population. The country's intellectual elite was the clergy—many of them foreigners, almost all foreign-trained. Very soon after the country became Christian, Hungarian and Croatian students were sent to the great universities of France, Italy, and England. Hungarian students made their mark very early at the universities of Paris, Padua and Bologna. Another interesting but less frequently quoted fact is that Hungary had early contact with Oxford. The earliest undergraduate of Oxford was Nicolaus clericus de Hungaria, who studied there from 1193 to 1196.[16] The cost of his education was defrayed by Richard the

Lionhearted who was distantly related to the Hungarian king; his sister-in-law was Queen Margaret of Hungary, the second wife of Béla III. Of the signatories of the Golden Bull one bishop was of English extraction, another fought with English barons in the Crusades. This even might have affected the content of the Golden Bull, which was signed merely seven years after the Magna Charta and dealt with the same issues.

Although the language of the clergy and the administration was Latin (and remained so for many centuries, well into modern times), soon also a literature in the vernacular appeared. The Latin alphabet was found to be entirely suitable for the notation of Hungarian sounds, while there was an increasing need for the translation of legends, hymns, and the like for beginners and for nuns whose education did not include Latin. We have fascinating records of the educational standards of the latter group. In 1273 an interrogation took place in the Dominican cloister of Rabbit Island, with regard to the beatification of Margaret, daughter of Béla IV, the order's most illustrious member. In all 110 witnesses were heard by the commission. And while the order housed the daughters of the oligarchy, the majority did not even know how old they were, or had been, at the time they had entered the convent. (One said, "I still had milk teeth"). Most of them did not know the names of the months, many could not read at all.

At the same time two major literary relics testify to the high quality of vernacular literature: *The Funeral Oration* (*Halotti Beszéd*), translated by a Dominican monk from Geofroi de Breteuil's Latin hymn,[17] is a prose piece, but *Mary's Lament* (Ó-Magyar Mária Siralom) proves that by the thirteenth-century poetry in Hungarian had reached a high level of artistry.[18] Alliteration, rhyme, and rhythm patterns attest to this. Its sophistication makes us believe that this was just one of the many works composed during that period, but the Tatar invasion which had left the country in ashes, had also destroyed those treasures.

Legends of saints (such as Margaret and Saint Francis) do not show a realistic portrayal of the surroundings, but reflect also the new strivings, a new theory of nature, recognition of beauty.

During the same century secular biographies were added to the lives of saints, and several chronicles recorded the history and deeds of the Hungarians.

The first schools were run by Fransiscans. The students learned to read and write and also to read musical scores. It seems that the burghers of Buda were in the vanguard of modern secular education. At least by the fifteenth century, most of them could read and write in Hungarian and in German, and many also in Latin. They also knew how to count and used both Roman and Arabic numerals. Their extensive trade with western Europe made them aware of the need for education and the learning of crafts. Owing to adverse historical circumstances, no medieval Hungarian university survived into modern times; 1367 Pécs, 1389 Óbuda, 1467 Pozsony were the landmarks of Hungary's attempts at higher education. None functioned for more than a few decades. Lower-level education was also manifested in the sports, of which every one was popular in medieval Buda. Tournaments imitated by the guilds' competitions provided for all-year entertainment. Music was very popular (many family names refer to musical instruments), and it is recorded that the city hired musicians. It is also known that Pietro Bono of Ferrara played his lyre for Beatrix.[19] Scores of medieval book illuminations show musical instruments.

Buda's intellectual and artistic blossoming started under the Árpád rulers. The palace was expanded during the Anjous and further enlarged by Sigismund who in the first quarter of the fifteenth century added the much admired Friss Palace. This was an enormous feudal castle with a sumptuous Hall of Knights and the famed Short Tower. Buda's significance is proven by the fact that it was chosen as the meeting place for many a crowned head at the time when Sigismund was acting as peacemaker between Poland and Venice. Three kings, three ministers of state, a Serbian despot, 13 dukes, 21 counts, 26 barons, 1,500 knights, one cardinal, a papal nuncio, 3 archbishops, and 11 bishops were housed within the walls of the Buda castle. We must add to this number at least 3,000 servants in order to arrive at the actual number of visitors staying in Buda at one time. It is known that in 1437, the royal dean, Monsignor Berrerius, intending Buda to host the Basle Council, gathered lodgings statistics regarding available housing. He established that Buda alone (not counting its public buildings) had 997 lodging houses, providing 3,276 heatable dwelling rooms, and stables for 4,705 horses. Many of the Hungarian and Croatian barons and lesser nobles had homes in Buda.[20]

While the earlier cultural centers of Hungary were seats of bishoprics, Buda, without a sea became the real cultural center of Hungary, owing to the presence of the royal residence. This was most obvious during the reign of Matthias Corvinus (1458–1490), whose splendid court was a meeting place of Europe's intellectual and artistic elite. This is the period when the city of Buda and the newly built Renaissance royal palace gained international significance. Of the historians, Galeotto Marzio (who also excelled in astronomy) and Antonio Bonfini represent Italy; Regiomontanus, the famed astronomer, Germany; Giovanni Dalmata (in the company of many lesser known Dalmatian and Croatian artist and artisans), the Southern Slavs.[21] Also, scores of foreign authors dedicated their work to the Hungarian king who was considered a generous Maecenas to the representatives of the New Learning. Even Ficino considered moving to Buda but later changed his mind.

Matthias' court could also take pride in its very own humanists who had made the chancery comparable to the most respected ones in the West. The concept of the "Hungarian quattrocento," which is frequently regarded as the most glorious period in the country's history, is clearly tied to the personae of Iohannes Vitéz, and his nephew Janus Pannonius.[22] Vitéz is often referred to as the father of Hungarian humanism. At his episcopal see at Várad, and later as archbishop of Esztergom and primate of Hungary-Croatia, Vitéz was a fountainhead and disseminator of humanist learning. He contributed to the spreading of humanist values far beyond the borders of the country and his own immediate political influence. Both he and Janus were of Slavonian origin, and archetypal for that Hungarian Renaissance personality which, ethnically Croatian, Serbian, Roumanian, Polish, or German, came to serve at the Buda court. A wealthy prelate, Vitéz began to send his relatives to study in Italy at his own expense, with the definite plan to educate them for future service in the royal chancery. The chancery itself, which from a relatively modest beginning, had evolved into a large administrative system by the mid-fifteenth century, needed the new kind of versatile humanist personalities who had the diplomatic and political expertise and the authority to deal with the newly arisen functions. Vitéz's own correspondence with people such as Enea Silvio and Poggio Bracciolini, collected and published as early as 1451 (*Epistolae*, edited by Paulus Iwanich), testify to this.[23] His nephew, Janus, who later became the pride of Hungarian-Croatian humanism, was sent to study in Italy, in the famous school of Guarino da Verona, for the same purpose.

Janus, although preparing for work in the chancery and in the church (he received doctoral degrees in law and in theology), presented us with an extra bonus, his marvelous poetry, unequaled "beyond the Alps" during his time. His career is fascinating, controversial, and very typically Renaissance.

Janus was still young when he became bishop of Pécs (a lucrative see), and the king's friend and confidant. Yet after his return from Italy, he permanently had the feeling of living far off the centers of Europe, and complained about being exiled in a barbarian land. He was—also in this sense—truly universal. He belonged to that international network of humanists who had no real country and no real mother tongue. His world was the antique world, his oeuvre has no truly Hungarian or Croatian characteristics but is determined by the intellectual universalism of Renaissance Europe. Yet, his rise and fall are typically Hungarian. In Hungary he—and his uncle—represented a new class, the lower nobility which is the actual carrying force of the Renaissance. Until his fall (he organized a plot against Matthias, had to flee and died on his way to Italy), Janus was an excellent example of the mobility of his class (as was actually, Matthias' own rise). Janus' career and that of his fellow humanists prove that although there was a hothouse character to the Buda Renaissance, there was also a definite need for the development of the class to which he belonged. His fall is also typically Hungarian and special for the period. Matthias' mistake was that he feudalized his humanists and then expected them to continue fighting for the aims of centralization, namely against their own vested interests.

After the plot was discovered (1472), Matthias lost his interest in humanist scholarship. Many of the aspiring scholars did not return from their Italian schools fearing the wrath of the king. Only after his marriage to Beatrix of Aragon (December 22, 1476), does a new influx of primarily Italian humanists reach Buda. The ensuing years until his death (1490) are the years of true splendor. We learn that at his wedding twenty-four courses were served and 983 dishes were on the tables (glasses and decanters not included). As opposed to this lavish feast, it has been recorded that in the 1520s, Louis II's court was so poor that often local burghers were asked to lend some wine for the royal table.

Matthias commissioned a large number of manuscripts which—in addition to those which he had confiscated from the rebels—made up the bulk of his famed Corvin Library. Already Sigismund had a valuable collection of books, but Matthias' out-shone it by far. Printing was also introduced into Hungary during Matthias' rule. The *Buda Chronicle* (*Chronica Hungarorum*, or *Chronicon Budense*) printed by Andreas Hess, and paid for by Ladislas Karai, *praepositus* of Buda, appeared in 1473 (there are ten extant copies of this title, the first book printed in Hungary proper).

While the flowering of the Buda Renaissance was the work and the pleasure of a select few, the town itself also flourished during the last quarter of the fifteenth century. Buda, with its surrounding settlements may have had twelve- to fifteen-thousand inhabitants; Pest possibly another ten thousand. Thus, together, they could be considered one of the large medieval cities. The thin layer of Renaissance erudition notwithstanding, that is what Buda actually remained until the Turkish onslaught: with a clear Hungarian majority, a medieval bi-ethnic city.

In spite of his opulent court, or perhaps also because of it, by the end of his rule Matthias' debts were approaching two million florins, while his income was only half. He permanently pressed the nobility, the peasants and the towns for more contributions.

In Nicolaus Olahus' *Hungaria,* which is one of the most moving examples of patriotism mixed with nostalgia, pre-Mohács Hungary is presented as the land of milk and honey. This was certainly not the case. The weak rule of the Jagiellonean kings and the newly arisen power of the barons further depleted the shrinking wealth of the country. During Wladislas' rule royal income decreased 60–80 percent, compared to Matthias'. By the second half of Matthias' rule German merchant settlers and merchant colonies were highly visible. The Hallers from Nuremberg, the Pemfflingers from Styria, and finally, from the 1490s on, the Augsburg Fuggers had permanent representation in Buda. The only area in which the South Germans did not get involved was cattle export, but even there, instead of merchandise bad money was funelled back to the country. During the Jagiello rule (actually between 1495–1526), the Fuggers, in partnership with the Thurzos, moved a million florins out of the country.[24] The 1514 peasant uprising reflected the dissatisfaction of the countryside, while the 1525 Buda pogrom directed against Jews and foreigners showed the growing tensions in the towns.

The Buda court suffered the results of weak kings and general mismanagement which manifested itself from lack of upkeep in the defense system to the gradual, thoughtless depletion of the Corviniana.

During the Jagiello period Buda increasingly became a trading place with no agriculture to back it. Its intellectuals, in addition to those active at court, were medical doctors, lawyers and teachers. The latter were teaching the children of the burghers. It seems that the townspeople also gained power in the face of a weakening kingdom. The merchant community's wealth was on the increase; their children were better educated. Even musicians were hired for them. Indeed, the citizens of Buda became so strong that by the early 1510s they were able to expel the Nuremberg merchant houses from the country, and succeeded—for a while—even to trade independently with the Turks.[25] Later some of the same people played leading roles in Buda's life under the rule of Zápolya.

Like their Italian colleagues, the citizens were just about to show muscle—when the Turks arrived. The burghers of Buda differed in one major aspect from their Italian counterparts: They did not pay enough attention to having safe walls surround their town. Buda fell without resistance, owing mostly to the fact that there was no defensible fortification to withstand a powerful attack (the same predicament forced Zápolya to flee in 1527). The burghers of Buda had no experience of foreign armies besieging their walls. They faced the Turkish attack and the ensuing many changes of power utterly unprepared. Suleiman occupied and set fire to an almost empty city.

In the following years, although the inhabitants slowly returned and the rebuilding of Buda began, the internecine struggles for the throne hampered any true development. After 1541 the Turks maintained the city council in place, but as the years went by the council members' actual authority decreased. Slowly the Hungarian population of the city left (the Germans were expelled by Zápolya), and more and more Turks moved in and settled in the deserted houses of the Buda patricians. The place of the Hungarian merchants was taken by new settlers from the Balkans (Orthodox Serbs, but also Catholic Bosnians, some Dalmatians, and Jews). At the 1686 recapturing of Buda (September 2), the Hungarian population of the earlier capital was estimated to be no more than 5 percent.

NOTES

1. Evlyia Čelebi, quoted by László Zolnay, *Az elátkozott Buda—Buda aranykora* (Budapest, 1982), 335.
2. Zolnay, *Az elátkozott Buda*, 133.
3. Ibid., 165.
4. Today Margitsziget, i.e., Margaret Island.
5. Also called *Kálti Márk Képes Krónikája* or *Bécsi Képes Krónika*.
6. *Ofner Stadtrecht*, also quoted by Zolnay in *Hétköznapok Budán*, 35.
7. László Gerő, *Gothic Houses in Buda* (Budapest, 1966), esp. 11–14.
8. Zolnay, *A budai vár*, 55.
9. Evlyia Čelebi, *Evlyia Čelebi török világutazó magyarországi utazásai*, I, 244.
10. Gerő, 14.
11. Zolnay was a principal member of the excavating team. Cf. his findings in *Buda középkori zsidósága* (Budapest, 1968).

12. It was translated from Hebrew into Hungarian by László Jólesz, and published in 1979.

13. Quoted by Zolnay in *Az elátkozott Buda*, 99.

14. Bertrandon de la Broquière was an expert horse breeder who had also investigated breeding in the stables of the famous Turkish cavalry. He visited the Balkans and explored much of the Levant, spoke Arabic and Turkish, and his travel accounts include the best description of medieval Damascus.

15. *Ofner Stadtrecht*, 158.

16. He is depicted in the bottom left corner of the traditional pictorial map of Oxford as "Nicholao Clerico de Hungaria, the earliest recorded undergraduate."

17. The *Funeral Oration* (26 lines and a 6 line supplication) was discovered in the *Pray Codex*. It was first described by György Pray in 1770.

18. *Mary's Lament* (37 lines) was discovered in a Latin codex housed in the University Library of Louvain. It was recently donated to Hungary by the Belgian government.

19. Jolán Balogh, *Művészetek Mátyás király udvarában* I:446.

20. Sándor Zaharias, and Sándor G. Lestyén, *2,000-Year-Old Budapest*, 19.

21. Balogh's work contains a thorough survey and rich bibliographic material on the subject. Cf. also *Schallaburg, 1982*.

22. More on the cultural and political environment of fifteenth century Hungary in my *Janus Pannonius: Poet and Politician*.

23. Iván Boronkai's new edition includes the material from the earliest collection, correspondence after the 1451 cut-off date, and stuff that was left out by Paulus Iwanich. It also contains eleven of Iohannes Vitéz's orations.

24. For more on this, see Zsuzsanna Hermann, *Az 1515. szerződés . . .*

25. There is a plethora of material on the subject. Most frequently quoted are: Lajos Fógel, *II. Lajos udvara* (Budapest, 1917), and an even earlier publication, Vilmos Fraknói, *Magyarország a Mohácsi Vész elött, a pápai követek jelentései alapján* (Budapest, 1884).

BIBLIOGRAPHY

Balogh, Jolán. *Művészetek Mátyás király udvarában* [The Arts in the Court of King Matthias]. Budapest: 1966.

Bibliotheca Corviniana. Budapest: 1967.

Birnbaum, Marianna D. *Janus Pannonius: Poet and Politician.* Zagreb, 1981.

Bjorkman, Walther. *Ofen zur türkischen Zeit, vornemlich nach türkischen Quellen.* Hamburg, 1920 (*Hamburg Universität. Abhandlungen aus dem Gebiet der Auslandskunde* 3).

Boemus, Ioannes Aubanus, *Mores, Leges, Ritus Omnium Gentium . . .* Lugduni, 1582.

Budapest régiségei. [The Antiquities of Budapest]. Budapest: 1889 (especially vols. 15–17).

Budapest története a későbbi középkorban és a török hódoltság idején [The History of Budapest During the Late Middle Ages and During the Period of Turkish Occupation]. By András Kubinyi, et al. Budapest: 1975 (*Budapest története,* 2).

Budapest története az őskortól az Árpádkor végéig [The History of Budapest From Prehistoric Times to the End of the Árpád Period]. By Tibor Nagy, György Györffy, and László Gerevich. Budapest: 1975.

Čelebi, Evlyia. *Evlia Cselebi török világutazó magyarországi utazásai, 1600–1664* [The Hungarian Journal of Evlia Cselebi, Turkish World Traveler]. Trans. and with notes by Imre Karácsony. Budapest, 1904 (*Török-magyarkori történelmi emlékek,* II. *Irók*) [Turkish-Hungarian Historical Monuments, Authors].

Csemegi, József. *A budavári főtemplom* [The Main Church of Castle Hill]. Budapest, 1955.

Czagány, István. *A budavári palota és a Szt. György téri épületek* [The Palace on Castle Hill and the Buildings of St. George's Square]. Budapest, 1966.

Elekes, Lajos. *Die Verbündeten und die Feinde des ungarischen Volkes in den Kampfen gegen die türkischen Eroberer.* Budapest: 1954 (*Studia historica,* 9).

Fekete, Lajos. *Budapest a törökkorban* [Budapest During the Turkish Occupation]. Budapest: 1944.

Fógel, József. *II Ulászló udvartartása (1490–1516)* [The Court of Wladislas II, 1490–1516]. Budapest: 1913.

Gerevich, László. *A budai vár feltárása* [The Excavation of the Buda Castle]. Budapest: 1966.

Gerő, László. *Gothic Houses in Buda.* Budapest: 1966.

Göllner, Carl. *Turcica,* Three vols. Bukuresti: 1961–1978.

Gyurky, Katalin. *Az egykori budai domonkos kolostor* [The One-Time Dominican Cloister of Buda]. Budapest: 1976.

Hermann, Zsuzsanna. *Az 1515. szerződés; adalék a Habsburgok magyarországi uralmának előtörténetéhez* [The Treaty of 1515. Notes on the

Prehistory of the Hapsburg Rule in Hungary]. Budapest: 1961 (*Értekezések a történeti tudományok köréből. Új sorozat*, 21).

Kristó, Gyula. *Az Aranybullák évszázada* [The Century of the Golden Bulls]. Budapest: 1976.

Kubinyi, András. "A mezőgazdaság története a Mohács előtti Budán" [The History of Agriculture in Pre-Mohács Buda]. *Agrártörténeti szemle.* (1964) nos. 3–4.

Buda története 1541–ig [The History of Buda Until 1514]. Budapest: 1969.

Kulcsár, Péter. *A Jagello-kor* [The Jagiello Period]. Budapest: 1981.

Lestyén, Sándor and Zahariás, Sándor G. *2,000-Year-Old Budapest.* Budapest: 1945.

Miskimin, Harry, A. *The Economy of Early Renaissance Europe, 1300–1600.* Cambridge: 1975.

Mollay, Karl, ed. *Das Ofner Stadtrecht: eine deutschsprachige Rechtssammlung aus Ungarn.* Weimar: 1959.

Olahus, Nicolaus. *Hungaria—Atila . . .,* Vindobonae: 1763.

Pauler, Gyula. *A magyar nemzet története az árpádházi királyok alatt* [The History of the Hungarian Nation During the Rule of the House of Árpád]. Two vols. Budapest: 1893.

Rózsa, György. *Budapest régi látképei* [Old Vistas of Budapest]. Budapest: 1963 (*Monumenta historica Budapestinensis*, 2).

Schallaburg '82; Matthias Corvinus und die Renaissance in Ungarn. Tibor Klaniczay et al., eds. Schallaburg: 1982.

Stavrianos, L. S. *The Balkans Since 1453.* Hinsdale, Illinois: 1958.

Szakály, Ferenc. *Magyar adóztatás a török hódoltságban* [Hungarian Taxation During the Turkish Occupation]. Budapest: 1981.

Vitéz, Iohannes. *Ioannes Vitez de Zredna Opera quae supersunt.* Edited by Iván Boronkai. Budapest: 1980.

Wernher, Georgius. *De admirandis Hungariae aquis.* Basle: 1549.

Zolnay, László. *Buda középkori zsidósága* [The Jews of Medieval Buda]. Budapest: 1968.

_____. *Az elátkozott Buda—Buda aranykora* [The Anathematized Buda—The Golden Age of Buda]. Budapest: 1982.

_____. *Kincses Magyarország: Középkori művelődésünk történetéből* [Treasurehouse: Hungary. From the History of Our Medieval Culture]. Budapest: 1977.

_____. *Ünnep és hétköznapok a középkori Budán* [Holidays and Weekdays in Medieval Buda]. Budapest: 1969.

4

Unfulfilled Autonomy: Urban Society in Serbia and Bosnia

Sima Ćirković

Recent research has shown that urban settlements, which are a prerequisite for the appearance of an urban society, have a long and complex history in the Balkans and that their origins cannot be derived from one common root. The statement that we have to differentiate between an eastern and a western component might sound monotonous, but we can hardly expect it to be otherwise in an area cut by many important borderlines, like the frontier between the Eastern and Western Roman Empire, between the zones of Greek and Latin languages, between the Catholic and the Eastern Orthodox churches.

The territory comprising Serbia and Bosnia in the late medieval period was part of a larger area in which urban life of late antiquity was destroyed and extinguished.[1] In the rare written sources there are accounts of devastations and catastrophes in Roman cities in the Balkan provinces. These accounts seem to be confirmed by archaeological excavations of many ruins that have not produced one single case of survival of urban life after the critical decades of the early seventh century. Discontinuity of urban life is an outstanding characteristic of the entire interior area of the Balkan peninsula, but considerable differences in the duration and completeness of the rupture can be observed. In the eastern part of the area, with which we are concerned, it is possible to notice a return to the remnants of old urban settlements and their later revival so that a number of well-known Roman cities continued to exist in the Middle Ages: Singidunum in Belgrade, Viminacium in Braničevo, Naissus in Niš, Ulpiana in Lipljan, Scupi in Skopje, Theranda in Prizren, etc. In the western part, which includes regions of what are now western Serbia, Bosnia, Herzegovina (Hercegovina) and Montenegro (Crna Gora), we are unable to cite one single example of this kind. Ruins of large Roman cities like Municipium Malvesatium, near Užička Požega, or the extensive ruins near the river Lim as well as those large Roman towns that had been situated in the region of Ilidža or Titograd, do not have any continuation. Some of them could not be identified and are called Municipium S or Municipium M. The longer the rupture lasted, the more complete was the oblivion.

In my opinion it is possible to reconstruct the line that divided the two areas and which helps us perceive the conditions that generated those differences. The clue for such a reconstruction is given by the charters of the Byzantine Emperor Basil II for the archbishopric of Okhrid issued in 1018 and 1020.[2] They contain the names of settlements considered suitable to become sees of bishoprics. Some of settlements had been centers of bishoprics during the previous period, a fact that has a bearing on our evaluation of their earlier development; but from our present standpoint the charters of Basil II are important primarily as indications of the impact of Byzantine rule. Namely, the charters were issued at a time when the territories in the interior of the peninsula, as far as the rivers Sava and Danube, came under Byzantine control. For almost two and a half centuries they remained within the frontiers of the Byzantine Empire which endeavoured to organize them according to its ideas, in which cities were intended to be the strongholds of the governmental system and the focuses of political and cultural influence.[3] Even a cursory examination could show that the results of the Byzantine revival of ancient towns were considerable in general terms, but were not the same for all the towns concerned. Belgrade, Niš, Skopje, and Prizren became towns once again and preserved their urban character for good. Braničevo was mentioned as *civitas munitissima* as late as 1437, while some others lost their importance, like Lipljan, or totally disappeared, like Ras. Sirmium underwent a substantial transformation in which, it seems, the Byzantine foundations did not play an important part: The medieval "Civitas Sancti Demetrii" arose from a settlement near the ancient monastery of the same name. Nevertheless a general conclusion may be drawn that the Byzantine element in the origins of medieval urban settlements must be taken into consideration, and we shall later return to the Byzantine urban heritage.

From the peripheral sees of bishoprics in 1018–1020, that is, from Sirmium, Ras, and Prizren westward there were no sees in any towns as far as Sisak and Zagreb, except on the Adriatic coast. When the bishoprics in Serbia were founded in 1220, their sees were located in large monasteries. Some years later, when attempts were made in Bosnia to reform the ecclesiastical organization, there was not a single town in which to place the cathedral.[4]

The unequal distribution of urban settlements, ascertained in 1018–1020, conspicuous around 1220, and visible even a century later, disappeared gradually during the second half of the fourteenth century. By the time both areas fell under Ottoman rule, there was hardly any difference in the degree of urbanization. On both sides of our borderline (Sirmium-Ras-Prizren) a late wave of newly emerged urban settlements produced a kind of balance.

The early beginnings of this wave date back to the mid-thirteenth century when German miners, called Saxons, came into Serbia and started the production of silver, copper, and lead. They appear for the first time in a source from 1254, then for a few decades all data are related to Brskovo, probably the first center of the mining industry. By the beginning of the fourteenth century three more mines appear, later seven, then the number increases suddenly so that around thirty mining places could be recorded in the entire territory of the Balkans for the entire medieval period including the beginning of Ottoman rule.[5] We should not attribute an urban character to every place where mining had been registered, but we have good reason to pay special attention to the mining settlements for they are sharply contrasted to their rural and dependent surroundings. By their very nature the mining settlements are distinctive from the feudal environment so they cannot be overlooked in any attempt to describe and characterize the urban society in Serbia and Bosnia.

It cannot be determined with accuracy whether the Saxons arrived in Serbia fleeing from the Tatars or as a group of colonists invited by the Serbian king, Stefan Uroš I (1243–1276).[6] In any case, the charters containing their privileges have not been preserved. From later sources referring to Saxons, it can be deduced that they enjoyed personal freedom, that they had the right to prospect for ore, dig pits, shafts, and build other necessary installations—and, being Catholics in an Eastern Orthodox surrounding, they enjoyed also the freedom of religion. The Saxons had also their own autonomous jurisdiction. Only for a short period of time could those privileges remain limited to the foreigners, to the Saxons or Teotonici as they sometimes had been referred to in Latin and Italian sources. The opening of new mines, or the expansion of production in existing ones, could be brought about only by a considerable increase of manpower which, in its turn, was possible only by including some of the native population in the process. The admission of native people into a mining settlement could be legalized in two ways: Workers could be treated as members of the "familia" of a Saxon enjoying autonomy who takes over responsibility for his men; such a practice is confirmed by a document dated 1302,[7] and it is easy to understand how restricted was its applicability. And the rights of the Saxon could also be transferred to all inhabitants of a mining settlement without regard to their origin.

Mining law, as it is known in medieval Europe in all its variants, including those that are preserved in Serbian and Turkish texts,[8] is very specialized and regulates a considerable number of areas: the delineation of the fields belonging to pits, relations among mines, their reciprocal services, the care for drainage and ventilation, and also the problems of groups of miners, laborers and entrepreneurs, especially questions concerning common ex-

penses and the partition of the profits of members of companies
(*gvarci,* from German *Gewerke*). The institutional technical and unin-
telligible to laymen, mining law had drawn together into a whole
all the participants in mining production, from common diggers
to entrepreneurs and financiers. The institutional expression of
this kind of unity was the assembly (*zbor, sborum*) which had a
number of responsibilities according to the rules of the mining
law. The integrative role played by the mining law helps us also
understand how it was possible to keep alive the name of Saxons
for centuries after the small group of true Germans had been
assimilated into the Slav environment. The appellation "Saxons"
had changed its meaning: Having lost its ethnic content, it denoted a status whose outstanding feature remained a high degree of autonomy.

Besides the just mentioned assembly, every settlement of this
category had a council consisting of twelve members called *purgari.* The term is a loanword from the German *Bürger,* or more
precisely, *die Geschworenen Bürger—cives iurati.* Seldom was the
term translated into old Serbo-Croatian or Italian: *gragjani, borgh-
esani, cittadini*—citizens, but never with the adjective "sworn."
The *purgari* had administrative as well as judiciary responsibilities. Sometimes they were characterized by contemporaries as
officiales or *maiores civitatis* or *anciani.*[9]

The individual head of a mining settlement was the count.
knez, comes civitatis. The fact that the first known *comes civitatis*
was a German, *comes Vreibergerius,* mentioned in 1280, is an
important indication that this function also belonged to Saxon
institutions.[10]

Institutions of Saxon origin are an essential characteristic of
urban settlements in all Balkan countries with an evolved mining
industry. Their importance is increased by the fact that they did
not remain limited exclusively to mining settlements. Nevertheless, all problems of the autonomy of urban settlements are not
exhausted with the Saxons, their rights, and their institutions.
In order to obtain a more realistic picture we must take into
account elements that strengthened as well as those that reduced
original Saxon autonomy.

Economic conditions from the early beginnings of the mining

settlements forced merchants and miners into close cooperation. The metals produced in the mines in Balkan countries (silver, silver with gold, copper, lead), being valuable articles and constantly in demand, attracted merchants who began to participate in the production especially of silver, in order to secure the costly metal for themselves. An increase in production required new capital for investment in larger and more expensive equipment and installations. So it happened that the miners were joined by a considerable number of merchants originating from the coastal cities, mainly from Dubrovnik and Kotor and in a lesser number from Bar, Split and other cities.[11] They all were citizens of autonomous communes who, while living for years or even for decades in the mining settlements of Serbia and Bosnia, remained subject to the laws and authorities of their native cities. The status of those merchants in the Balkan countries was determined by the general privileges granted to their cities. Best-known are the rights of the Ragusans, inhabitants of Dubrovnik (Ragusa), established and confirmed by political treaties which the *commune,* later the republic, concluded and renewed with the rulers of Serbia and Bosnia for more than two and a half centuries.[12]

The Ragusans enjoyed freedom of trade and business activity and were guaranteed the security of their property. Their mutual disputes were settled either by law courts in Dubrovnik or by a Ragusan *consul* who used to visit the urban settlements in Serbia. After 1396 the Minor Council of Dubrovnik appointed an ad hoc body consisting of one consul and two judges for every single lawsuit. Disputes between Ragusans and native inhabitants, who were divided into two categories—Serbs and Saxons—were settled by a joint court consisting of an equal number of judges from both groups to which the litigants belonged. From the end of the fourteenth century those Ragusans who were owners of mining installations, landed properties and houses, were obligated to participate in the defense of the town and to pay taxes. Because of the fact that Ragusans were members of companies for the exploitations of mines (*gvarci, Gewerke*) and farmers of taxes from the mining industry, they were included in that part of the population subject to the mining law. Thus they enjoyed autonomy on a twofold basis: They were citizens of Dubrovnik and, as mining entrepreneurs, they acquired also the status of Saxons. The Ragusans, like other merchants from Dalmatian cities, of course remained subject to the laws of their native cities and, outside the sphere of mining, they behaved as foreigners who insisted on their separate jurisdiction. The situation was complicated by the fact that among local residents in Serbian and Bosnian towns there were also native people who were merchants not related to the mining industry. To some of them, Ragusan citizenship had been granted with the rights and immunities of native Ragusans.[13]

The government of Dubrovnik usually directed its instructions to "Ragusans and to those who consider themselves Ragusans" (*Raguseis et tamquam Raguseis se habentibus*). In such a variety of legal distinctions abuses could hardly have been avoided. There are cases when the origin or, more precisely, the legal status of some individuals who went under the guise of Saxons, Serbs or Ragusans, according to their interests, had to be established by a formal lawsuit. Even rulers were sometimes at a loss in regard to the persons and numbers of their subjects. Despot Djuradj Branković ruled in 1433 that all Ragusans in the town of Srebrnica had to be registered in order to avoid further uncertainties.

The plurality of groups of town residents living according to separate legal systems had far-reaching consequences for the conditions of the urban settlements and their inhabitants. In a certain sense it made their autonomy safer and more stable. It is always difficult to change the status of a social group, but it must have been extremely difficult to change the status of foreigners whose rights had been sanctioned by treaties concluded and confirmed successively by several generations of rulers, especially when those foreigners were not guests, but permanent residents performing important economic functions. But the same plurality had also a negative impact on the development of the urban autonomy because it prevented the formation of a unified community of citizens comparable to that kind of *universitas* or *commune* which had been known not only in Italy and in most West European countries, but also in the cities situated on the Adriatic coast.

In the context of the present paper I cannot offer a detailed account of the terminology relating to urban settlements in the South Slav area. I shall only stress the fact that all terms used to denote the urban settlements were deduced from the place, from topography, and not from a community of inhabitants. The basic term *grad*, common to all Slav languages, had "fortification" in the core of its meaning and was used at the same time for large urban settlements and for solitary fortresses and even for walls. The second, and perhaps most often used, appellation for this category of settlements, *trg*, was originally the place where sellers and buyers used to meet. Later it denoted a part of a settlement and, finally, a type of settlement.[14] The chronologically latest and puzzling term *varoš*, is a loanword from the Hungarian whose original meaning, "a settlement under a fortress (*vár*)," has a parallel in the Slav *podgradije* and Latin *suburbium*. This term appeared in the fifteenth century and later spread over the entire Balkan peninsula, reaching even the Aegean Islands with a changed meaning. Latin and Italian sources were following the Slav terminology using, for the urban settlements in Serbia and Bosnia, the terms: *civitas, zitade, mercato, borgho*, the latest being used mostly for unfortified settlements. Noticeable is the absence of the term *opština* or *opkina* (community),[15] which was well-known and used hundreds of times, but related to Dubrovnik, Kotor, or Venice, never to a settlement in the interior of the peninsula.

This difference in use was by no means accidental. It is, in my opinion, an important witness to the fact that medieval people were aware that those settlements belonged in different categories. Some essential differences can be perceived by a cursory comparative procedure. The Dalmatian cities and Dubrovnik will be discussed by Professor Krekić. I shall limit myself to some points which seem to be appropriate in elucidating the incompleteness of the autonomy of the mining settlements, an autonomy that was otherwise the broadest in the Balkan hinterland.

The communes of the Adriatic coast and the mining settlements in Serbia and Bosnia had in common three general features: the personal freedom of their inhabitants, the circumstance that both categories of settlements were separated from their rural and feudal environments, and the capability of the inhabitants to settle their internal affairs by themselves. The first two points do not need further discussion, while the third demands some additional remarks concerning the various degrees of self-government. As a matter of fact, there were differences among communes and even among various periods in the life of a single commune. Some of them were independent to an extent that enabled them to pursue their own foreign policy, either permanently, like Dubrovnik after 1358, or occasionally in particular circumstances like other cities. Something like that is inconceivable as far as the urban settlements of Serbia and Bosnia are concerned.

Even the coastal communes had representatives of their overlords in some periods of their history. Dubrovnik was receiving its *comes* from Venice before 1358, Kotor and the towns in the south had a count appointed by the Serbian king. But a kind of inexorable trend led to the reduction of the rights of such representatives and finally to their elimination. It is characteristic of the juridical independence of those cities that they were allowed to appeal against the sentences issued by their own highest law courts to the courts of other cities or to Italian universities, bypassing their overlord.[16] In the settlements with Saxon autonomy the ruler's representatives (*kefalije, vojvode*) were permanently present. In Novo Brdo they took part in judicial procedures concerning objects of a more substantial value and in cases of criminal law. The mining towns had special mediators between the local autonomy and the central authority. Officially they were called *carinici* (customs officials), but actually they were tax farmers, collectors of taxes emanating from the ruler's regal rights (part of ore, part of refined metal, incomes of the mint, market taxes etc.). Tax farmers were recruited mostly from among merchants and mining entrepreneurs. They were private persons with considerable public powers during the terms of their leases because they were substitutes for the nonexisting institutions and apparatuses which had to care for the finances of the state. They had jurisdiction even in the sphere of mining law.

There is no reason to consider tax farmers as factors that aimed in principle to restrict the towns' autonomy, but some cases from the largest towns, such as Novo Brdo and Srebrenica, show that the tax farmers (individuals or companies) were inclined to force their will upon the citizens and to introduce innovations especially when contracts of the lease were being changed. Obliged to pay a larger assessment of annual taxes with every lease renewal, they tried to increase their incomes by raising taxes or changing the terms of tax collection. The citizens' quick answer was to appeal to the government of Dubrovnik for protection. The Ragusan government in principle favored the maintenance of traditional order and demanded the abolition of all innovations. Protests were directed to the ruler and, at the same time, orders were issued to the tax farmers if they happened to be Ragusans. All known conflicts of this kind ended in restoration of the previous order. Only one case of an uprising of citizens which turned into bloodshed is recorded, but the real causes of the conflict remain unknown.[17]

Important indications of the differences in the degree of self-government are the city statutes. The communes on the Adriatic coast codified their statutes in the thirteenth and early fourteenth centuries. They contained numerous and varied regulations beginning with the responsibilities of governing bodies and the judicial procedure and ending with technical specifications for housing construction. In the older literature the consensus was that the towns in the interior did not have their statutes and that the occasional mention of *zakon* (law) had to be related to common law or to decrees of the ruler. Since the discovery and publication in 1962 of the Code of Mining of Despot Stefan Lazarević (1389–1427) dated 1412, which contains in its final part twenty articles concerning the city of Novo Brdo,[18] a contrary opinion seems to prevail, namely that the mining settlements had their statutes and that the twenty articles are indeed an excerpt from the Statute of Novo Brdo.

I have some doubts whether such a revision is justified. There is no need to emphasize that the Code of Mining, as a typical *Bergordnung* cannot be considered by any means analogous to a city statute. On the one hand, it did not cover the whole of urban life despite its complex content. On the other hand, it is only a hypothesis, without support in the existing part of the text, that the twenty articles are only a part of a larger legal code. Considered as an excerpt from a more extensive legal source, the twenty articles contain, in part, regulations similar to those known from the statutes of Dalmatian communes. In any case we have to bear in mind an important difference in the general circumstances: The coastal communes had created a law for themselves in a kind of legal vacuum, while the mining towns, existing in an environment regulated by the law of the Byzantine codes and the Code of Stefan Dušan (1349, 1354), had opportunities for only highly specialized legislation.

Almost all of our sources come from the archives of the coastal cities; nevertheless, there is no evidence that citizens of Dubrovnik or Kotor, living and working for years in one of the mining towns, would have severed their ties with the native city where their families were left with the bulk of their property. On the contrary, native inhabitants of mining towns who accepted foreign citizenship, make up, as we have seen, an entire category of those who "considered themselves Ragusans." There is no reason to be captivated by the hypothesis that Dalmatian citizens could have contributed to the formation of a kind of mining commune: As individuals they could not have been inclined to double their burdens and duties; even less willing were their native communes to share the loyalty of their citizens.

The businessmen from the coast who performed the functions of town counts or, as tax farmers, had control of public finances, did not contribute to the improvement of the administrative technique making use of the experiences of their cities. The counts and the councils of *purgari* had a modest apparatus: a town crier with the appellation *putal* (from the German, *Bütell*, bailiff), a kind of clerk (*pristav*), and some servants. The chancellor is not mentioned, but the town seal, *bulla del luogo*, is recorded.[19] The town authorities disposed with some financial means and were able to pay servants and to hire couriers when needed, but there was no town hall, or *Rathaus*, or *palacium regiminis*, or anything analogous. The count of Srebrenica, the second largest mining center in our area, carried out his duties and dispensed justice in his home. We know by accident that the ruler had granted a piece of land *pro honore comitatus* but no public or communal building was constructed.[20] The house of the count, who was a citizen of Dubrovnik, was later included in the total estate that was divided among his heirs. At the same time, the ruler's income from Srebrenica had been leased for an annual sum of between 24,000 and 30,000 gold ducats.

In a certain sense this fact reveals the frailty and incompleteness of the autonomy of mining towns more than many legal records. The considerable wealth created on the spot was divided among the ruler, the mining entrepreneur, and the merchants, avoiding completely the rest of the community, powerless in its public functions. It also becomes clear why archaeological excavations reveal only two kinds of public buildings: fortifications and churches. The walls and towers result from rulers' investments, the churches from pious endowments of citizens. But we cannot say that the churches embody the solidarity of the urban community, because there were two varieties of churches for both religious groups among the inhabitants, Catholic and Orthodox. The Catholic churches deserve special attention owing to the fact that they symbolized Saxon autonomy. Around them were gathered the descendants of the Saxons, who did not change their religion, and Dalmatian merchants who, without exception, were regarded as "Latins" by their Orthodox Slav environment. The wills of Ragusans explain how it was possible, in that remote "schismatic" part of the Balkans, to support not just individual priests, but groups of priests, chaplains and canons.[21] Some humanistic intellectuals originated in the Catholic clerical milieu of the mining towns, among them Djuradj Dragišić-Benignus in Srebrenica and Martin Segonus in Novo Brdo.[22]

The prosperity of the mining towns also influenced Orthodox church life. Novo Brdo, *Novomonte,* whose German name Neue Berge was not forgotten, became, in the fifteenth century, the see of an Orthodox bishop. He was the successor of the bishop of Roman Ulpiana, whose see was earlier in Lipljan (eleventh to thirteenth centuries) and successively in the royal monastery of Gračanica (fourteenth century). In the fifteenth century Novo Brdo was the cradle of three authors (Dimitrije Kantakuzin, Vladislav Gramatik and Konstantin Janjičar).[23] I mention them only in order to call attention to the fact that by the end of the medieval period, the urban centers in Serbia took over the role of cultural focuses played previously by monasteries. The mining settlements, which must have been extremely crude and uncivilized in their early beginnings, came closer to their Adriatic counterparts whose cultural takeoff dates also from the fifteenth century.

Speaking about features that make the essential difference between coastal and mining towns, we cannot bypass the role of the patriciate. Even before it formally closed its ranks and monopolized decision making and public functions, the patriciate was the social force that carried out and achieved the urban autonomy in coastal cities. Hence it seems justified to ask whether the mining towns had a similar social stratum with a similar function. All that has been said in passing makes it appear doubtful. People attracted by mining were heterogeneous, including extremes on both sides: manual laborers, paid by shifts or living on credit until the discovery of the ore, on the one hand, and top entrepreneurs, who were able to combine the business of mining with trade and tax farming, on the other, with many in between.

The technology of the time warns us that we have to reckon with a high percentage of laborers and their suppliers in the total population of a mining town. There were, of course, people who could be compared to a kind of middle class: mining technicians, various supervisors, better-off craftsmen whose production was based on the use of metal, like goldsmiths, silversmiths, etc. The fact that the most successful ones were assimilated by the Ragusans through the granting of citizenship did not favor their possible melting into a local social elite. There is one document which could clarify the situation, but there are also problems concerning that unique piece of evidence. It is a letter dated 1481 in Dubrovnik, addressed to the Duke of Ferrara. Its author, a Ragusan nobleman, informs the duke of the high quality of some fragments of ore brought from the duke's territory, and recommends two experts in the "mining art," a *ser* Nicola Change, obviously a Saxon descendant, and *ser* Gan Lapor, without doubt an Albanian, who both are referred to as *cintilomeni de Nova Monte* (noblemen of Novo Brdo). This is a private letter, written twenty-five years after the fall of Novo Brdo to Ottoman rule, and directed to a completely uninformed person in circumstances in which it might have been advantageous for the writer to elevate the social rank of the persons he recommended.[24] In any case, against this disputable document we have only a huge *argumentum ex silentio*. The problem must, in my opinion, remain open until some conclusive evidence appears.

The urban landscape of medieval Serbia and Bosnia was marked by the presence of the mining towns, although they were not the only types of urban settlements. A new wave followed them, not so distinct, but also not insignificant. It was a relatively massive wave of small settlements, which shot up like mushrooms on the fertile soil of the increased population and the need for diversified labor. In Germany a specific term, *Minderstädte* ("towns stunted in their development"), was created to characterize this kind of urban formation. In the Balkans they emerged in the late fourteenth and early fifteenth centuries and gave birth to almost all the urban settlements that became important during Ottoman rule. Because of ignorance as to their medieval roots, those settlements have been attributed wrongly to an alleged oriental incentive brought in by the Ottomans. According to recent literature, local trade was the economic basis for the rise or transformation of settlements belonging to this group. They appear at the foothills of castles, intersections of roads, stopping places for caravans, and places of occasional fairs.

In Bosnia the "suburbs," in the original meaning of the word, were especially frequent. Their origins are reflected in the names adopted from the castles or fortresses in whose shadow they had arisen: Podvisoki-Subvisochi-Sottovisochi, underneath the royal castle Visoki; Podsoko-Sotosochol, below the fortress Soko; Podborač-Subtusborach-Sotoborach, under Borač, the principal castle of the family Pavlović; then Podprozor, Subvisegrad, Sotodobrun, Podblagaj, Podkonjic, etc. One curious case reveals how usual and natural seemed the genesis of an urban settlement of this type. In eastern Bosnia, close to the river Drina, in the late fourteenth century a Franciscan monastery was built and provided with a bell tower, *zvonik* in Slav. A road to Serbia passed nearby. These facts gave birth to a settlement whose name was then created according to the known model: Podzvonik-Sotosuonich, but sometimes also *civitas Campane*.[25]

These types of settlements did not have miners; foreign merchants visited them only occasionally. Did they enjoy some kind of autonomy and, if so, what kind? Evidence concerning the organization and internal life of these settlements seems to suggest that their autonomy and administration were modeled on the mining towns. For two urban settlements without mining industry, the *purgari*, are recorded. One was the just-mentioned Podzvonik, the second, the little marketplace Goražde. Are we justified in generalizing on the base of only two cases? Anyway, the special attention is due to the fact that the councils of sworn citizens did not remain limited to the mining towns. Town counts are attested to in a larger number of suburbs and marketplaces.[26]

Serbia has known this type of settlement which was not connected with castles and fortresses but with markets and fairs. The early Ottoman tax registers (*defters*) show that this category of *trgovi* ("marketplaces") differed from the neighbouring villages more by their size than by the occupations of their inhabitants. On the average, the *trgovi* consisted of 100 families, whereas the average for each village was 20. However, the sultans' incomes from such marketplaces were usually ten or more times larger than from an average village.[27]

In Serbia the most puzzling are those towns mentioned in the beginning of this paper, which make up the Byzantine heritage. As a matter of fact, we must limit our interest only to those among them that were "inherited" or conquered in the twelfth and thirteenth centuries, of which we already spoke; those acquired later had been, and remained, purely Byzantine towns.[28] The Law Code of Tsar Dušan expressly confirmed the rights of the newly acquired Greek towns.

The towns inherited or conquered from the Byzantine Empire differed, both in their urban organization and in their social structure, from all types of urban settlements discussed here.

They were all fortified with walls and towers; some also had a citadel (*akropolis, kula*)²⁹ where the garrison of the city guard were lodged. In this, the strongest part of the fortress, the residence of the governor (*kefalija, vojvoda*) and of the military commander (*kefalija kulski, vojvoda kulski*) were also located. Our scant sources occasionally mention arsenals, storehouses, and jails in that section of the town. In the citadel were concentrated some of the functions that we find in communal buildings in coastal cities.

The name *amborij*, from Greek *emporion*, used for the civilian part of the settlement, belongs to the Byzantine heritage. In one of the charters concerning the town of Štip in Macedonia, the term *amborij* and the Slavic term *podgradije* are used alternatively. Towns belonging to this category do not show economic specialization which could be compared to mining or trade centers. Various craftsmen appear among the town dwellers. Only in Prizren, silk manufacture, an ancient Byzantine urban trade which survived in the later period, was developed.³⁰

A characteristic feature of the old towns of Byzantine origin is the presence of an influential aristocracy.³¹ The exploitation of large-scale landed properties and livestock raising provided them with economic means for their political aspirations. It was from among the members of such landed aristocracy that the ruler recruited the personnel for provincial and local administration. Naturally, such a social elite was Greek in origin or became Greek through assimilation under the prevailing circumstances in the Balkans. Previous development had as a consequence a high degree of concentration of Greek elements in towns, surrounded by a Slavic rural environment. Skopje and Prilep were Greek towns at the time of the Serbian conquest.³² In a single charter granted to a monastery located near Prilep, we find among the former owners a *protonobilissimus*, a *stratopedarches*, a *sebastos*, a son of a *sebastokrator* (*sevastokratorović*) and a *kastrophylaks*.³³ The Greek element preserved its influential position even under the Serbian rulers. In Skopje, after twenty years of Serbian rule, a philo-Byzantine party was strong enough to attempt to surrender the city to John VI Kantakouzenos during his offensive against Stefan Dušan in 1350. However, in towns whose growth came later—as in the case of Štip[34]—the inhabitants were almost entirely of Slavic origin judging by their names.

In this category of towns, as elsewhere in the Byzantine Empire, we find families that had been donated to churches or monasteries. In Greek documents these families are called *paroikoi*, as were dependent peasants throughout the Byzantine world.[35] In a Serbian charter concerning Štip, the donated families were called *otroci*, a term used generally for slaves.[36] Such evidence permits one to reach the conclusion that some of the inhabitants of this category of towns did not enjoy personal freedom and that the well-known European principle of *Stadtluft macht frei* did not apply here. There was no sharp line dividing free citizens in towns from servant peasants in rural surroundings. We have to take into account, however, some distinctive features of the landed estate (*seigneurie*), especially the monastic estate in the Byzantine world. Here it was possible and usual that people were granted to monasteries and obliged to serve in accordance with their condition.[37]

Consequently, the fact that some town dwellers belonged to a monastery or church does not mean per se that they were of servile condition and that they did not enjoy personal freedom. We always have to consider their duties and obligations. In the few extant documents, we find among the people donated to monasteries, town inhabitants who owned hereditary properties, such as houses, fields, vineyards, water mills etc. In such cases the gain for the church consisted in the transfer to the ecclesiastical institution of taxes, duties, and services that those people previously paid to the ruler or to his functionaries. By the same act, such town dwellers were exempted from the jurisdiction of the civil authorities and submitted to the jurisdiction of the church or monastery which thenceforth received judiciary taxes, fines, etc.

All extant charters concerning the possessions of churches or monasteries in towns mention also villages with servant peasants so that lists of granted immunities refer to both categories. Only in the charter issued by King Milutin in 1299/1300 to the monastery of Saint George near Skopje are immunities for its possessions in Skopje enumerated separately. To our regret, however, this charter repeats only immunity formulas from an earlier Bulgarian charter (about 1258).[38] Such formulas give us some evidence on the functionaries who were expected to affect the monastic possessions. The earlier charters contain long lists of various fiscal functionaries, while the later ones—issued during Serbian rule—mention only the *kefalija* and *knez*. The former functionaries belonged to the Byzantine administrative system in the epoch of the Palaeologoi, which was taken over by the Serbs in conquered territories and later expanded throughout the whole Serbian state.[39]

The area governed by a *kefalija* varied in size, but his seat was always in his most important town. The *kefalija* was appointed by the ruler in whose name he governed. In the area administered by the *kefalija*, the town in which he resided had a small district called "the *metochion* of the town." It comprised villages in the immediate vicinity of the town (*metoh gradski*). It is impossible to tell, however, how the regime in this district differed from the remaining territory of the *kefalija*.

There is no trace in the surviving evidence of any kind of local autonomous body. Only the Orthodox Church enjoyed autonomy, first, "in all spiritual matters"—a definition that covered an area broader than canon law in the western church—and second, in general jurisdiction over people subordinate to individual churches or monasteries.[40] Because of that, the church played a very important role in the administration of justice in these types of towns, especially when the town was the seat of a bishop or of a metropolitan.[41]

The appearance of the *knez* among the local authorities is the only link that connects this category of towns with the urban settlements discussed earlier in this paper. We do not know the sphere of activity and the legal competences of the *knez* and are, therefore, unable to find out whether he was a local autonomous official or not. In any case, the *knez* was not inherited from the Byzantine administrative system but was introduced into the towns by their new masters. In the Serbian administrative system, as far as it is known, the *knez* was an official in mining or merchant settlements and also the head of a village.[42] The *knez* was not brought in from outside, but recruited (imposed from above, or selected) from the resident population, even from temporary inhabitants, like the Dalmatians. Based on these facts, we may be allowed to guess that the *knez* in Skopje, Štip, and Strumica was a local resident whose authority, unknown to us, was in reality limited to the town and its district.

It might seem curious to the modern mind to find such a variety of types and difference of degrees of urban autonomy within one state, like the Serbian kingdom of the Nemanjićes. However, under the circumstances of medieval political organization, it seems quite normal: Because of its inefficiency and incompetence, the state was doomed to play a passive role and was forced to accept the results of a spontaneous development.

NOTES

1. Recent literature on Roman urban settlements is noted in Yugoslav historical bibliographies: *Ten Years of Yugoslav Historiography 1945–1955* (Belgrade: National Committee for Historical Studies, 1955); *Historiographie yougoslave 1955–1965* (Belgrade: Fédération des Sociétés Historiques de Yougoslavie, 1965); *The Historiography of Yugoslavia 1965–1975* (Belgrade: The Association of Yugoslav Historical Societies, 1975). Surveys of more extensive areas: Esad Pašalić, *Antička naselja i komunikacije u Bosni i Hercegovini* (Sarajevo: Zemaljski Muzej, 1960); Fanula Papazoglu, *Makedonski gradovi u rimsko doba* (Skopje: Filozofskiot Fakultet, 1957); Miroslava Mirković, *Rimski gradovi na Dunavu u Gornjoj Meziji* (Belgrade: Arheološko Društvo Jugoslavije, 1968).

2. Heinrich Gelzer, "Ungedruckte und wenig bekannte Bistümerverzeichnisse der orientalischen Kirche," *Byzantinische Zeitschrift* 2(1893) 22–72.

3. On Byzantium's struggles see Georg Ostrogorsky, *History of the Byzantine State* (Oxford, Blackwell 1968); *Vizantijski izvori za istoriju naroda Jugoslavije*, Vols. III and IV (Belgrade, Vizantološki Institut, Srpska akademija nauka i umetnosti, 1966, 1971).

4. Constantin Jireček, *Geschichte der Serben*, Vol. I (Gotha, 1911), pp. 298–300.

5. A short survey based on extensive literature: Sima Ćirković, "The Production of Gold, Silver, and Copper in the Central Parts of the Balkans from the 13th to the 16th Century," in *Precious Metals in the Age of Expansion* (Stuttgart: Klett-Cotta, 1981), pp. 41–69.

6. On Saxons see Mihailo Dinić, *Za istoriju rudarstva u srednjovekovnoj Srbiji i Bosni* I (Belgrade: Srpska akademija nauka i umetnosti, 1955), pp. 1–27.

7. Ljubomir Stojanović, *Stare srpske povelje i pisma*, I (Belgrade: 1929), pp. 36–37

8. *Zakon o rudnicima despota Stefana Lazarevića*, edited by Nikola Radojčić (Belgrade: Srpska akademija nauka i umetnosti, 1962); N. Beldiceanu, *Les actes des premiers sultans conservés dans les manuscrits turcs de la Bibliothèque Nationale à Paris* II (La Haye: Mouton, 1964), pp. 245–254; Fehim Spaho, "Turski rudarski zakoni," *Glasnik Zemaljskog muzeja u Sarajevu* 25(1913) 133–194.

9. M. Dinić, *Za istoriju rudarstva*, I: 14–19, proved that *purgari* does not mean "citizens" but members of the council.

10. Gregor Čremošnik, *Kancelariski i notariski spisi 1278–1301* (Belgrade: Srpska kraljevska akademija, 1932), pp. 36–37. Aleksandar Solovjev, "Prebegar u Brskovu," *Jugoslovenski istoriski časopis* 3(1937), pp. 270–275.

11. Bariša Krekić, *Dubrovnik in the 14th and 15th Centuries: A City between East and West* (Norman: University of Oklahoma Press, 1972).

12. Treaties between Dubrovnik and rulers of Serbia and Bosnia as well as charters with privileges granted to Dubrovnik are preserved from the end of the twelfth to the middle of the fifteenth century.

13. Jovanka Mijušković, "Dodeljivanje dubrovačkog gradjanstva u srednjem veku," *Glas SANU* 246(1961) 89–130.

14. Desanka Kovačević-Kojić, *Naselja srednjovekovne bosanske države* (Sarajevo: Veselin Masleša, 1978), pp. 133–142 (chapter on terminology).

15. Sima Ćirković, "Seoska opština kod Srba u srednjem veku," *Simpozijum Seoski dani Sretena Vukosavljevića* 5(1978)pp. 81–88.

16. The citizens of Kotor had the right to appeal against the sentences of their own law court to the colleges of Perugia, Padua, and Bologna, and those of Bar to Dubrovnik and Venice.

17. Material from the archives in Dubrovnik concerning quarrels with tax farmers is presented especially in the works on individual mining centers. Cf. Dinić, *Za istoriju rudarstva*, Vols. I–II (on Srebrenica, Rudnik and Novo Brdo).

18. *Zakon o rudnicima despota Stefana Lazarevića*, edited by N. Radojčić, pp. 51–57.

19. Dinić, *Za istoriju rudarstva* I: 106.

20. Historijski arhiv Dubrovnik, *Sentenze di Cancellaria* 9, fol. 161v.

21. Dinić, *Za istoriju rudarstva* I: 95–96, II: 92–95.

22. K. Krstić, "Dragišić, Juraj," *Enciklopedija Jugoslavije* 3 (Zagreb: Jugoslavenski leksikografski zavod, 1958) 68–69; Agostino Pertusi, *Martino Segono di Novo Brdo vescovo di Dulcigno. Un umanista serbodalmata del tardo Quattrocento* (Roma: Istituto storico italiano per il medio evo, 1981).

23. Dimitrije Bogdanović, *Istorija stare srpske književnosti* (Belgrade: Srpska književna zadruga, 1980), pp. 225–229, 237–240.

24. Jorjo Tadić, "Nove vesti o padu Hercegovine pod tursku vlast," *Zbornik Filozofskog fakulteta u Beogradu* VI/2 (1962) 144–145. With the term "gintilomini" Ragusans used to denote the towns' aldermen, e.g., in a document from 1430: "chon guarentizia de voivoda Bogdam (*sic*) e chon chonte Dobruscho e de Vochosau purgar e de Radiuoi purgar e de Divoie purgar e de Nichut purgar e chon altri gintilomini segondo la usanza de Srebruniza." See Dinić, *Za istoriju rudarstva* I, p. 106.

25. D. Kovačević-Kojić, "Zvornik(Zvonik) u srednjem vijeku," *Godišnjak Društva istoričara BiH* 16(1965) 19–35.

26. Idem., "O knezovima u gradskim naseljima srednjovjekovne Bosne," *Radovi Filozofskog fakulteta Sarajevo* 6 (1971) 333–345.

27. The most useful for this purpose is the register dated 1455, compiled immediately after the Ottoman conquest: *Oblast Brankovića, Opširni katastarski popis iz 1455. godine*, edited by Hamid Hadžibegić, Adem Handžić, Ešref Kovačević (Sarajevo: Orijentalni institut, 1972).

28. On the late Byzantine town see, Ljubomir Maksimović, "Charakter der sozialwirtschaftlichen Struktur der spätbyzantinischen Stadt (13.–15.Jh.)." *Jahrbuch der österreichischen Byzantinistik* 31(1981) 149–188.

29. Jovanka Kalić, "Byzanz und die mittelalterlichen Städte in Serbien," *Jahrbuch der österreichischen Byzantinistik* 32/4 (1982) 595–604.

30. S. Ćirković, "Štip u XIV veku," *Zbornik u čast akademika Mihajla Apostolskog* (Skopje: Makedonska akademija nauka i umetnosti, 1986), 25–36.

31. Lj. Maksimović, "Koreni i putevi nastanka gradskog patricijata u Vizantiji," *Gradska kultura na Balkanu (XV–XIX vek). Zbornik radova* (Beograd: Balkanološki institut, 1984) 19–57.

32. C. Jireček, *Geschichte der Serben* II (Gotha: 1918) 27–28.

33. The charter for monastery Treskavac: Djura Daničić, "Tri srpske hrisovulje," *Glasnik Društva srpske slovesnosti* II (1859) 129–136.

34. Some 150 names of inhabitants of Štip are known. Only a small minority are unequivocal Greeks, but we must make allowances for the names of Christian saints which are common in both languages.

35. Božidar Ferjančić, "Posedi vizantijskih provincijskih manastira u gradovima," *Zbornik radova Vizantološkog instituta* 19(1980) 209–250.

36. As I hope to have demonstrated in the paper quoted in note 30, slaves cannot be meant here, because some of those *otroci* had their own horses and were exempted from the obligation of carriage. The same exemption occurrs in other charters as a privilege of warriors and lesser noblemen. Cf. Rade Mihaljčić, "Vojnički zakon," *Zbornik radova Filozofskog fakulteta u Beogradu* 12/1(1974) 305–309.

37. Miloš Blagojević, "Zakon svetoga Simeona i svetoga Save," *Sava Nemanjić. Istorija i predanje* (Beograd: Srpska akademija nauka i umetnosti, 1979) 157–164.

38. *Spomenici za srednovekovnata i ponovata istorija na Makedonija* (Skopje: Arhiv na Makedonija, 1975) 185–187, 200–204, 211–214.

39. M. Dinić, "Vlasti za vreme Despotovine," *Zbornik Filozofskog fakulteta u Beogradu* 10/1 (1968) 237–243; Lj. Maksimović, *Vizantijska provincijska uprava u doba Paleologa* (Beograd: Vizantološki institut, 1972) 70–100.

40. *Zakonik cara Stefana Dušana 1349 i 1354,* edited by N. Radojčić(Beograd: Srpska akademija nauka i umetnosti, 1960), articles 4, 12, 33, pp. 44, 45, 49.

41. A. Solovjev, "Sudije i sud po gradovima Dušanove države," *Glasnik Skopskog naučnog društva* 7–8(1930) 147–162.

42. *Knez* as head of town or marketplace in Article 141 of the Code of Law of Stefan Dušan. *Zakonik cara Stefana Dušana 1349 i 1354,* edited by N. Radojčić, p. 70.

BIBLIOGRAPHY

Andjelić, Pavo. "Trgovište, varoš i grad u srednjovjekovnoj Bosni. Prilog tipologiji naselja" [Market, Town and Fortress in Medieval Bosnia: Contribution to the Typology of Settlements]. *Glasnik Zemaljskog muzeja* 18(1963) 179–194.

———. *Bobovac i Kraljeva Sutjeska. Stolna mjesta bosanskih vladara u XIV i XV stoljeću* [Bobovac and Kraljeva Sutjeska. Residences of Bosnian Rulers in the XIVth and XVth Centuries]. Sarajevo 1973.

180   *Sima Ćirković*

Božić, Ivan. "Srpsko gradjanstvo u srednjem veku" [Medieval Serbian Citizenry]. *Nastava istorije u srednjoj školi* I,2(1951) 106–117.

_____. "Grad i selo na Zetskom primorju u XV veku" [Town and Village in the Coastal Region of Zeta in the XVth Century]. *Istorijski glasnik* 2 (1973) 63–70.

_____. *Nemirno Pomorje XV veka* [The Troublesome Pomorje in the XVth Century]. Beograd: Srpska Književna Zadruga, 1979.

Ćirković, Sima, *Istorija srednjovekovne bosanske države* [History of the Medieval Bosnian State]. Beograd: Srpska Književna Zadruga, 1964.

_____. "Civitas Sancti Demetrii." In *Civitas Sancti Demetrii, Sremska Mitrovica*. Sr. Mitrovica: 1969, pp. 59–71.

_____. "Smederevo-prestonica Srpske Despotovine" [Smederevo— The Capital of the Serbian Despotate]. In *Oslobodenje gradova u Srbiji od Turaka 1862–1867, Zbornik radova prikazanih na naučnom skupu SANU, održanom 22–24. maja 1967*. Beograd: 1970, pp. 61–69.

_____. "Šabac u srednjem veku" [Šabac in the Middle Ages]. In *Šabac u prošlosti* I. Šabac: 1970, pp. 83–114.

_____. "Prijepolje u srednjem veku" [Prijepolje in the Middle Ages]. In *Simpozijum Seoski dani Sretena Vukosavljevića* III. Prijepolje: 1976, pp. 211–223.

_____. "Production of Gold, Silver and Copper in the Central Parts of the Balkans" In *Precious Metals in the Age of Expansion*, Vol. 2. Stuttgart: Beiträge zur Wirtschaftsgeschichte, 1979, pp. 41–69.

_____."Sviluppo e arretratezza nella penisola balcanica fra il XIII e il XVI secolo." In *Sviluppo e sottosviluppo in Europa e fuori Europa dal secolo XIII alla rivoluzione industriale*. Firenze: Atti della Decima Settimana di Studio. Istituto Internazionale di Storia Economica "Francesco Datini." 1983, pp. 291–311.

Čremošnik, Gregor. Dubrovački konzulati u Srbiji do Dušanovog vremena [Ragusan Judicial Boards in Serbia until Dušan (1331–1355)], *Glasnik Zemaljskog muzeja* 41(1929) 81–94.

Dinić, Mihailo, "Trg Drijeva i okolina u Srednjem veku" [The Borough Drijeva and Its Surroundings in the Middle Ages]. *Godišnjica Nikole Čupića* 47(1938) 109–147.

_____. "Zemlje hercega Svetoga Save" [The Lands of the Duke of St. Sava], *Glas SANU* 182(1940) 151–257.

_____. *Za istoriju rudarstva u srednjovekovnoj Srbiji i Bosni* [Contributions to the History of Mining in Medieval Serbia and Bosnia]. I–II. Beograd: Srpska Akademija Nauka, 1955–1962.

_____. "Nastanak dva naša srednjovekovna grada. I Peć do turskih vremena, II Ribnica-Podgorica" [The Origins of Two Medieval

Towns: Peć and Podgorica]. *Prilozi za književnost, jezik, istoriju i folklor* 31(1965) 195–203.

_____. "Trepča u srednjem veku" [Trepča in the Middle Ages]. *Prilozi za književnost, jezik, istoriju i folklor* 33(1967) 3–10.

_____. *Srpske zemlje u srednjem veku* [Serbian Lands in the Middle Ages]. Beograd 1978.

Ferjančić, Božidar. "Kruševac i okolina do 1371. godine" [Kruševac and Surroundings up to 1371]. *Kruševac kroz vekove. Zbornik referata sa simpozijuma održanog od 4. do 9. oktobra 1971.* Kruševac: 1972, pp. 3–8.

Handžić, Adem. "Rudarstvo i rudarski trgovi u drugoj polovini XV vijeka" [Mining and Mining Boroughs in the Second Half of the XVth Century]. *Radovi sa simpozija "Istorija rudarstva i metalurgije od praistorije do XX veka."* Zenica: Izdanja Muzeja grada Zenice, Vol. VIII, 1978.

Hrabak, Bogumil. "Dubrovačka naseobina u kopaoničkom rudniku u Belom Brdu" [The Ragusan Settlement in the Mine Belo Brdo in the Mountain Region of Kopaonik]. *Ogledi* 1(1952) 52–58.

_____. "Prošlost Pljevalja po dubrovačkim dokumentima do početka XVII stoleća" [History of the Town Pljevlja to the Beginning of the XVIIth Century According To Ragusan Documents]. *Istorijski zapisi* 1–2(1955) 1–38.

_____. "Rujna—trg u oblasti Užica u XV veku" [Rujna—a Borough in the Region of Užice in the XVth Century]. *Istoriski pregled* 1(1954) 48–50.

_____. "Srednjovekovni rudnik i trg Rudišta pod Avalom" [Medieval Mine and Borough Rudišta near Mountain Avala], *Godišnjak Muzeja grada Beograda* 3(1956) 99–106.

_____. "Trg Valjevo u srednjem veku" [Borough Valjevo in the Middle Ages]. *Istorijski glasnik* 3–4(1953) 91–102.

_____. "Dubrovački trgovci u Valjevu u feudalno doba" [Ragusan Merchants in Valjevo in the Feudal Age]. *Glasnik Arhiva u Valjevu* 2–3(1967) 5–13.

Jireček, Konstantin. *Die Heerstrasse von Belgrad nach Constantinopel und die Balkanpässe. Eine historisch-geographische Studie.* Prag: 1877.

_____. *Die Handelsstrassen und Bergwerke von Serbien und Bosnien während des Mittelalters.Historisch-geographische Studien.* Prague: 1879.

_____. "Die Bedeutung von Ragusa in der Handelsgeschichte des Mittelalters." In *Almanach der Kaiserlichen Akademie der Wissenschaften in Wien.* 1899, 367–452.

_____. "Staat und Gesellschaft im mittelalterlichen Serbien. Studien zur Kulturgeschichte des 13.–15. Jahrhunderts." *Denkschriften der*

Kaiserlichen Akademie der Wissenschaften in Wien 56(1912), 58(1913), 64(1919).

Kalić, Jovanka. *Beograd u srednjem veku* [Belgrade in the Middle Ages]. Beograd: Srpska Književna Zadruga, 1967.

————. Byzanz und die mittelalterlichen Städte in Serbien, *Akten des XVI. Internationalen Byzantinistenkongresses II, Jahrbuch der österreichischen Byzantinistik* 32,4(1982) 595–604.

————. Niš u srednjem veku [Niš in the Middle Ages]. *Istorijski časopis.* 31(1984) 5–40.

Klaić, Nada. Prilog pitanju postanka slavonskih varoši [The Problem of the Origin of Boroughs in Slavonija]. *Zbornik radova filozofskog fakulteta u Zagrebu* 3(1955) 41–59.

————. "Die Stadt in den kroatischen Ländern im XIV. Jahrhundert." *Studia Balcanica III. La ville balkanique XVᵉ–XIXᵉ siècles.* Sofia: 1970, 111–116.

Kovačević, Desanka. Dans la Serbie et la Bosnie médiévales: Les mines d'or et d'argent." *Annales. Économies, sociétés, civilisations.* Mars-avril: 1960, 248–258.

Kovačević-Kojić, Desanka. "Dubrovačka naseobina u Smederevu u doba Despotovine" [Ragusan Settlement in Smederevo in the Age of the Serbian Despotate]. In *Oslobođenje gradova u Srbiji od Turaka 1862–1867. Zbornik radova prikazanih na naučnom skupu SANU, održanom 22–24. maja 1967.* Beograd: 1970, pp. 103–120.

————. "Dubrovčani zanatlije u srednjovjekovnoj Srebrnici" [Ragusan Craftsmen in Medieval Srebrnica]. *Godišnjak Društva istoričara Bosne i Hercegovine* 15(1966) 25–45.

————. "O knezovima u gradskim naseljima srednjovjekovne Bosne" [On the Counts in the Urban Settlements of Medieval Bosnia]. *Radovi Filozofskog fakulteta u Sarajevu* 6(1971) 333–345.

————. "Uloga rudarstva u privrednom razvoju gradskih naselja Srbije i Bosne tokom prve polovine XV vijeka" [The Role of Mining in the Economic Development of Urban Settlements in Serbia and Bosnia in the First Half of the XVth Century]. *Godišnjak Društva istoričara Bosne i Hercegovine* 18(1970) 257–263.

————. "Zvornik(Zvonik) u srednjem vijeku" [The Town Zvornik in the Middle Ages]. *Godišnjak Društva istoričara Bosne i Hercegovine* 16(1965) 19–35.

————. "O srednjovekovnom trgu na mjestu današnjeg Sarajeva" [On the Medieval Borough on the Location of Today's Sarajevo]. *Zbornik Filozofskog fakulteta u Beogradu* 10, 1(1970) 353–362.

_____. "Priština u srednjem veku" [The Town Priština in the Middle Ages]. *Istorijski časopis* 22(1975) 45–74.

_____. *Gradska naselja srednjovjekovne bosanske države* [Urban Settlements in the Medieval Bosnian State]. Sarajevo: Veselin Masleša, 1978.

Krekić, Bariša. *Dubrovnik in the 14th and 15th Centuries: A City between East And West*. Norman: University of Oklahoma Press, 1972.

_____. *Dubrovnik, Italy and the Balkans in the Late Middle Ages*. London: Variorum Reprints, 1980.

Maksimović, Ljubomir. "Charakter der sozialwirtschaftlichen Struktur der spätbyzantinischen Stadt 13.–15. Jh." *Akten des XVI. internationalen Byzantinistenkongresses I, Jahrbuch der österreichischen Byzantinistik* 31,1(1981) 149–188.

_____. "Koreni i putevi nastanka gradskog patricijata u Vizantiji" [The Roots and Ways of Genesis of the Urban Patriciate in Byzantium]. *Gradska kultura na Balkanu(XV–XIX vek)*. Beograd: 1984, pp. 19–55.

Novaković, Stojan. "Grad, trg, varoš, k istoriji reči i predmeta koji se njima kazuju" [Town, Market, Borough; Contribution to the History of Words and Objects Related to Them]. *Nastavnik* 1892; reprinted in *Iz srpske istorije*. Beograd: 1966, pp. 144–161.

Spremić, Momčilo. "Kruševac u XIV i XV veku" [Kruševac in the XIVth and XVth Centuries]. *Kruševac kroz vekove. Zbornik referata sa simpozijuma održanog od 4. do 9. oktobra 1971*. Kruševac 1972, pp. 9–24.

Šufflay Milan. "Städte und Burgen Albaniens hauptsächlich während des Mittelalters." *Denkschriften der Akademie der Wissenschaften in Wien*. Phil.-hist. Klasse 63(1924) 3–81.

Tadić, Jorjo. "Privreda Dubrovnika i srpske zemlje u prvoj polovini XV veka" [The Economy of Dubrovnik(Ragusa) and Serbian Lands in the First Half of the XVth Century]. *Zbornik Filozofskog fakulteta u Beogradu* 10,1(1968) 419–439.

Thalloczy, Lajos. *Povijest banovine, grada i varoši Jajca* [History of the Banate, Fortress and Town Jajce]. Zagreb: 1916.

Tošić, Djuro. "Brštanik u srednjem vijeku" [Brštanik in the Middle Ages]. *Godišnjak Društva istoričara Bosne i Hercegovine* 21–27(1976) 37–50.

_____. "Uredjenje srednjovjekovnog trga Drijeva" [Administration of the Medieval Marketplace of Drijeva]. *Godišnjak Društva istoričara Bosne i Hercegovine* 34(1983)123–137.

Voje, Ignac. *La structure de la classe des marchands en Bosnie et en Serbie pendant la deuxième moitié du XVe siècle*. Association internationale d'études du Sud-est européen. Sofia: 1969, pp. 627–632.

_____. "Prilog proučavanju domaćih trgovaca Srbije u XIV i XV veku, kao i trgovačkih veza sa Dubrovnikom" [Contribution to the Study of Domestic Merchants in Serbia in the XIVth and XVth Centuries and of Commercial Ties with Dubrovnik]. In *Oslobođenje gradova u Srbiji od Turaka 1862–1867, Zbornik radova prikazanih na naučnom skupu SANU, održanom 22–24. maja 1967.* Beograd: 1970, pp. 87–102.

5
Developed Autonomy: The Patricians in Dubrovnik and Dalmatian Cities

Bariša Krekić

The first important fact to keep in mind when descending from the hinterland to the coast of the Adriatic Sea is that "discontinuity of urban life is an outstanding characteristic of the entire interior area of the Balkan Peninsula," as Professor Sima Ćirković put it.[1] This is, also, the first major difference between the urban society of the hinterland and that of Dubrovnik and the Dalmatian cities. True, the coastal area had undergone interruptions of urban life in the early Middle Ages, but those disruptions were usually short-lived and generally affected the physiognomy of the cities, rather than interrupting the continuity of the tradition of autonomy. This tradition in many instances quickly recovered and resumed life under different physical circumstances (as in the case of Epidaurus-Ragusium-Dubrovnik and Salona-Split).

Another important fact about the coastal cities and some aspects of their development in the late Middle Ages is that the cities of the Adriatic coast, usually discussed as a whole by historians, "in reality never constituted a unit until the nineteenth century, nor were they territorially connected."[2] The third element that must be mentioned is the difference between the historical evolution of Dubrovnik and that of the cities of northern Dalmatia, from Zadar to Split. Because of later similarities in some aspects of their development, it is frequently forgotten that in the earlier period there existed certain geographic, political and economic realities that clearly marked the difference between them and that left a lasting imprint on the evolution of the society in each city.

The paths of development between Dubrovnik and the northern Dalmatian cities began to diverge rather clearly in the eleventh century. After the first Venetian conquest of the eastern Adriatic coast in the year 1000, and the rapid collapse of the Venetian presence there, the cities returned for a short time to Byzantine sovereignty. Then the northern cities switched allegiance again and accepted Croatian and, later, Hungarian and Venetian authority, while Dubrovnik remained under Byzantine domination with brief interruptions until the year 1205. Thus it was in the first half of the eleventh century that Dubrovnik and the northern Dalmatian cities separated politically, although this did not prevent the development of many similarities in their economic, social and cultural lives.

The distinctions between Dubrovnik and the other Dalmatian cities were caused not only by the different political conditions, but also by geographic factors. These differences affected, among other things, the development of local autonomies, as shaped by the patriciate of the various cities. The power of the patricians depended much more on the economic development of the city than on any other element. There can be no doubt, for example, that Dubrovnik's geographic location very much favored its economic growth: On the one hand, it was situated at the end of the chain of islands on the main north-south navigational route along the eastern coast of the Adriatic Sea; on the other hand, it stood at the outlet of main continental roads which brought Balkan products and people from the hinterland to the seacoast, thus connecting east and west. No other city on the eastern coast of the Adriatic had such a favorable position.

Another geographic advantage for Dubrovnik was the fact that in the eleventh and twelfth centuries it was too far removed to the northwest for its sovereign, the Byzantine Empire, to exercise any real power and control over the city; at the same time it was too far away to the south for the Hungarians and the Venetians to succeed in imposing permanent authority over it. Thus Dubrovnik was able, with a few brief intermissions, to live practically on its own throughout most of the eleventh and twelfth centuries, at a time when the other Dalmatian cities were under foreign domination, whether Hungarian, Venetian or other.[3]

All of this means that Dubrovnik and the other cities were not in similar political positions at the time of the dramatic events which shook the area with the appearance of the Crusaders of the Fourth Crusade in 1203–1204. The single most important fact to be remembered from this period is, of course, the emergence of Venice as the overwhelming, dominating power on the eastern Adriatic coast, which became part of the Venetian colonial empire. The Venetians established themselves as the masters of all important cities and islands of Dalmatia, including Dubrovnik. However, while the northern Dalmatian cities came under a more or less total and direct Venetian occupation and control, Dubrovnik managed to preserve a degree of internal autonomy and considerable flexibility in its international trade. Once again one observes the difference in the political status between the northern and southern cities of the coast.

Further differentiation among them was largely the result of developments in the Balkan hinterland, over which neither Venice nor the coastal cities had any control. Indeed, Venice had imposed limitations on the naval trade of all its subjects, including Dubrovnik, but exactly at that time Dubrovnik was fortunate and wise enough to profit immensely from the development of mining, first in Serbia in the mid-thirteenth century, then in Bosnia, in the first half of the fourteenth century.[4] No other Dalmatian city was able to do the same simply because of their geographic remoteness from the mining areas and because of the lack of roads that might have given relatively easy access there. It is interesting to note that the Venetians themselves, shrewd merchants that they were, had little or no interest in engaging in the increasingly profitable metal trade—especially silver trade—in the Balkan hinterland. There were certainly good reasons for that and I have tried elsewhere to sort them out; suffice it to say here that the neglect of the Balkan mineral market was one of the few, but nonetheless one of the major errors of judgment of the otherwise prudent and experienced Venetian political leaders.[5]

The wealth extracted from the metal trade between the hinterland and Dubrovnik, and through Dubrovnik with Italy, became the main source of Dubrovnik's prosperity and greatly contributed to the social stratification and to the development of the political structures within the city. Here we touch once again upon the patricians. The rather poor and not very powerful patricians of the other Dalmatian cities in later centuries very much envied the rich and powerful patricians of Dubrovnik. The roots of the growing difference in the strength and position of various patrician groups go back to the thirteenth and fourteenth centuries, the period of Venetian domination in Dalmatia and of the development of silver and other mining in the hinterland.

The Venetian period was also decisive for the evolution of administrative structures in the Dalmatian cities, which were strongly influenced by Venice. At the same time, the Venetians did not want to have competition in Dalmatia and imposed substantial controls and limitations on the cities. This led to a series of confrontations and even uprisings, especially in the case of Zadar, in the thirteenth and fourteenth centuries.[6] And, as has been already mentioned, since the northern Dalmatian cities did not have the added dimension of a strong and profitable trade with wider areas in the Balkan hinterland to sustain them, their resistance to Venetian pressure was weaker and the development of their patriciate and of their autonomy in general less dynamic than in Dubrovnik. This can be seen from some comparative numbers for the sixteenth century that reflect a situation that goes back a few hundred years. Thus we see that in the mid-sixteenth century in Zadar there were 17 patrician households and 70 male members of the city council; in Trogir there were 10 households; and in Split 16. In Dubrovnik, at the same time, there were 30 households and about 300 patrician councillors.[7]

Who were these patricians and how did they manage to occupy leading positions in the cities? Our information on their origins is scarce even in a city like Dubrovnik which has preserved its archives, one of the richest collections of documents in the entire Mediterranean world.[8] Some of those who became patricians were probably descendants of the early Roman population of the cities, others were wealthy merchants, and still others descendants of families whose members had distinguished themselves in the service of the city or of the church but were not necessarily rich.

Regardless of origin, the patricians were, as is to be expected, the main force driving towards autonomy in all Dalmatian cities as well as Dubrovnik. They called themselves *nobiles, maiores, seniores, meliores* and such. To ensure the monopoly of their power they imitated Venice in effecting the closure of their ranks with the *serrate* in various cities during the fourteenth century. Of course, the introduction of a monopoly of power and of an oligarchy provoked very negative reaction on the part of the rest of the population, especially of those who felt that they should have been included within the ranks of the patriciate but were left out. The form and intensity of this reaction varied from place to place. In Dubrovnik, for example, it seems to have been very small, partly, no doubt, because the relative prosperity of the city was less conducive to rebellion.

One should also bear in mind that there was a lot of similarity in the interests of the patricians and their main nonpatrician competitors—rich merchants, shipowners, captains, and craftsmen. The patricians of Dubrovnik, and many noblemen in other Dalmatian cities, were not rich landowners; they derived their subsistence principally from commerce. This is illustrated very vividly in the case of Dubrovnik by Philippus de Diversis de Quartigianis from Lucca, the high-school principal in Dubrovnik from 1434 to 1441, in his work *Situs aedificiorum, politiae et laudabilium consuetudinum inclytae civitatis Ragusii:*

> Some of the merchants are called *plebei*, others are called *nobiles;* among the first the lowest ones are the *perlabuchii,* who sell and buy the lowest goods: eggs, chicken and similar merchandise. Mediocre merchants are called *comardarii* and they sell and buy cheese, salted meat, fresh meat and such. The supreme merchants buy and sell gold, silver, lead, wax, corals, pepper, textiles made of wool, silk,

cotton . . . and similar merchandise of great value. The nobles also do all of this and I call them supreme merchants, although there are some who live only from rents, but those are few.[9]

One of the differences between the patricians of Dubrovnik and those of other Dalmatian cities was that the Ragusan patricians had become rich early and this helped them withstand Venetian pressures more effectively than the patricians in the northern Dalmatian cities could do, with the result that Venetian political control in Dubrovnik was limited, although a Venetian *comes* did reside in the city and represent the Doge. His power, however, was gradually curtailed by the increasingly dynamic local nobility. The Venetians, aware of the situation, rarely tried to enforce their will and control in Dubrovnik in a brutal or aggressive manner. That is another reason that conflicts between Dubrovnik and Venice during the Venetian overlordship of the city never took drastic forms such as one frequently finds, for example, between Venice and Zadar. Still, controversies between the Venetian count and the local patriciate, organized in three governmental councils, did take place from time to time.

For example, in 1266 one Venetian count of Dubrovnik was involved in events which led to a rather serious crisis between the two cities. Indeed, in a letter of November 1266, the Venetians described how the former count of Dubrovnik, Giovanni Quirino, upon his return to Venice, had complained that during his tenure in Dubrovnik "enormous and grave deeds against him had taken place." According to the Venetian letter, the count had been busy persecuting those Ragusans who had been banished from the city, when they, "having obtained support from others in that land . . . attacked with arms in their hands the count and those who were with him." In this attack one of the count's companions was killed, others wounded, "and the count himself was in mortal danger, for they wanted to strike him, not his companion." These dramatic events had taken place outside the city and when the count executed one of the malefactors, implementing the sentence of the Ragusan court, the Ragusans prevented him from entering the city. The count waited for five days and then was forced to go to Venice, leaving all his possessions in Dubrovnik.

Not surprisingly, the Venetian government was extremely angry and offended by such Ragusan behavior, stressing that the attitude taken towards the count was considered hostile to Venice itself. The Venetians threatened that should Dubrovnik fail to send ambassadors to Venice "to obey all our orders," they would "proceed as necessary . . . as required by such an outrage."[10] From the fact that the Venetian letter was addressed *universitati communitatis Ragusine*, it seems obvious that Quirino had not yet been replaced. Dubrovnik may have remained without a Venetian count for a short time after these events, but it seems fairly certain that things calmed down pretty soon and there is proof of normal Veneto-Ragusan relations soon after.[11]

Another instance of a conflict between the count and the local patricians of Dubrovnik occurred in the early fourteenth century, when the Venetian count refused to honor the ancient agreements between Dubrovnik and Serbia regarding murders committed by Ragusans against Serbs and vice versa. These agreements provided for the payment of a monetary fine, *vražda*, of 500 hyperpers, instead of the death penalty. When the Venetian count of Dubrovnik insisted on enforcing the death penalty and was supported by the doge in that decision, the Ragusans did not hesitate to take their case to Venice itself and to challenge—in a respectful but firm manner—the Venetian attitude. The Venetians, for their part, pointed out that when the counts of Dubrovnik assumed office, they were given a *commissio* by the doge to which they had to adhere and whose clauses could be altered only by the doge himself. Among the instructions in the commission was one stating that "he who kills another must die." After further negotiations and after the categorical refusal of the Serbian King Milutin to abolish the *vražda* and to start enforcing the death penalty, the Venetian attempt to impose their views in this important and delicate matter failed.[12]

Mention of the commission that the Ragusan count received from the doge at the time he left Venice to assume his duties in Dubrovnik is found again in 1313. During a long and tortuous debate between Dubrovnik and Venice concerning the right of the count to enjoy special *regalia* from the island of Lastovo, it was stated that "our Counts' commissions cannot be diminished or modified without your (sc., the Doge's) and your Major Council's authorization."[13] The fact that the count's commission could not be modified without assent from Venice certainly meant a considerable limitation on the Ragusan patricians' freedom to make decisions, but it was possible for them to argue and to negotiate and, as has been shown, the Venetians did not always have their way.[14]

Looking at the economic side of things, while one can say without hesitation that the patricians were, as a whole, the most powerful sector of the population, one also can recognize immediately the considerable differences in wealth that existed within that group in all Dalmatian cities and in Dubrovnik. One indication of the importance of the patricians in the economic life of a city is the amount of their participation in moneylending. In the case of Dubrovnik, for which we have rich documentation, the patricians acted as creditors in about two-thirds of the loans to individuals between 1280 and 1400. Another sign is their participation in public loans, exacted and regulated by the government. The average contribution of patricians in five such loans for which we have data in the early fourteenth century, was 46.10 percent, while the average number of patricians participating in those operations amounted to only 10.47 percent. All of this is clearly indicative of the economic importance of the patricians, but when one analyzes the sources more closely, one discovers that it was, in fact, a small group of patrician families, eleven of them, which consistently made the highest contributions to those loans and can consequently be considered the richest of the group.[15]

It is difficult to compare the relative wealth of the patricians in various Dalmatian cities simply because there are insufficient data for the fourteenth and fifteenth centuries. The situation is somewhat better for the sixteenth century, thanks to reports of various Venetian functionaries in Dalmatia. Thus in 1528, Vittore Barbarigo, formerly Venetian count in Zadar, wrote in his report:

> This city and its territory is generally very poor, in particular the nobles, who—because they refuse to diminish their nobility and

disdain to engage in any industry—live in great misery and poverty
and few of them can live decently, because their possessions—that
is to say their estates—are all derelict and uncultivated because of
the fear of the Turks. . . . The citizens still survive because they
engage in activities, some in shops, some in trade and navigation.
The rest of the population fares much better because they become
adept in various skills, above all navigation.[16]

A quarter of a century later, in 1553, Giovanni Battista Giustiniani in his most interesting *Itinerario* remarked on the same
subject: "The wealth of the nobles (of Zadar) is not great, because
the largest incomes existing among them are of 400 ducats, 500,
and until 700, (as) for example the Tetrici, Rosa, Civallelli (families); and others have incomes of 100 ducats, 200 [ducats,] and
up to 300. Many of those nobles are very poor."[17] Speaking of
Šibenik, Giustiniani noted: "There are sixty noble households,
few rich and many poor ones."[18] In Trogir he found ten noble
families, which are "very poor, except for three which can be
said to be decently provided for in respect to the situation existing in Dalmatia."[19] In Split, "the richest (noble families) do
not surpass the income of 200 ducats a year, and the majority
are poor. Similarly, the wealthiest plebians do not top 200 ducats
of annual income and the major portion is very poor."[20] In Dubrovnik, however, Giustiniani encountered a completely different
situation: "There are many individuals and families that have
100,000 ducats and more of income. They navigate all over the
world and have altogether one hundred merchant ships, so that
it is thought that there is an infinite quantity of money in Dubrovnik. . . . All the nobles over the age of twenty enter their
council and now they are three-hundred. There are no more
than thirty noble families, because many are extinct."[21] The difference between Dubrovnik and the northern Dalmatian cities
is very striking, even admitting that Giustiniani exaggerated
things somewhat.

Not very dissimilar is the comparison between Dubrovnik and
the coastal cities to the south. Domenico Gritti, the former *rector
et provisor* of Kotor, wrote in a report in 1528 that "most of the
people from that city and from the district are very poor and
they survive with difficulty, except for those who have a few

ducats for trafficking, because from wine incomes—and they have no other—there are big expenses even before they collect them."[22] A few years later, in 1533, another former *provisor Cathari*, Triphone Gradonico, wrote that people there are "very poor."[23]

The very perceptive Giustiniani, in his *Itinerario* from 1553, gives a lengthy description of Kotor and notes, among other things, that

> there is extreme poverty among the nobles, this because they lost the major and better portion of their territory . . . at the time of the wars, for reasons they themselves created, because they treated their laborers so badly, that they [sc., the nobles] led them to desperation so that they [sc., the laborers] were forced to surrender to the Turks . . . There are no more than ten [noble] houses that live from income, but they take advantage of some trade. It is true that some of them have much money because of the commerce they exercise. The plebeians are, for the most part, similarly poor; there are five or six houses that are well off and the others live from their skills, some from navigation, and many among them trade and participate in traffics. All of them, nobles as well as plebeians, have barbarous habits, more so the plebeians, who are of a malignant nature.[24]

Giustiniani gives the names of fifteen noble families, with the remark that "there were many others, up to forty, but when the land was burned, some disappeared and some went to live in Dubrovnik."[25]

In Giustiniani's *Itinerario* one finds interesting information on Budva, Bar and Ulcinj, too. Of the inhabitants of Budva he says: "They have barbarous habits and they live sordidly, the way Gypsies do, dwelling in the same room with their animals, as almost all Albanians do, which proceeds from the extreme poverty which exists in that province."[26] In Ulcinj things are more complex: "The inhabitants are divided into nobles, citizens and laborers . . . In older times nobles and citizens used to have very ample incomes, but in 1405 they lost the large and fertile territory where there were many important villages, which are now dominated by the Turks."[27] Remnants of distinguished families from nearby cities, now occupied by the Turks, like Scutari, Alessio,

Durazzo etc. took refuge in Ulcinj. They "are mostly engaged in trade and visit the Turkish ports, they live very comfortably, but one does conclude that there is extreme poverty among the nobles, citizens and inhabitants of Ulcinj."[28] In Bar, according to Giustiniani, "the wealth (of the nobles) is minimal and similarly that of the plebeians, because they live off the small incomes they have, since there is no commerce, except for some of little importance."[29]

Let us return to the fourteenth century. When the Venetian authority in Dalmatia collapsed in 1358 under the attack of the powerful King Louis of Hungary and Croatia, Dubrovnik was the only city that managed not only to preserve its local autonomy, but to become a completely independent city-state, while the other Dalmatian cities were incorporated into the Hungarian kingdom. Dubrovnik negotiated a separate treaty with King Louis which ensured for the city total self-government and freedom of action in the international field, against a symbolic payment of an annual tribute and acceptance of the protection of the Hungarian kingdom. Such an outcome was possible due to Dubrovnik's wealth, its well-organized and very profitable trade, and its already rich and politically very experienced patrician class. The political sophistication of the Ragusan patricians manifested itself increasingly from this time on, especially in the field of international diplomacy. Their conduct of foreign policy under delicate and precarious circumstances, particularly after the appearance of the Ottomans in Dubrovnik's immediate vicinity in the mid-fifteenth century, was a masterpiece of wisdom, caution, foresight and pragmatism. And it is in this particular area that the differences between Dubrovnik and the northern Dalmatian cities become more visible than anywhere else. The other cities simply had no foreign policy, with the exception of occasional and shortlived attempts. They had no chance to have one, because they were constantly under foreign administration, Hungarian and Venetian, which made it impossible for them to fashion a foreign policy of their own. Thus, they lacked an essential attribute of autonomy: freedom of activity in the international arena.

The longtime Venetian domination of the northern Dalmatian

cities makes it hard to gauge another important aspect of the patrician government in those cities: concentration of power. Constant Venetian intervention in the internal affairs of the cities and the nonexistence of independent international policy make it more difficult for us to see who the main movers in the city affairs were. Did they belong to a small group of powerful families or was there a wider spectrum of patricians participating in the leadership of the city? One can see rather dimly in Split, for example, a certain continuity in the role played by a few families (Madi, Jancii, Cindri, Papali) over a protracted period of time. But that is not enough to draw clear conclusions on the concentration of power.[30]

Things are somewhat better in Zadar. Professor Tomislav Raukar has shown that as early as the twelfth century, authority in Zadar was concentrated in the hands of a group of families that would evolve later on into the local patriciate. The Venetian domination over the city between 1205 and 1358 slowed down this trend, but between 1358 and the reimposition of Venetian authority in 1409, "we can consider the process of concentration of communal functions in the hands of the most powerful families as completed."[31] This is visible from an incomplete list of rectors of the city between 1382 and 1409. There were twelve rectors from the Grisogono family, seven Matafari, six Nassi, six Zadulini and five each from the Sopa, Begna, Fanfogna and Georgi. These were the eight most prominent families in Zadar at the time, but some other rich families were represented with only two rectors (Rosa) or even one (Civalele, Bartolazi).[32] Some families participated in the supreme position only thanks to distinguished individuals. Thus the Detrizi and Petrizo families each held the position of rector three times, but it was always one and the same person from each family that occupied the position. Finally, some families never had rectors from their ranks. Professor Raukar concluded that there was a group of about fifteen economically most powerful families in Zadar and that "the power in the commune was held by these economically strongest patrician families," but that the patricians lost a great deal of their clout during the Venetian period after 1409, because Venetian policy was hostile to the patriciate of Zadar.[33]

It is interesting to note that in Dubrovnik, the other city where one can see things even more clearly and over an even longer period of time, one finds a situation rather similar to that in Zadar. During the fourteenth and fifteenth centuries there was a substantial decline in the number of patrician families in Dubrovnik, but at the same time there was a significant increase in the number of individual patricians in the city.[34] The Ottoman conquest of vast areas in the Balkan hinterland might have induced some of the Ragusan patricians trading there to return home, and this could explain part of the substantial growth of their numbers, especially in the first half of the fifteenth century, but the full explanation must be sought in the development of the city itself.

The first half of the fifteenth century was a period of great growth and prosperity in Dubrovnik generally and was perceived as such by the local patricians themselves. Numerous contemporary documents reflect this view. Let me cite just two to illustrate my point. The first is from March 1427 and it states: "By God's grace the land has grown and is multiplying from good to better."[35] The second document is from 1432 and is even more explicit: "Our city, more by the grace of almighty God than through our efforts and merits, has grown and multiplied as much in temporal goods and possessions, as it has in people and inhabitants."[36] There are also documents which refer directly to the increase in numbers of patricians. Thus in 1426 it was decided to start the elections of next year's functionaries on December 6, rather than on December 15, as was usual, "because the functionaries to be elected annually have multiplied by God's grace."[37] Even more conspicuous evidence of this growth is a decision in 1436 to reform the administration of the Ragusan possessions, which opens with the words: "Since by the grace of almighty God noblemen have multiplied in our city."[38] In 1452 it was declared that the Major Council from now on would be considered "in sufficient numbers" when one-hundred councillors were present, instead of sixty, as was the rule earlier.[39] Finally, in 1477 it was established that the Senate would have fifty-one members, instead of forty-five, and that the *quorum* would be thirty-five, instead of thirty-one, "because by the grace of God the number of noblemen has grown and multiplied."[40] Let us now turn to the problem of concentration of power in the political life of Dubrovnik. In a letter to King Louis of Hungary and Croatia in 1361, the Ragusans proudly wrote: "The decisions in this land of yours are not made by one citizen, but by many citizens assembled in councils."[41] This was true, but those "citizens assembled in our councils" were, of course, limited to patricians only, a sort of "patrician democracy." And even within that class, a careful analysis of data proves—as I have demonstrated elsewhere—that a small group of prominent families controlled the top positions in the city. Ten leading families in the fourteenth century occupied 52.87 percent of the positions in the four most important government bodies: the Senate, the Minor Council, the judgeship and rectorship. They were:

Menčetić/Menze	Bunić/Bona
Sorkočević/Sorgo	Crijević/Crieva
Djurdjević/Georgio	Lukarević/Luccari
Gundulić/Gondola	Bobaljević/Babalio
Gučetić/Gozze	Budačić/Bodaza

In the fifteenth century the ten leading families occupied no fewer than 68.86 percent of the positions in the aforementioned goverment bodies. They were:

Gučetić/Gozze	Sorkočević/Sorgo
Gundulić/Gondola	Pucić/Pozza
Bunić/Bona	Crijević/Crieva
Djurdjević/Georgio	Menčetić/Menze
Restić/Resti	Zamanjić/Zamagna

The seven families that appear on both lists can be considered the leading group of the Ragusan patriciate in the fourteenth and fifteenth centuries.[42] They were:

> Gučetić/Gozze,
> Gundulić/Gondola
> Bunić/Bona
> Sorkočević/Sorgo
> Djurdjević/Georgio

Menčetić/Menze
Crijević/Crieva

The interesting question is: Does the Ragusan patricians' political hierarchy correspond to the economic power of those families? The information I have at this time—although incomplete—indicates that there is no one-to-one correspondence between wealth and participation in political control of the city.[43] This was certainly due, at least in part, to changing fortunes of individual families, but it was also a consequence of the very important role that a number of strong and able patricians played in the administration of Dubrovnik, as was the case with some of the Zadar patricians. Fourteen such men occupied high positions in Dubrovnik for between thirty four and fifty six years. Seven from among them were sole representatives for their families in those positions for all that time. It was principally and sometimes exclusively due to the efforts and the prestige of these individuals that their families managed to participate and even to play important roles at the uppermost level of the political structure of Dubrovnik. Some of these men were rich and one can assume that their political role was at least in part a corollary of their wealth, but others were not rich at all, as is evident from their wills.[44] In these cases there can be no doubt that personal ability was the source of their influence and success.

Another problem connected with the closing of the ranks of the patricians, with their taking over exclusive control of political life, and with the growing concentration of power in the hands of a limited group of families within that class, is the question of political dissent in the Dalmatian cities and in Dubrovnik. The process of social stratification took place in each commune with a great many similarities in their respective institutions, although they grew under different circumstances and their economic development varied greatly. The outside powers which at various times dominated the Dalmatian cities did not prevent the growth of the communal system and, indeed, all the cities of Dalmatia considered themselves communes.

Of course, the influence of the Venetian model in all of this was enormous and acted in many ways as an equalizing force.

Paradoxically, although it was under the control of Venice only a relatively short time, much shorter than the northern Dalmatian cities, Dubrovnik was the place where the Venetian model was imitated in the most consistent way. This can be explained by the fact that Dubrovnik was economically the strongest city and that it did not suffer much from foreign interference in its internal affairs. The adoption of many aspects of the Venetian governmental mechanism by the Ragusan patriciate had as a consequence a remarkable stability and continuity in the political life of that city, as was the case in Venice itself.

This does not mean, however, that the situation was idyllic and that there were no problems. As a matter of fact, in the year 1400 Dubrovnik survived an outright attempt to subvert its political order by a group of young patricians and a number of local craftsmen with outside support from the nearby Bosnian area. The plot was discovered at the last moment and its leaders were beheaded.[45] There were other cases that confirm the existence of discontent in Dubrovnik at this time. In March of 1407 a tailor approached a patrician near the cathedral and said to him: "Thank you, sir, for hitting me last night on my face and for drawing your dagger three times to strike me. Tell me the reason. . . . Beware that I could beat you up three times better than you could do it to me . . . because I do not own either a house or a vineyard." Then he added: "O noblemen, do not offend and beat the plebeians this way, because God will make you lose your reign . . . and if you persist in humiliating the plebeians this way you will not govern any more."[46] In another case, from 1409, during a fistfight between two plebeians and a patrician, one of the men said to the patrician: "Son of a jackass, tadpoles, everybody is fed up with you."[47]

These were serious offenses and grave menaces. To make things worse, in addition to conflicts between plebeians and patricians, there were frequent cases where the behavior of the patricians themselves was far less than praiseworthy. A good example was ser Basilius de Basilio who, at the beginning of the fifteenth century while count of the islands belonging to Dubrovnik north of the city, did his best to seduce young servant girls and to rape young women. At the same time he humiliated and mistreated elderly men, quarreled with the rector, and so on.[48] Clearly, such behavior could not enhance respect for the patricians nor endear them to their subjects.

Clashes among patricians took place sometimes in the meetings of the councils and even the rector was occasionally insulted. For example, in July 1418 a patrician complained that he had been insulted in the hall of the Major Council by a colleague in the presence of the rector and of the Minor Council.[49] Even worse, the rector himself complained that he had been insulted by a distinguished patrician in the chambers of the Minor Council and in the presence of nine members of that body, while he, the rector, was sitting in the Council.[50] The existence of dissent, cliques and conflicts among patricians can be seen also from many other indications. Suffice it to mention one: in Dubrovnik the rector was changed every month, after 1358, and the elections by secret ballot usually took place in the Major Council in the last two or three days of the previous month for the coming month. However, sometimes the rector could not be elected that easily and the voting went on for days and the impasse and inability of the councilors to agree on the person of the new rector became quite a problem. One of the more dramatic of such cases took place in 1395. It took three days and no less than thirty-one ballots to elect ser Andreas de Sorgo rector for November of that year. Things became so heated in the Major Council that, on October 30 an order was issued that all members must attend next day's meeting of the Council under penalty of fines and "that nobody from the Major Council may bring weapons into the said Council under penalty of jail."[51] Finally, some of the painstakingly elected rectors were chosen with only a relative majority of the votes, all of which confirms the existence of groups and factions among the patricians and of bitter tensions and conflicts inside the governmental institutions.

Dissent among the patricians and conflicts with the plebeians took place in other Dalmatian cities as well. The famous historian of Split, Thomas the Archdeacon, wrote of the situation in that city in 1226:

> In the first place, such a plague of arrogance prevailed in Split that those who felt themselves powerful, rectors and consuls, paid little

attention to the general good and for small personal profits were ready to sell the most valuable assets of the commune. In addition to that, thefts, robberies, murders and all sorts of evil went unpunished. He who valued moderate behavior above everything else was no friend, but the common people of the whole city elected their chieftains by their own free will from among the more powerful ones, and under their maleficent protection many crimes were committed. The chieftains themselves quarreled with one other and competed with one other as to who would commit worse things. He who could boast of having done more evil was considered to be greater and better.[52]

This situation persisted and Thomas writes, under the year 1238: "The whole city was in a terrible state because dissensions were so great that there was nobody—as usually happens—who did not fight on the side of one or another party. Parents started to fear for their children, for their property, and for their lives. Everyone was so prone to crime that it seemed that the general ruin was threatening the citizens."[53] Of course, Thomas's assertions must be taken with some reservations because of his own political biases in the case, but even with that there can be no doubt that his text gives an interesting and vivid description of a very bad internal situation in Split in the thirteenth century.

During the bitter fighting around the city of Zadar between the Venetians and the Hungarians in 1345–1346, a popular rebellion exploded inside the city. A chronicle from Zadar tells us that in the city

> disorders took place because of a rebellion of richer plebeians against the nobles. But also, from within the ranks of the lowest populace, very many became traitors to their own country out of greed. . . . There was a lot of noise in the city streets and the common people rebelled very violently. No noble was completely safe . . . and none dared to move around town, nor did any have the courage to scold them (i.e., the populace) publicly because of their irascible heart. Indeed, whenever the leaders of the populace spotted a distinguished man, they unloaded a lot of insults on him. One day the lowest populace, armed with all sorts of weapons, gathered in very large numbers in a big square. They screamed loudly and started attacking nobles with violent and menacing words, saying that they

would rather surrender the city to the doge than remain in such a difficult situation.[54]

As we learn from the text, some patricians also participated in the movement which was crushed a few days later and ended with the decapitation of two patricians and two plebeians, the blinding of four and life imprisonment of five other plebeians.[55]

Problems and conflicts persisted and we have more information on them from the sixteenth century. Disregarding information on such events on Dalmatian islands, including the famous rebellion on the island of Hvar in the early 1500s, we shall consider here first a few examples of the situation in the northern Dalmatian cities. The above-mentioned Vittore Barbadigo, former count of Zadar, says in his report of 1528: "There is very great discord between the nobles and the citizens, and this because of their great competition . . . and one does not want to yield to the other and they spend lots of money on this."[56] Giovanni Battista Giustiniani, in his *Itinerario* of 1553, speaking of Zadar, noted: "The nobles live together amiably. There is no other hatred among them except between the Tetrici and the Civallelli. In addition to their being against each other in their councils, it has happened recently that a son of messer Battista Tetrici had died, murdered by Francesco Civallello, who was then mortally wounded . . . by a servant of messer Niccolo Tetrici."[57]

Moving on to Šibenik, Giustiniani wrote: "There are many secret and open hatreds and bad feelings among the noble households. There is old and bitter hatred between the nobles and the plebeians because of the many murders of nobles by plebeians, which happened because of plebeian women who were harassed and molested beyond measure, principally by the young (noblemen)."[58] Of the situation in Trogir, Giustiniani tells us: "There are ten noble families . . . among whom there is little trust, and between them and the plebeians there is ancient and very great hatred, because they (sc. the plebeians) do not like to be ordered around by the nobles,"[59] while in Split "there is old and inextinguishable hatred between nobles and citizens."[60]

The situation in the cities south of Dubrovnik had similar

characteristics. In Kotor, in the spring of 1380, the plebeians overthrew the patrician government and, although the patricians obtained help from their fellow-patricians of Dubrovnik and from the ban of Dalmatia and Croatia, unrest in the city lasted for several months. Eventually the patrician authority was re-established, but the relations between patricians and plebeians remained strained for a long time to come.[61] As late as 1536 Andrea Valerio, former *rector et provisor* of Kotor, reported that "there are great hatreds between nobles and plebeians in Kotor,"[62] and Giustiniani, in 1553, wrote that "the hatred and the hostility which exists between nobles and plebeians (in Kotor) is caused by the city government, in which the plebeians would like to participate, and by unrestrained arrogance and haughtiness of the nobles, who want to dominate the people in a hundred ways."[63]

There is no mention of social conflicts in Budva.[64] In Ulcinj the main problems seem to have stemmed, not from the opposition between the nobles—who were not even fully developed—and the people, but from certain habits of the Albanian population of the city. Indeed, Giustiniani says that "these Albanians have barbarous customs, they speak the Albanian language, totally different from the Dalmatian, but they are worthy of praise because they are very loyal to their leader. There are no extreme persecutions or internal hatreds among them, although they are very quick with rage . . . but this natural disposition of theirs' quickly disappears. They do not like foreigners, in fact they have a natural passion against all of them. . . . They thus remain enemies of foreigners, but I tend to believe that this happens from an inborn barbarism which exists in their souls, for they are little disposed to love themselves, let alone others."[65]

Giustiniani's rather simplistic explanation of the situation in Ulcinj could not be applied to the city of Bar. The situation there was much more complex and difficult. Although somewhat less advanced than Kotor, Bar had had a basically similar political development. Early conflicts between the nobles and the plebeians took place in Bar in the 1440s and were provoked by attempts of the plebeians to constitute a parallel assembly, and also by problems pertaining to the division of communal land. The Venetian overlords tried to curb local rivalries and used them to keep both sides in check. In the sixteenth century the situation was still very bitter as ancient hatreds lingered between the nobles and the plebeians and problems remained unsolved.[66]

Giustiniani asserted that there used to be seventy-four noble families in Bar, only thirteen of which he mentions as existing at his time, and all of them very poor.[67] "The old and inextinguishable hatred which lives even today between the nobles and the plebeians of that city originates in the government of the city, which rests only with the nobles." Giustiniani describes how the plebeians rebelled in 1507 against the nobility, which led to the creation of two councils in 1512. However, new armed disturbances broke out in 1512 and Giustiniani tells us that "sixty-two (men) fell on both sides . . . many homes of nobles were sacked by the plebeians who—to achieve this effect—introduced through a side door (of the city) . . . five-hundred Albanians who committed this crime."[68] Finally, the Venetian *proveditore* from Kotor intervened with two hundred men and "after much dissension of the nobles and the plebeians" managed to make peace "with which the nobles were not very satisfied, but they calmed down by force, to avoid civil war which . . . had harmed them."[69]

Giustiniani offers a very intelligent and exceptionally perceptive general evaluation of the Dalmatian nobility of his day: "In the whole of Dalmatia a haughty arrogance and insolence is flourishing among the nobility, and it is located amidst ignorance and poverty, which are the two extremes of this Dalmatian nobility."[70] In view of these sharp observations, it is interesting to note that in Giustiniani's lengthy description of Dubrovnik, there is not a single word on conflicts within the patrician class or between the patricians and the plebeians.

It seems pretty clear that in most coastal cities there were social conflicts and that those conflicts lasted for centuries with varying degrees of intensity. However, they rarely menaced either the privileged position of the patricians or the overall Venetian domination. Dubrovnik in this area again was different from the other Dalmatian cities and—free from Venetian control after 1358—enjoyed mostly political stability and social peace.

In conclusion, let me state some of the conditions that in my opinion, a city should meet to be considered autonomous:

1. Fully developed institutions as reflected in city statutes, and general acceptance of these institutions by the governed and the governing as representing the state, the state itself being seen as an institution independent from individuals who occupy one or another leading position.
2. The existence of a patrician class, strong and effective enough to act as a driving force toward autonomy and as the sole ruling group inside the city.
3. Personal freedom of the inhabitants and independence in internal affairs, as outlined in city statutes and other laws.
4. Independence in external affairs, even though the city might recognize overall authority or protection of a foreign ruler or state.

If we use these four principles to measure the degree of autonomy of Dubrovnik and of the Dalmatian cities, it becomes quickly evident that Dubrovnik was the only city which, from the eleventh century on, was moving ever closer to fulfilling those requirements. By the fourteenth century Dubrovnik had fully met all of them and, after 1358, it can be considered not only a fully autonomous city, but an independent city-republic, which will, indeed, soon begin using that denomination for itself.[71]

All the other Dalmatian cities achieved some of the attributes of autonomy but never all of them. They had statutes and institutions and patricians as well, but the authority of the patricians was severely limited—with short-lived exceptions—by the presence of external dominant powers that imposed direct controls through their own functionaries, the presence of their armies, fleets etc. For the same reasons those cities could never obtain full independence in their internal affairs, into which the foreigners interfered constantly. And, of course, the Dalmatian cities could least of all have had an independent foreign policy, being themselves under foreign domination.

Thus, in the end, one has to say that although in all the Dalmatian cities and in Dubrovnik forms of autonomy were present, it was only in Dubrovnik that one finds the substance of real autonomy. The other cities had what one might call a semi-autonomous status, the degrees of which varied during the turbulent events from the eleventh to the fifteenth centuries. With the establishment of Venetian domination in Dalmatia at the beginning of the fifteenth century, the situation of the cities and of their autonomies stabilized and remained unchanged for centuries to come, while Dubrovnik embarked on the road of independence.

NOTES

1. Sima Ćirković, "Continuity and Rupture of Hierarchies: The Case of the Dalmatian Cities and Their Hinterland"; article to be published soon in Italy, the manuscript of which Professor Ćirković gracefully allowed me to use. See also Ćirković and Desanka Kovačević-Kojić, "L'économie naturelle et la production marchande aux XIIIe–XVe siècles dans les régions actuelles de la Yougoslavie." *Balcanica* Vol. XIII–XIV (Belgrade 1982–1983) 47–49.

2. Ćirković, "Hierarchies."

3. Josip Lučić, "Povijest Dubrovnika od VII stoljeća do godine 1205," in *Povijest Dubrovnika*, Vol. II (Zagreb: Historijski institut Jugoslavenske akademije znanosti i umjetnosti u Dubrovniku, 1973), 55–131. Nada Klaić, *Povijest Hrvata u razvijenom srednjem vijeku*, (Zagreb: Školska knjiga, 1976), 68–80. Vinko Foretić, *Povijest Dubrovnika do 1808*, Vol. I (Zagreb: Nakladni zavod Matice hrvatske, 1980), 26–54. See also Bariša Krekić, *Dubrovnik in the 14th and 15th Centuries: A City between East and West*, (Norman: Oklahoma University Press, 1972), 7–15. Jadran Ferluga, *L'amministrazione bizantina in Dalmazia*, (Venice: Deputazione di storia patria per le Venezie, 1978), 198–199, 202–204, 211–214, 236–238.

*I wish to express my gratitude to Miss Joan Dusa for carefully reading and editing my text.

Maren M. Freidenberg, *Dubrovnik i Osmanskaia Imperia*, (Moscow: Nauka, 1984) 17.

4. On Balkan mining, see most recently, S. Ćirković, "Dubrovčani kao poduzetnici u rudarstvu Srbije i Bosne," *Acta historico-oeconomica Iugoslaviae*, Vol. 6/1979 (Zagreb, 1979) 1–20; Idem, "The Production of Gold, Silver and Copper in the Central Parts of the Balkans from the 13th to the 16th Century," *Beiträge zur Wirtschaftsgeschichte: Precious Metals in the Age of Expansion* (Stuttgart, 1981), 41–69; Ćirković and Kovačević-Kojić, "L'économie naturelle" 50–51; D. Kovačević-Kojić, "O rudarskoj proizvodnji u srednjevjekovnoj Bosni," *Godišnjak društva istoričara Bosne i Hercegovine*. Vol. XXXIV (Sarajevo 1983), 113–122.

5. B. Krekić, "Venetian Merchants in the Balkan Hinterland in the Fourteenth Century," in B. Krekić, *Dubrovnik, Italy and the Balkans in the Late Middle Ages*, (London: Variorum Reprints, 1980), no. XIV; idem, "Mleci i unutrašnjost Balkana u četrnaestom veku," *Zbornik radova Vizantološkog instituta Srpske akademije nauka i umetnosti*, Vol. XXI (Belgrade 1982), 143–158.

6. On Zadar see Grga Novak, Presjek kroz povijest grada Zadra, in *Grad Zadar—Presjek kroz povijest* (Zadar: Institut JAZU u Zadru, 1966), 17–35.

7. Ćirković, "Hierarchies."

8. Fernand Braudel, *The Mediterranean and The Mediterranean World in the Age of Philip II*, Vol. II (New York: Harper Colophon Books, 1976), 1258: "The Ragusa Archives are far and away the most valuable for our knowledge of the Mediterranean."

9. The only publication of De Diversis' original text in Latin is the old and rare edition by Vitaliano Brunelli in *Programma dell' I. R. Ginnasio Superiore in Zara*, nos. xxiii, 1880; xxiv, 1881; and xxv, 1882, which is extremely hard to find. My quote is from the recent excellent translation of De Diversis into Serbo-Croatian by Ivan Božić in *Dubrovnik* vol. 3 (1973), 11–74.

10. *Diplomatički zbornik Kraljevine Hrvatske, Dalmacije i Slavonije*, ed. Tade Smičiklas. Vol. V (Zagreb: JAZU, 1907), 399–400.

11. See Konstantin Jireček, *Geschichte der Serben*, Vol. I (Gotha, 1911), 324–325.

12. See B. Krekić, "An International Controversy over the Death Penalty in the Balkans in the Early Fourteenth Century," *Byzantine Studies/Etudes byzantines*, vol. 5, pts. 1–2, (1978) 171–176.

13. Historical Archives in Dubrovnik (hereafter HAD), *Reformationes*, Vol. IV, 12–13.

14. For a controversy between the government of Dubrovnik on one side, and the Venetian count and government on the other, over the fate of some members of the Bardi Company in Dubrovnik in 1330 see B. Krekić, "Four Florentine Commercial Companies in Dubrovnik (Ragusa) in the First Half of the Fourteenth Century," in Krekić, *Dubrovnik, Italy and the Balkans*, no. I.

15. These calculations are based on the data I myself collected in HAD and on those found in Ignacij Voje, *Kreditna trgovina u srednjovjekovnom Dubrovniku*, (Sarajevo: Akademija nauka i umjetnosti Bosne i Hercegovine, 1976), especially Tables X and XI. A more detailed analysis of these problems will be found in Krekić, "Influence politique et pouvoir économique à Dubrovnik (Raguse) du XIIIe au XVIe siècle," forthcoming in *Atti della XIIa Settimana di Studio (1980)*, Istituto di storia economica "Francesco Datini," Prato.

16. *Commissiones et relationes venetae*, Šime Ljubić, ed., Vol. II (Zagreb: JAZU, 1877), 45.

17. Ibid., 197.
18. Ibid., 204.
19. Ibid., 208.
20. Ibid., 215.
21. Ibid., 249.
22. Ibid., 48.
23. Ibid., 86.
24. Ibid., 245–246.
25. Ibid., 246.
26. Ibid., 238–239.
27. Ibid., 226.
28. Ibid., 227.
29. Ibid., 234.

30. Grga Novak, *Povijest Splita*, Vol. I (Split: Matica hrvatska, 1957), passim. Giustiniani gives a list of sixteen noble families in Split in the mid-sixteenth century. *Commissiones*, 215.

31. Tomislav Raukar, *Zadar u XV stoljeću, ekonomski razvoj i društveni odnosi* (Zagreb: Sveučilište u Zagrebu, Institut za hrvatsku povijest, 1977), 56.

32. Ibid., 56 n. 15. See also Giustiniani's list of seventeen noble families in Zadar. *Commissiones*, 197.

33. Raukar, *Zadar* 57–58. On Zadar patricians and society see also Nada Klaić and Ivo Petricioli, *Zadar u srednjem vijeku do 1409* (Zadar, Sveučilište u Splitu, Filozofski fakultet Zadar, 1976), 222–241.

34. Krekić, "Influence politique."

35. HAD, *Liber viridis*, 158; also *Liber viridis*, Branislav Nedeljković, ed. (Belgrade: SANU, 1984), 171.

36. Ibid., 173v; Nedeljković, 204.

37. HAD, *Consilium Majus*, Vol. III, 132v. *Liber viridis*, 152v–153; Nedeljković, 160.

38. *Consilium Majus*, Vol. V, 194.

39. Ibid., Vol. IX, 247.

40. Ibid., Vol. XI, 30v.

41. *Pisma i uputstva Dubrovačke Republike*, edited by Jorjo Tadić, (Belgrade: Srpska kraljevska akademija, 1935), 40.

42. These lists and calculations are based on materials I assembled in the Historical Archives in Dubrovnik (HAD). For details see: B. Krekić, "O problemu koncentracije vlasti u Dubrovniku u XIV i XV vijeku," forthcoming in *Zbornik radova Vizantološkog instituta*.

43. More on this problem in Krekić, "Influence politique."

44. Lists of names and details of participation of these individuals in governmental bodies in Krekić, "O problemu koncentracije."

45. See B. Krekić, "Prilozi unutrašnjoj istoriji Dubrovnika početkom XV veka," *Istoriski glasnik*, nos. 1–2 (Belgrade, 1953) 63–70.

46. HAD, *Lamenta de criminali*, Vol. II, detached sheet.

47. "Puloglauzi, doiedoste suemu suietu." *Ibid*. On verbal violence in Venice at this time see Guido Ruggiero, *Violence in Early Renaissance Venice* (New Brunswick: Rutgers University Press, 1980), 125–127.

48. B. Krekić, Ser Basilius de Basilio, *Zbornik radova Vizantološkog instituta SANU*, Vol. XXIII (Belgrade 1984), 172–182.

49. HAD, *Lamenti politici*, Vol. II, 182v.

50. Ibid., 183.

51. *Reformationes*, Vol. XXX, 115v. On electoral schemes and manipulations in Venice see Robert Finlay, *Politics in Renaissance Venice* (New Brunswick: Rutgers University Press, 1980), 61–64, 94–96. On the violent behavior of the patricians see Ruggiero, *Violence in Venice*, 65–81.

52. As quoted in Novak, *Povijest Splita*, Vol. I, 105–106.

53. Nada Klaić, *Izvori za hrvatsku povijest do 1526. godine*, (Zagreb: Školska knjiga, 1972), 128.

54. Ibid., 204–205.

55. Ibid., 206–207. Raukar, *Zadar*, 29. See also Klaić-Petricioli, *Zadar u srednjem vijeku*, 242–246.

56. *Commissiones*, 45–46.

57. Ibid., 197.

58. Ibid., 204.
59. Ibid., 208.
60. Ibid., 215.
61. S. Ćirković, in *Istorija Crne Gore*, Vol. II, t. 1 (Titograd: Redakcija za Istoriju Crne Gore, 1970), 86–87.
62. *Commissiones*, 110.
63. Ibid., 245.
64. Ćirković, *Istorija Crne Gore*, 87.
65. *Commissiones*, 227.
66. S. Ćirković, "Srednji vijek," in *Bar, grad pod Rumijom*, Ćirković and others, eds. (Bar: Izbor, 1984), 19–29; Bogumil Hrabak, "Pod okriljem mletačkog lava," ibid., 45–53.
67. *Commissiones*, 234.
68. Ibid., 234–235.
69. Ibid., 235.
70. Ibid., 222.
71. In a decision of March 7, 1385, the Major Council of Dubrovnik speaks of *nostra res publica ragusina. Reformationes*, Vol. XXVI, 116v. Mihailo Dinić, *Odluke veća Dubrovačke Republike*, Vol. II (Belg. ade: SANU, 1964), 120. The opinion of Edith Ennen, *The Medieval Town* (Amsterdam-New York-Oxford: North-Holland Publishing Co., 1979), 119, that "a superficial indication of the existence of a free town community is the appearance of consuls" does not seem to apply to Dubrovnik, as it does not to Venice.

For additional recent opinions on Dalmatian cities see: Maren M. Freidenberg, "Social Connections and Antagonisms in Dalmatian Towns of the XV–XVI Centuries," *Studia Balcanica*, Vol. III: *La ville balkanique XVe–XIXe ss.*, Blgarska akademia na naukite (Sofia: Institut za balkanistika, 1970), 117–123; idem, "Gorodskaia obschina, X–XI v. v Dalmacii i ee antichnii analog." *Etudes balkaniques*, no. 2 (Sofia, 1977), 114–125; idem, "Dinamika gradske strukture u Dalmaciji u XIV–XVII stoljeću," *Radovi Centra JAZU u Zadru*, vol. 24 (Zadar, 1977), 71–95; idem, "Gorodskaia obschina v srednevekovnoi Dalmacii i drevnegrecheskii polis," *Prilozi povijesti umjetnosti u Dalmaciji*, vol. 22, *Fiskovićev zbornik*, Vol. II (Split 1980), 68–85. T. Raukar, "Venecija i ekonomski razvoj Dalmacije u XV i XVI stoljeću," *Radovi*, vol. 10 (Zagreb: Institut za hrvatsku povijest, 1977), 203–225; idem, "Društvena struktura dalmatinske komune u srednjem vijeku," *Jugoslovenski istorijski časopis*, vols. 3–4, (Belgrade, 1978), 102–110; idem, "Komunalna društva u Dalmaciji u XIV stoljeću," *Historijski zbornik*, vols. 33–34, (Zagreb 1980–1981), 139–209. J. Lučić, "Komunalno uredjenje dalmatinskih gradova u XI stoljeću," *Zbornik Zavoda za povijesne znanosti Istraživačkog centra JAZU,* vol. 10 (Zagreb 1980), 209–235.

BIBLIOGRAPHY

(This bibliography contains only the most important books pertaining to the history of Dubrovnik and the Dalmatian cities during the Middle Ages and the Renaissance, published after the Second World War. Articles and minor works have not been included because of their large number).

Aymard, Maurice. *Venise, Raguse et le commerce du blé pendant la seconde moitié du XVI*ᵉ *siècle.* Paris: S.E.V.P.E.N. 1968.

Beritić, Lukša. *Utvrdjenja grada Dubrovnika* [The Fortifications of the City of Dubrovnik]. Zagreb: Jugoslavenska akademija znanosti i umjetnosti (hereafter JAZU), 1955.

_____. *Urbanistički razvitak Dubrovnika* [The Urbanistic Development of Dubrovnik]. Zagreb: Zavod za arhitekturu i urbanizam Instituta za likovne umjetnosti JAZU.

Beritićev zbornik, Društvo prijatelja dubrovačkih starina, Dubrovnik 1960.

Biegman, Nicolas H. *The Turco-Ragusan Relationship according to the Firmans of Murad III (1575–1595) Extant in the State Archives of Dubrovnik.* The Hague-Paris: Mouton, 1967.

Bošković, Djuradj. *Stari Bar* [Old Bar]. Beograd: Savezni institut za zaštitu spomenika kulture, 1962.

Božić, Ivan. *Dubrovnik i Turska u XIV i XV veku* [Dubrovnik and Turkey in the Fourteenth and Fifteenth Centuries]. Beograd: Srpska akademija nauka i umetnosti (hereafter SANU), 1952.

Carter, Francis W. *Dubrovnik (Ragusa), A Classic City-State.* London and New York: Seminar Press, 1972.

Čremošnik, Gregor, ed. *Spisi dubrovačke kancelarije* [Documents from Dubrovnik's Chancellery]. Vol. I. Zagreb: JAZU, 1951.

Deanović, Mirko. *Anciens contacts entre la France et Raguse.* Zagreb: Institut français de Zagreb, 1950.

Demović, Miho. *Glazba i glazbenici u Dubrovačkoj Republici od početka XI do polovine XVII stoljeća* [Music and Musicians in the Republic of Dubrovnik from the Beginning of the Eleventh to the Middle of the Seventeenth Century]. Zagreb: JAZU, 1981.

Dinić, Mihailo, ed. *Odluke veća Dubrovačke Republike* [The Decisions of the Councils of the Republic of Dubrovnik]. 2 Vols. Beograd: SANU, 1951, 1964.

————, ed. *Iz Dubrovačkog arhiva* [From Dubrovnik's Archives]. 3 vols. Beograd: SANU, 1957, 1963, 1967.

Dinić-Knežević, Dušanka. *Položaj žena u Dubrovniku u XIII i XIV veku* [The Position of Women in Dubrovnik in the Thirteenth and Fourteenth Centuries]. Beograd: SANU, 1974.

————. *Tkanine u privredi srednjovekovnog Dubrovnika* [Textiles in the Economy of Medieval Dubrovnik]. Beograd: SANU, 1982.

————. *Dubrovnik i Ugarska u srednjem veku* [Dubrovnik and Hungary in the Middle Ages]. Novi Sad: Filozofski fakultet u Novom Sadu, Institut za istoriju, Vojvodjanska akademija nauka i umetnosti, 1986.

Djurić, Vojislav. *Dubrovačka slikarska škola* [Dubrovnik's School of Painting]. Beograd: SANU, 1963.

Fisković, Cvito. *Prvi poznati dubrovački graditelji* [The Earliest Known Builders of Dubrovnik]. Dubrovnik: JAZU, 1955.

Foretić, Vinko. *Povijest Dubrovnika do 1808* [The History of Dubrovnik until 1808]. 2 vols. Zagreb: Nakladni zavod Matice hrvatske, 1980.

Freidenberg, Maren M. *Dubrovnik i Osmanskaja Imperija* [Dubrovnik and the Ottoman Empire]. Moscow: Izdatelstvo Nauka, 1984.

Han, Verena, ed. *Arhivska gradja o staklu i staklarstvu u Dubrovniku (XIV–XVI vek)* [Archival Sources on Glass and Glassmaking in Dubrovnik from the Fourteenth to the Sixteenth Centuries]. Beograd: SANU, 1979.

————. *Tri veka dubrovačkog staklarstva (XIV–XVI vek)* [Three Centuries of Glassmaking in Dubrovnik, Fourteenth to Sixteenth Centuries]. Beograd: SANU, 1981.

Hrabak, Bogumil. *Izvoz žitarica iz Osmanlijskog Carstva u XIV, XV i XVI stoljeću. Udeo Dubrovčana u prometu "turskim" žitom* [Exports of Grains from the Ottoman Empire. The Participation of Ragusans in the Traffic of "Turkish" Grains]. Zajednica naučnih ustanova Kosova. *Studije.* Vol. 20. Priština 1971.

Kečkemet, Duško. *Židovi u povijesti Splita* [Jews in the History of Split]. Split: Jevrejska općina u Splitu, 1971.

Klaić, Nada and Petricioli, Ivo. *Zadar u srednjem vijeku do 1409, Prošlost Zadra* [Zadar in the Middle Ages, The Past of Zadar]. Vol. II. Zadar: Sveučilište u Splitu, Filozofski fakultet u Zadru, 1976.

Kostić, Veselin. *Dubrovnik i Engleska, 1300–1650* [Dubrovnik and England, 1300–1650]. Beograd: SANU, 1975.

Krekić, Bariša. *Dubrovnik i Levant (1280–1460)* [Dubrovnik and the Levant, 1280–1460]. Beograd: SANU, 1956.

————. *Dubrovnik (Raguse) et le Levant au Moyen Age*. Paris-La Haye: Ecole Pratique des Hautes Etudes, Sorbonne, 1961.

————. *Dubrovnik in the 14th and 15th Centuries. A City between East and West.* Norman: Oklahoma University Press, 1972.

————. *Dubrovnik, Italy and the Balkans in the Late Middle Ages.* London: Variorum Reprints, 1980.

Lučić, Josip. *Prošlost dubrovačke Astareje* [The Past of Dubrovnik's Astarea]. Dubrovnik: Matica hrvatska, 1970.

————. *Povijest Dubrovnika* [History of Dubrovnik]. Vol. II. Zagreb: JAZU, 1973.

————. *Obrti i usluge u Dubrovniku do početka XIV stoljeća* [Crafts and Services in Dubrovnik until the Beginning of the Fourteenth Century]. Zagreb: Sveučilište u Zagrebu, 1979.

————, ed. *Spisi dubrovačke kancelarije* [Documents from Dubrovnik's Chancellery]. Vol. II. Zagreb: JAZU, 1984.

Luetić, Josip. *1000 godina dubrovačkog brodarstva* [One-Thousand Years of Dubrovnik's Shipping]. Zagreb: Zora, 1969.

————. *Mornarica Dubrovačke Republike* [The Navy of the Republic of Dubrovnik]. Dubrovnik 1962.

————. *Pomorci i jedrenjaci Republike Dubrovačke* [The Seamen and Sailboats of the Republic of Dubrovnik]. Zagreb: Nakladni zavod Matice hrvatske, 1984.

Mahnken, Irmgard. *Dubrovački patricijat u XIV veku* [The Patricians of Dubrovnik in the Fourteenth Century]. 2 vols. Beograd: SANU, 1960.

Medini, Milorad. *Dubrovnik Gučetića* [Dubrovnik of the Gučetić]. Beograd: SANU, 1953.

Mitić, Ilija. *Konzulati i konzularna služba staroga Dubrovnika* [Consulates and Consular Services of Old Dubrovnik]. Dubrovnik: JAZU, 1973.

Nedeljković, Branislav, ed. *Liber viridis.* Beograd: SANU, 1984.

Novak, Grga. *Povijest Splita* [The History of Split]. Vol. I. Split: Matica hrvatska, 1957.

Petrović, Djurdjica. *Dubrovačko oružje u XIV veku* [Dubrovnik's Weapons in the Fourteenth Century]. Beograd: Vojni muzej, 1976.

Popović, Toma. *Turska i Dubrovnik u XVI veku* [Turkey and Dubrovnik in the Sixteenth Century]. Beograd: SANU, 1973.

Rad JAZU. vol. 384. *Radovi sa medjunarodnog simpozija u povodu šestote obljetnice dubrovačke karantene* [Papers Presented at the International Symposium on the Occasion of the Six-Hundredth Anniversary of the Quarantine in Dubrovnik]. Zagreb: JAZU, 1980.

Raukar, Tomislav. *Zadar u XV stoljeću, Ekonomski razvoj i društveni odnosi* [Zadar in the Fifteenth Century. Economic Development and Social Relations]. Zagreb: Sveučilište u Zagrebu, 1977.

Roller, Dragan. *Dubrovački zanati u XV i XVI stoljeću* [Crafts in Dubrovnik in the Fifteenth and Sixteenth Centuries]. Zagreb: JAZU, 1951.

————. *Agrarno-proizvodni odnosi na području Dubrovačke Republike od XIII do XV stoljeća* [Agrarian Conditions in the Territory of the Republic of Dubrovnik from the Thirteenth to the Fifteenth Century]. Zagreb: JAZU, 1955.

Samostan Male Braće u Dubrovniku [The Franciscan Monastery in Dubrovnik]. Kršćanska sadašnjost Zagreb and Samostan Male Braće u Dubrovniku, 1985.

Sindik, Ilija. *Komunalno uredjenje Kotora od druge polovine XII do početka XV stoleća* [The Communal Structure of Kotor from the Second Half of the Twelfth to the Beginning of the Fifteenth Century]. Beograd: SANU, 1950.

Spremić, Momčilo. *Dubrovnik i Aragonci (1442–1495)* [Dubrovnik and the Aragonese, 1442–1495]. Beograd: Zavod za izdavanje udžbenika SRS, 1971.

Steindorff, Ludwig. *Die dalmatinischen Städte im 12. Jahrhundert.* Cologne-Vienna: Böhlau Verlag, 1984.

Tadić, Jorjo. *Dubrovački portreti* [Portraits from Dubrovnik]. Beograd: Srpska književna zadruga, 1948.

————, ed. *Dubrovačka arhivska gradja o Beogradu* [Dubrovnik's Archival Materials Concerning Belgrade]. Beograd: Gradja za istoriju Beograda, 1950.

————, ed. *Gradja o slikarskoj školi u Dubrovniku* [Sources on the School of Painting in Dubrovnik]. 2 vols. Beograd 1952.

Tenenti, Alberto and Branislava. *Il prezzo del rischio. L'assicurazione mediterranea vista da Ragusa (1563–1591).* Rome: Jouvence, 1985.

Voje, Ignacij. *Kreditna trgovina u srednjovjekovnom Dubrovniku* [Loan Operations in the Trade of Medieval Dubrovnik]. Sarajevo: Akademija nauka Bosne i Hercegovine, 1976.

Grad Zadar—Presjek kroz povijest [The City of Zadar—A Cross-Section through Its History]. Zadar: JAZU, 1966.

Zbornik, Studije i gradja o Jevrejima u Dubrovniku [Studies and Materials concerning Jews in Dubrovnik]. Vol. I. Beograd: Jevrejski istorijski muzej, 1971.

Zjačić, Mirko, ed. *Spisi zadarskih bilježnika* [Documents of Zadar Notaries]. Vol. I. Zadar: Državni arhiv, 1959.

Index